GW00420479

MALCOLM MARSHALL

by

Vic Isaacs and Dave Allen

Published by the Association of Cricket Statisticians and Historians, West Bridgford, Nottingham
2000
Typeset by Limlow Books
Printed by Tranters, Derby
ISBN: 1 902171 29 2

Hampshire in 1993

Marshall is fourth from the right on the front row

TRIBUTE
by Victor Isaacs

For a few years I often spoke to Malcolm about producing a statistical book on his achievements. Malcolm, a hidden stattophile, often asked me how his career was shaping and in the years before the Internet, he often assisted me in keeping his figures up to date by putting me in contact with friends in the West Indies and latterly South Africa.

I first saw Malcolm Marshall on April 27th 1979 when, with Gordon Greenidge, he walked into the hotel at Derby where the team were dining together, a sort of bonding exercise for the first match of the season. He was introduced to his new team-mates and I remember my old pal, Dave Turner, remarking to me and a couple of the players: "Isn't he skinny".

The following morning, in Arctic conditions, he warmed up with the team in preparation for the opening Benson & Hedges match of the season. The records show that he dismissed just one batsman, but he made a few spectators sit up and notice. That skinny fast bowler Denzil had started his Hampshire career.

At Oxford the following week, I noticed Malcolm sitting alone in the bar of the hotel, and he approached me to ask where there was a good eating spot. We went out together to a Chinese restaurant and talked about his ambitions. He had already represented the West Indies, and hoped that his career would be extended in that vein. I had to ask him to try and speak slower as his rapid Barbadian talk was difficult to understand. It was probably the last time I ate with Malcolm on a one to one basis but, although socially we did not mix, he was a good friend and always had good words to say about my work with Hampshire.

Malcolm's will to win was shown to me, to my detriment, one year when we decided to play pool in the hotel bar whilst the team were watching a World Cup soccer game. I was reasonably good at pool, but still, to my surprise, I took a 6-1 lead. We stopped for some Kentucky (his treat), and just when I was thinking of retiring for the night, Malcolm insisted we continue our contest. I was tired and drained as he won six straight and, with the score now on 7-6 in his favour, we retired.

I will miss Malcolm, he became a good friend and supporter, but I am grateful to have known him, to have scored every one of his Hampshire matches, and I am grateful for the memories.

MALCOLM MARSHALL

Friday 10 September 1999 was a beautiful late summer day. At Northlands Road the Hampshire and Somerset bowlers were unable to find any life in a pitch which was responsible for the most turgid of drawn matches.

Hampshire's coach, Malcolm Marshall watched the cricket from the players' balcony and during the tea interval took his ten year old son Mali onto the outfield and bowled to him. The young man hit the tennis ball very hard and very cleanly – the older man expected and encouraged a proper performance. That was Malcolm Marshall's last appearance at a Hampshire match. In less than two months he was dead.

It is a fault of cricket that it can be over sentimental and excessively nostalgic. In such circumstances as these however, we recognise that memories are so precious that they must be treated with respect. Anyone who has followed cricket over the past twenty years will have recollections of Malcolm Marshall and for those of us fortunate enough to have been involved with his main sides, Barbados, West Indies, Hampshire or Natal the memories will be particularly vivid.

This is partly because Malcolm Marshall was a great cricketer and in particular a great fast bowler. It does not matter whether we can call him the greatest, it is enough to observe that he shared a platform with every great fast bowler from David Harris, the first great fast bowler of the Hambledon era, to Curtley Ambrose. In the particular context and circumstances of international cricket in the 1980s his bowling was as fine as any player has ever produced. Because he was physically strong, skilful, intelligent, determined and aggressive he would have achieved as much in any other circumstances or period.

Malcolm Marshall grew up in the demanding but fundamentally gentle society of Barbados at the time when cricket was the dominant cultural activity for young men. By his own account he toyed with wicket-keeping and generally preferred batting but learned to bowl fast because that was the only way to claim occupation of the crease. He was never built like a fast bowler but developed his crucial shoulder action at a young age. He bowled with open-chested action which helped his inswinger and, even as a coach would suggest that this 'natural' action was an insurance against the back injuries suffered by many bowlers with classic side-on actions.

Through intelligence he knew or deduced his opponents' weaknesses, loved setting traps and added variations of movement, length and pace to his typical delivery. As a human being Marshall was as friendly and obliging as any cricketer I have met – until he stepped onto a cricket field. Then, whatever the circumstances or status of the match, he was a fearsome opponent.

No cricketers knew this better than the English batsmen of the 1980s although he reserved some of his most venomous performances for the Indians, believing that they had cheated him out for a duck in his first Test innings. Vengsarkar in particular lived to regret his vociferous appeal at Bangalore in 1978.

Just occasionally the aggression would overwhelm the intelligence but as he matured this was less and less likely to happen. Two matches at Portsmouth illustrate the point. In the first in 1983 Hampshire forced Gloucestershire to follow on. Marshall's 3-29 included Gloucestershire's star batsman Zaheer Abbas. In the second innings Marshall clearly felt that Zaheer was frightened and attacked him with a succession of short balls. Zaheer ducked and weaved, playing a number of extravagant but uncomfortable shots. Marshall persisted with his attacking ploy but Zaheer reached 87 before Malone dismissed him. Gloucestershire just saved the game.

Seven years later, Derbyshire were 140-1 requiring just 95 more to win with time to spare. Marshall then took seven wickets in 51 balls to bowl Hampshire to a relatively comfortable victory. The local newspaper described this as his "Finest Hour" and allowing for a certain parochialism in the judgement it was as precisely a Masterclass in the arts of fast bowling as one could hope to see. It was also the performance of a mature performer where the earlier display had suffered from a certain irrational aggressiveness.

Marshall's intelligence enabled him to make the transition from player to coach. In addition to his fellow countrymen cricketers in South Africa and Southern England have reason to be grateful for his thinking and teaching. He took on difficult tasks with West Indies and Hampshire, coaching two sides in significant decline following years of success. In Hampshire in particular, there is a feeling that players like Jason Laney, Derek Kenway, Will Kendall, Alex Morris and Dimitri Mascarenhas might constitute a living memorial to a great cricketer and a great man.

Early Years

Malcolm Denzil Marshall was born in St Michael, Barbados on 18th April 1958, the son of Denzil and Eleanor. His father, a policeman, died in a motorcycle crash in 1959 and Malcolm was brought up by his mother, who worked as a store cashier, and grandparents, Lillian and Oscar. Eleanor later remarried and Malcolm had a half-brother, Michael and half-sister, Cheryl-Anne. Malcolm was educated at St Giles Boys School where he first played organised cricket and at Parkinson Comprehensive School, Barbados. Leaving school at 15, he joined Spartan Cricket Club and Texaco Cricket Club. In 1975 he was selected for Barbados Youth and played against England Youth. In April 1977 he took a job with Banks Brewery and began playing for their club side.

1977/78

Marshall made his first-class debut at the age of 19 in the final match of the season and took 6-77 in the first innings. Barbados were Shell Shield Champions and repeated the success in the next two seasons plus 1981/2; 1983/4; 1985/6 and 1990/1 (as the Red Stripe Cup). Despite this success with his home side after one match, Marshall never won a Championship in England.

	Own Team Total	O	M	R	W		Opp Total	Ct
1. Barbados v Jamaica, Bridgetown, January 17, 18, 19, 20 (Match drawn)								
run out	0 447	28.4	7	77	6	A.B.Williams b	341	
						M.L.C.Foster b		
						H.G.Gordon c D.A.Murray		
						E.A.Campbell c D.A.Murray		
						L.N.G.Wright c D.A.Murray		
						S.A.Francis b		
did not bat	- 225-5d	5	0	20	1	H.S.Chang c A.E.Greenidge	103-2	

SEASON'S AVERAGES

Batting and Fielding	M	I	NO	Runs	HS	Ave	100	50	Ct
Shell Shield	1	1	0	0	0	0.00	-	-	-

Bowling	O	M	R	W	BB	Ave	5i	10m
Shell Shield	33.4	7	97	7	6-77	13.85	1	-

1978/79 – West Indies in India and Sri Lanka

After one first-class match, Marshall was selected to tour the sub-continent with the full West Indies side who were lacking Lloyd, Richards, Roberts, Holding and others. He scored his first half-century v West Zone and took 13 wickets in the first three matches winning a place in the first Test. As on his first-class debut, he was dismissed without scoring although he always protested the decision and the Indians' behaviour. He took just three wickets in his first three Test matches.

	Own Team Total	O	M	R	W		Opp Total	Ct
2. West Indians v Indian Colts, Pune, November 22, 23, 24 (Match drawn)								
c K.Srikkanth b G.Sharma 12	388	29	12	50	4	R.Lamba c J.R.Lyon	257-9d	
						K.Srikkanth lbw		
						R.Sethi c J.R.Lyon		
						M.D.Gunjal lbw		
did not bat	- 254-2							
3. West Indians v West Zone, Baroda, November 26, 27, 28 (Match drawn)								
c sub b K.D.Ghavri 59	315-9d	19	0	46	1	N.Y.Satham c sub	299-6d	1
did not bat	- 192-4							
4. West Indians v South Zone, Hyderabad, December 9, 10, 11 (Match drawn)								
c and b M.V.Narasimha Rao 20	278	21	7	45	4	Sajjad Akbar c and b	283-8d	1
						V.Sivaramakrishnan c S.F.A.F.Bacchus		
						B.P.Patel c H.A.Gomes		
						T.E.Srinavasan lbw		
did not bat	- 281-4d	18	2	71	4	Sajjad Akbar b	169-6	
						V.Sivaramakrishnan lbw		
						S.B.Jung c S.Shivnarine		
						R.M.H.Binny c J.R.Lyon		
5. WEST INDIES v INDIA, Bangalore, December 15, 16, 17, 19, 20 (Match drawn)								
lbw b B.S.Chandrasekhar 0	437	18	2	53	1	C.P.S.Chauhan c D.R.Parry	371	
b K.D.Ghavri 5	200-8							
6. West Indians v East Zone, Jamshedpur, December 23, 24, 25 (West Indians won by an innings and 61 runs)								
did not bat	- 500-4d	19	5	71	6	R.Panda lbw	317-9d	2
						H.Gidwani c and b		
						Jodh Singh b		
						Daljit Singh b		
						Paramjit Singh b		
						R.Burman b		
		16.3	5	54	5	R.Panda b	122	
						H.Gidwani c J.R.Lyon		
						R.C.Saxena lbw		
						Paramjit Singh c J.R.Lyon		
						R.Burman b		
7. WEST INDIES v INDIA, Calcutta, December 29, 30, 31, January 2, 3 (Match drawn)								
c R.M.H.Kirmani b Kapil Dev 1	327	12	3	44	1	A.D.Gaekwad c D.A.Murray	300	1
lbw b B.S.Bedi 1	197-9	14	3	45	0		361-1d	
8. West Indians v North Zone, Jullundur, January 20, 21, 22 (Match drawn)								
lbw b R.C.Shukla 12	167	14	4	41	2	V Sunderam c D.A.Murray	311-3d	
						S.C.Khanna c H.S.Chang		
not out 26	343-6							
9. WEST INDIES v INDIA, Kanpur, February 2, 3, 4, 6, 7, 8 (Match drawn)								
not out 1	452-8	34	3	123	1	S.M.Gavaskar c D.A.Murray	644-7d	
10. West Indians v Karnataka, Ahmedabad, February 10, 11, 12 (Karnataka won by 11 runs)								
c and b B.Vijaykrishna 9	220	15	4	42	6	R.M.H.Binny c J.R.Lyon	219	1
						H.Chandrasekhar c H.S.Chang		
						B.P.Patel c J.R.Lyon		
						G.R.Viswanath c J.R.Lyon		
						B.Vijakrishna lbw		
						K.Tandon b		
c B.S.Chandrasekhar b B.Vijaykrishna 2	280	15	4	32	2	R.M.H.Binny lbw	292-8d	
						H.Chandrasekhar lbw		

11. West Indians v Sri Lanka Board President's XI, Colombo Cricket Club Ground, Colombo, February 16, 17, 18 (Match drawn)

b R.S.Abeysekera	0	212	4	0	16	1	R.G.C.E.Wijesurija b	190
c and b S.Jeganathan	3	201	8	3	19	0		122-5

12. West Indians v Sri Lanka, P.Savaravanamuttu Stadium, Colombo, February 22, 23, 24 (Match drawn)

run out	9	402-8d	21	10	32	4	N.D.P.Hettiaratchy	
							c J.R.Lyon	266
							A.N.Ranasinghe c J.R.Lyon	
							D.S.deSilva c A.T.Greenidge	
							A.R.M.Opatha c J.R.Lyon	
			9	3	26	0		133

SEASON'S AVERAGES

Batting and Fielding	M	I	NO	Runs	HS	Ave	100	50	Ct
Test matches	3	5	1	8	5	2.00	-	-	1
Other matches	8	10	1	152	59	16.88	-	1	5
Tour	11	15	2	160	59	12.30	-	1	6
Career	12	16	2	160	59	11.42	-	1	6

Bowling	O	M	R	W	BB	Ave	5i	10m
Test matches	78	11	265	3	1-44	88.33	-	-
Other matches	208.3	59	545	39	6-42	13.97	3	1
Tour	286.3	70	810	42	6-42	19.28	3	1
Career	320.1	77	907	49	6-42	18.51	4	1

1978/79

Marshall returned to play a full part in the Barbados season including another six-wicket return against Jamaica.

	Own Team Total	O	M	R	W		Opp Total	Ct

13. Barbados v Jamaica, Kingston, March 16, 17, 18, 19 (Match drawn)

c E.A.Campbell
b J.A.Gordon 9 416-9d 24 4 82 6 A.B.Williams c D.A.Murray 340
H.S.Chang c D.A.Murray
M.C.Neita c D.A.Murray
E.A.Campbell c A.E.Greenidge
J.A.Gordon c H.A.Braithwaite
E.E.Brown b
9 1 59 1 P.J.L.Dujon c C.S.Beckles 329-4

14. Barbados v Combined Islands, St John's, March 23, 24, 25, 26 (Barbados won by four wickets)

c I.Cadette b G.C.Shillingford 1 209 12 1 54 4 E.E.Lewis c N.A.Johnson 220
U.V.C.Lawrence lbw
I.Cadette lbw
G.C.Shillingford b
not out 7 154-6 14 3 39 2 V.A.Eddy c D.A.Murray 139
N.Phillip c D.A.Murray

15. Barbados v Trinidad & Tobago, Bridgetown, April 14, 15, 16, 17 (Match drawn)

c R.S.Gabriel b R.Nanan 4 405 40.1 9 103 3 R.S.Gabriel c D.L.Haynes 541
H.A.Gomes c C.G.Greenidge
D.E.Audain c C.G.Greenidge
did not bat - 50-0

16. Barbados v Guyana, Bridgetown, April 21, 22, 23 (Barbados won by an innings and 140 runs)

run out 17 362-7d 13.1 4 25 4 S.F.A.F.Bacchus
c T.R.O.Payne 136 1
G.S.Camacho c T.R.O.Payne
M.R.Pydanna c T.R.O.Payne
S.Matthews c D.A.J.Holford

12.1	0	39	5	S.F.A.F.Bacchus c and b	86	1
				M.A.Harper c S.T.Clarke		
				S.Shivnarine c T.R.O.Payne		
				D.I.Kallicharran c T.R.O.Payne		
				S.Matthews b		

SEASON'S AVERAGES

Batting and Fielding	M	I	NO	Runs	HS	Ave	100	50	Ct
Shell Shield	4	5	1	38	17	9.50	-	-	2
Career	16	21	3	198	59	11.00	-	1	8

Bowling	O	M	R	W	BB	Ave	5i	10m
Shell Shield	124.3	22	401	25	6-82	16.04	2	-
Career	444.4	99	1308	74	6-42	17.67	6	1

1979

Marshall had signed for Hampshire before the tour of India when their cricket chairman Charlie Knott made good use of his contacts in the Caribbean. Marshall made his debut for his third first-class side in fifteen months and avoided a third successive debut duck by the narrowest margin. Hampshire had been one of the strongest counties in the mid-1970s but were in a transitional phase, having just lost the captain Gilliat, Richards and Roberts. Marshall made a good impression with the ball and topped the county's averages but he was less successful as a batsman. He missed some weeks in mid-season as a member of the West Indies World Cup squad but did not appear in their winning team.

		Own Team Total	O	M	R	W		Opp Total	Ct
17. Hampshire v Glamorgan, Southampton, May 2, 3, 4 (Hampshire won by 116 runs)									
b A.H.Wilkins	1	237	21	5	45	3	E.W.Jones b	138	
							R.N.S.Hobbs b		
							A.H.Wilkins c M.N.S.Taylor		
did not bat	-	117-6d	15.3	8	23	4	A.Jones lbw	100	2
							G.Richards lbw		
							A.E.Cordle lbw		
							A.H.Wilkins c T.E.Jesty		
18. Hampshire v Oxford University, The Parks, May 9, 10, 11 (Match drawn)									
c J.L.Rawlinson									
b S.M.Clements	25	251-7d	6	2	12	0		59	
19. Hampshire v Worcestershire, Worcester, May 16, 17, 18 (Match drawn)									
did not bat	-	202-4d	18	3	53	1	B.J.R.Jones c C.G.Greenidge	254	
did not bat	-	90-4	4	2	4	0		145-8d	
20. Hampshire v Kent, Canterbury, May 26, 28, 29 (Match drawn)									
did not bat	-	309-3d	20	8	34	3	C.J.C.Rowe c T.E.Jesty	126	2
							C.J.Tavare b		
							C.S.Cowdrey c and b		
			-	-	-	-		229	
21. Hampshire v Somerset, Taunton, June 2, 4, 5 (Match drawn)									
b V.J.Marks	2	236	11	6	10	1	P.A.Slocombe lbw	200-5d	1
			7	1	19	0		201-6	
22. Hampshire v Indians, Southampton, July 4, 5, 6 (Match drawn)									
b M.Amarnath	1	315-9d	13	0	67	0		369-3d	
not out	3	145-7	8	2	15	1	D.B.Vengsarkar c and b	235-4d	2
23. Hampshire v Gloucestershire, Southampton, July 7, 9, 10 (Gloucestershire won by 130 runs)									
b M.J.Procter	0	219	20	5	53	1	M.D.Partridge c J.M.Rice	337	
c A.J.Hignell b B.M.Brain	9	186	18	2	56	5	A.W.Stovold b	198-7d	
							Sadiq Mohammad c C.G.Greenidge		
							J.C.Foat b		
							P.Bainbridge lbw		
							A.J.Hignell c G.R.Stephenson		

24. Hampshire v Derbyshire, Basingstoke, July 11, 12, 13 (Hampshire won by six wickets)
c and b P.N.Kirsten   0   328   11   5   14   1   A.Hill b   209   1
did not bat   -   158-4   17   4   46   1   A.Hill lbw   275   1

25. Hampshire v Yorkshire, Bradford, July 14, 16, 17 (Match drawn)
b G.B.Stevenson   4   297   21   6   48   2   R.G.Lumb   c T.E.Jesty   171-7d
              J.H.Hampshire   c G.R.Stephenson
did not bat   -   158-4d   6   2   16   2   K.Sharp b   59-4
              C.W.J.Athey b

26. Hampshire v Essex, Bournemouth, July 25, 26, 27 (Essex won by an innings and 33 runs)
c G.A.Gooch b J.K.Lever   5   128   30   8   93   4   G.A.Gooch
              c G.R.Stephenson   380   1
              K.S.McEwan   c G.R.Stephenson
              K.W.R.Fletcher b
              N.Phillip b

c M.S.A.McEvoy b R.E.East 16   219

27. Hampshire v Warwickshire, Nuneaton, July 28, 30, 31 (Hampshire won by 290 runs)
c C.Maynard b S.P.Perryman 2   200   12   8   8   0   111
did not bat   -   271-4d   11   5   14   2   D.L.Amiss   c N.G.Cowley   70
              T.A.Lloyd   c D.J.Rock

28. Hampshire v Somerset, Southampton, August 1, 2, 3 (Match drawn)
b J.Garner   0   225-7c   26   2   74   0   336-6d
did not bat   -   23-2

29. Hampshire v Glamorgan, Cardiff, August 4, 6, 7 (Match drawn)
c A.E.Cordle b R.C.Ontong   3   204   11   2   24   1   E.W.Jones   c G.R.Stephenson 205
              15   8   23   2   A.Jones   c C.G.Greenidge   49-2
              J.A.Hopkins   c G.R.Stephenson

30. Hampshire v Surrey, Portsmouth, August 11, 13, 14 (Surrey won by ten wickets)
c G.R.J.Roope b P.I.Pocock   9   207   25   7   63   2   A.R.Butcher
              c G.G.Greenidge   303
              G.R.J.Roope   c J.M.Rice
b P.I.Pocock   0   157   3   2   3   0   62-0

31. Hampshire v Middlesex, Portsmouth, August 15, 16, 17 (Match drawn)
c M.W.Gatting
   b N.G.Featherstone   10   403   16   5   43   3   M.J.Smith   c M.N.S.Taylor   140
              C.T.Radley   c G.G.Greenidge
              R.O.Butcher   c G.R.Stephenson
              6   5   1   1   M.W.Gatting   c C.G.Greenidge   8-2

32. Hampshire v Lancashire, Old Trafford, August 18, 20, 21 (Match drawn)
run out   26   254   32   16   40   4   G.E.Trim   c C.G.Greenidge   287-9d
              J.Abrahams   c C.G.Greenidge
              B.W.Reidy   c K.Stevenson
              D.P.Hughes   c D.R.Turner
not out   20   207   9.3   0   40   1   D.Lloyd lbw   94-2   1

33. Hampshire v Kent, Bournemouth, August 25, 27, 28 (Kent won by an innings and 56 runs)
c and b D.L.Underwood   14   144   19   5   43   0   282-7d
c G.W.Johnson
   b D.L.Underwood   3   82

34. Hampshire v Sussex, Bournemouth, August 29, 30, 31 (Sussex won by nine wickets)
lbw b Imran Khan   1   123   22   8   40   1   A.C.S.Pigott   c N.G.Cowley   282
c T.J.Head b Imran Khan   0   179   -   -   -   -   24-1

35. Hampshire v Surrey, Kennington Oval, September 5, 6, 7 (Surrey won by eight wickets)
lbw b S.T.Clarke   5   243   13   4   27   1   A.R.Butcher lbw   432   1
lbw b A.R.Butcher   38   228   -   -   -   -   41-2

SEASON'S AVERAGES

Batting and Fielding	M	I	NO	Runs	HS	Ave	100	50	Ct
County Championship	17	22	1	168	38	8.00	-	-	10
Other matches	2	3	1	29	25	14.50	-	-	2
Season	19	25	2	197	38	8.56	-	-	12
Career	35	46	5	395	59	9.63	-	1	20

Bowling	O	M	R	W	BB	Ave	5i	10m
County Championship	420	142	957	46	5-56	20.80	1	-
Other matches	27	4	94	1	1-15	94.00	-	-
Season	467	146	1051	47	5-56	22.36	1	-
Career	911.4	245	2359	121	6-46	19.49	7	1

1979/80 – West Indies in Australia and New Zealand

Marshall's tour figures were respectable but with Roberts, Holding, Croft, Garner and King in the side he was unable to win a Test place.

	Own Team	O	M	R	W		Opp	Ct
	Total						Total	

36. West Indians v Tasmania Invitation XI, Devonport, November 23, 24, 25 (West Indians won by 260 runs)

b P.R.Sleep	1	374	12	4	25	1	G.J.Cosier c D.L.Murray 144	
did not bat	-	202-4d	13	3	32	2	S.J.Howard c C.G.Greenidge 172	
							C.L.Broadby c D.L.Murray	

37. West Indians v Western Australia, Perth, January 5, 6, 7 (Western Australia won by eight wickets)

not out	23	169	18	3	66	3	G.M.Wood c D.A.Murray 396-6d	
							C.S.Serjeant c D.A.Murray	
							M.D.O'Neill c D.A.Murray	
c M.F.Malone								
b T.M.Alderman	15	313	9	4	21	1	G.M.Wood c A.I.Kallicharran 87-2	

38. West Indians v Northern Districts, Hamilton, February 3, 4, 5 (Match drawn)

c G.W.Howarth								
b C.W.Dickeson	7	377-6d	14	3	39	0		277-7d
did not bat	-	132-8	8	1	27	0		252-7d

39. West Indians v Wellington, Lower Hutt, February 16, 17, 18 (Wellington won by six wickets)

b E.J.Chatfield	0	102	16	3	43	5	B.A.Edgar c J.Garner 93	1
							R.H.Vance c D.A.Murray	
							J.F.M.Morrison c C.L.King	
							R.B.Reid b	
							E.J.Gray lbw	
not out	13	143	17	6	40	2	B.A.Edgar b 155-4	1
							G.A.Newdick c and b	

SEASON'S AVERAGES

Batting and Fielding	M	I	NO	Runs	HS	Ave	100	50	Ct
Other matches	4	6	2	59	23*	14.75	-	-	2
Career	39	52	7	454	59	10.08	-	1	22

Bowling	O	M	R	W	BB	Ave	5i	10m
Other matches	107	27	293	14	5-43	20.92	1	-
Career	1018.4	272	2652	135	6-42	19.64	8	1

1979/80

Marshall enjoyed a successful Shell Shield season, recording his best bowling figures against Trinidad & Tobago and batting consistently in the last three matches.

	Own Team	O	M	R	W		Opp	Ct
	Total						Total	

40. Barbados v Guyana, Georgetown, March 21, 22, 23, 24 (Barbados won by ten wickets)

c Timur Mohamed								
b C.E.H.Croft	5	340	12	5	23	1	T.R.Etwaroo b 145	
did not bat	-	32-0	14	4	34	2	R.C.Fredericks b 226	
							R.A.Harper lbw	

41. Barbados v Trinidad & Tobago, Port of Spain, March 28, 29, 30, 31 (Barbados won by five wickets)

not out	41	410-9d	15.4	5	38	6	R.S.Gabriel c T.R.O.Payne 259
							A.L.Logie c sub
							D.L.Murray c T.R.O.Payne
							B.D.Julien c D.L.Haynes
							R.Nanan b
							R.R.Jumadeen lbw
did not bat	-	104-5	16	4	28	2	H.A.Gomes c sub 251 1
							R.R.Jumadeen b

42. Barbados v Jamaica, Bridgetown, April 11, 12, 13, 14 (Barbados won by an innings and 6 runs)

c sub b J.A.Williams	41	456	8	0	28	0	155
			19	7	38	4	A.B.Williams b 295
							P.J.L.Dujon lbw
							M.A.Tucker b
							J.A.Gordon c D.A.Murray

43. Barbados v Combined Islands, Bridgetown, April 25, 26, 27, 28 (Barbados won by an innings and 19 runs)

run out	55	555	14	2	58	1	S.I.Williams c J.Garner 257
			6.3	2	26	2	U.V.C.Lawrence
							c D.A.Murray 279
							W.W.Davis c E.N.Trotman

SEASON'S AVERAGES

Batting and Fielding	M	I	NO	Runs	HS	Ave	100	50	Ct
Shell Shield	4	4	1	142	55	47.33	-	1	1
Career	43	56	8	596	59	12.41	-	2	23

Bowling	O	M	R	W	BB	Ave	5i	10m
Shell Shield	105.1	29	273	18	6-38	15.16	1	-
Career	1123.5	301	2925	153	6-38	19.11	9	1

1980 – West Indies in England, and for Hampshire

Marshall made an immediate impression with his first seven-wicket success at Worcester and was generally impressive in county matches. He established himself in the Test side where Roberts, Holding and Croft took the new-ball but Marshall's 15 wickets contributed to West Indies' dominance over Botham's side. Poor weather limited them to a single victory but they led on first innings in four of the five Tests.

Hampshire were deprived of the services of Marshall and Greenidge for most of the season and finished bottom of the table for the first time since 1905. Both players appeared in a few matches from mid-August under the new captain Nick Pocock and Marshall did enough to finish top of the county's bowling averages.

	Own Team Total	O	M	R	W		Opp Total	Ct
44. West Indians v Worcestershire, Worcester, May 10, 11, 12 (West Indians won by seven wickets)								
c N.Gifford b V.A.Holder	52 266	17	3	56	2	G.M.Turner		
						c S.F.A.F.Bacchus	252	
						J.A.Ormrod c D.L.Murray		
did not bat	- 134-3	17.1	3	56	7	A.P.Pridgeon		
						c I.V.A.Richards	144	
						B.J.R.Jones lbw		
						E.J.O.Hemsley b		
						Younis Ahmed c I.V.A.Richards		
						D.J.Humphries b		
						V.A.Holder b		
						N.Gifford c I.V.A.Richards		
45. West Indians v Northamptonshire, Milton Keynes, May 17, 18, 19 (West Indians won by six wickets)								
c T.J.Yardley b R.M.Tindall	17 369	17	4	34	3	R.G.Williams lbw	260	
						T.J.Yardley b		
						R.M.Carter lbw		

b R.G.Williams   2 60-4   7 1 29 3 G.Cook c D.L.Murray   166
                                            W.Larkins c S.F.A.F.Bacchus
                                            R.G.Williams c sub

46. West Indians v Derbyshire, Chesterfield, May 24, 25, 26 (West Indians won by nine wickets)
c P.N.Kirsten b M.Hendrick 11 290   22   7 52 4 B.Wood b   229
                                          P.N.Kirsten b
                                          A.J.Borrington lbw
did not bat   G.Miller b
                  - 11-1   11.5 5 20 2 M.Hendrick c D.L.Murray   68
                                          A.J.Mellor b

47. WEST INDIES v ENGLAND, Trent Bridge, June 5, 6, 7, 9, 10 (West Indies won by two wickets)
c C.J.Tavare b G.A.Gooch 20 308   19 3 52 1 P.Willey b   263
b R.G.D.Willis   7 209-8 24 8 44 2 P.Willey b   252
                                          A.P.E.Knott lbw

48. West Indians v Sussex, Hove, June 14, 15, 16 (Match drawn)
lbw b G.G.Arnold   5 227-8d 15 4 40 3 Imran Khan c I.V.A.Richards 143
                                          C.P.Phillipson c I.V.A.Richards
                                          G.S.le Roux b
                             4 0 18 0   191-4

49. West Indians v Glamorgan, Swansea, June 28, 30 July 1 (Match drawn)
did not bat   - 327-5d 19 5 54 6 A.Jones b   242
                                          J.A.Hopkins b
                                          R.C.Ontong c D.L.Murray
                                          Javed Miandad c I.V.A.Richards
                                          N.G.Featherstone c D.L.Murray
did not bat   - 60-0   G.C.Holmes c J.Garner

50. West Indians v Somerset, Taunton, July 5, 6 , 7 (Match drawn)
not out   2 400-7d 7   2 21 0
                                                              77-0

51. WEST INDIES v ENGLAND, Old Trafford, July 10, 11, (12), 14, 15 (Match drawn)
c G.A.Gooch b G.R.Dilley 18 260   12 5 36 3 B.C.Rose b   150
                                          M.W.Gatting c I.V.A.Richards
                                          P.Willey b
                         35   5 116 2 G.A.Gooch c D.L.Murray   391-7
                                          W.Larkins c D.L.Murray

52. West Indians v Yorkshire, Headingley, July 19, 20, 21 (West Indians won by 58 runs)
did not bat   - 342-3d -   -   -   -
did not bat   - 119-1d -   -   -   -   194-5d
                                                              209

53. WEST INDIES v ENGLAND, Kennington Oval July 24, 25, (26), 28, 29 (Match drawn)
c B.C.Rose b J.E.Emburey 45 265   29.3 6 77 2 A.P.E.Knott c C.H.Lloyd   370
                                            J.E.Emburey c M.A.Holding
                         23   7 47 0   209-9d

54. West Indians v Warwickshire, Edgbaston, August 2, 3, 4 (Match drawn)
not out   32 315   16 5 29 3 J.Whitehouse lbw   223
                                          A.M.Ferreira lbw
                                          R.G.D.Willis b
did not bat   - 227-7d 11 5 19 1 G.W.Humpage c D.L.Murray 180-3

55. WEST INDIES v ENGLAND, Headingley, August (7), 8, 9, (11), 12 (Match drawn)
c D.L.Bairstow b G.R.Dilley 0 245   11 3 22 2 D.L.Bairstow lbw   143   2
                                            C.M.Old c J.Garner
                         19   5 42 3 G.A.Gooch lbw   227-6
                                          W.Larkins lbw
                                          I.T.Botham lbw

56. Hampshire v Northamptonshire, Wellingborough, August 16, 18, 19 (Northamptonshire won by eight wickets)
c and b R.G.Williams   29 119   15 3 39 2 G.Cook c R.J.Parks   301
                                          B.J.Griffiths b
not out   72 247   9 3 15 0   66-2

57. Hampshire v Somerset, Bournemouth, August 20, 21, 22 (Match drawn)
c N.F.M.Popplewell
        b V.J.Marks 31 294-9c 19   7 34 3 P.A.Slocombe c R.J.Parks 280-7c
                                          V.J.Marks c R.J.Parks
                                          D.J.S.Taylor lbw
b N.F.M.Popplewell   67 278   12 3 27 0   147-5

58. Hampshire v Worcestershire, Bournemouth, August 23, 25, 26 (Hampshire won by four wickets)

		Own Team Total	O	M	R	W	Opp		Ct

c G.M.Turner b H.L.Alleyne 4 236 28 9 53 4 P.A.Neale c R.J.Parks 219 1
Younis Ahmed b
E.J.O.Hemsley c N.E.J.Pocock
A.P.Pridgeon b

c G.M.Turner
 b E.J.O.Hemsley 10 142-6 19 4 39 5 Younis Ahmed c C.L.Smith 155 2
D.N.Patel b
J.D.Inchmore lbw
H.L.Alleyne b
N.Gifford b

59. Hampshire v Nottinghamshire, Trent Bridge, August 30, September 1 (Nottinghamshire won by an innings and 22 runs)

c E.E.Hemmings
 b P.J.Hacker 19 100 21 5 49 3 P.A.Todd c R.J.Parks 180
C.E.B.Rice c R.J.Parks
R.E.Dexter c N.E.J.Pocock

b C.E.B.Rice 3 58

60. Hampshire v Leicestershire, Southampton, September 3, 4 (Leicestershire won by an innings and 34 runs)

lbw b N.G.B.Cook 13 182 18 8 50 0 333 1
c D.I.Gower b L.B.Taylor 3 117

SEASON'S AVERAGES

Batting and Fielding	M	I	NO	Runs	HS	Ave	100	50	Ct
Test matches	4	5	0	90	45	18.00	-	-	2
Other tour matches	8	7	2	121	52	24.20	-	1	-
County Championship	5	10	1	251	72*	27.88	-	2	4
Season	17	22	3	462	72*	24.31	-	3	6
Career	60	78	11	1058	72*	15.79	-	5	29

Bowling	O	M	R	W	BB	Ave	5i	10m
Test matches	172.3	42	436	15	3-36	29.06	-	-
Other tour matches	164	44	428	34	7-56	12.58	2	-
County Championship	141	42	306	17	5-39	18.00	1	-
Season	477.3	128	1170	66	7-56	17.72	3	-
Career	1601.2	429	4095	219	7-56	18.69	12	1

1980/81 – West Indies in Pakistan

Clarke and Croft were now the opening partnership and Marshall appeared in all four Tests. His second innings bowling was decisive in the only match with a positive result as West Indies won a second successive series 1-0. His batting was less impressive.

	Own Team Total	O	M	R	W		Opp Total	Ct

61. West Indians v N.W.F.P.Governor's XI, Peshawar, November 9, 10, 11, 12 (West Indians won by ten wickets)

c Sarfraz Nawaz
 b Amin Lakhani 13 267 6.2 1 14 1 Amin Lakhani b 91 1
did not bat - 40-0 8 0 44 0 215

62. West Indians v Sind Governor's XI, Sukkur, November 14, 15, 16 (West Indians won by 64 runs)

b Mudassar Nazar 20 213 18 4 30 4 Mansoor Akhtar b 228
Salim Yousuf lbw
Wasim Raja c D.A.Murray
Tahir Naqqash lbw

b Mudassar Nazar 24 149 5.3 1 9 5 Mansoor Akhtar b 70
Wasim Raja lbw
Tahir Naqqash lbw
Ilyas Khan b
Abdul Raquib b

63. WEST INDIES v PAKISTAN, Lahore, November 24, 25, (27), 28, 29 (Match drawn)
b Sarfraz Nawaz   9   297   21.5 5   88 3 Sadiq Mohammad
                                                c D.A.Murray   369
                                              Imran Khan lbw
                                            Iqbal Qasim b
                    15   4   30 0
                                                 156-7   1
64. WEST INDIES v PAKISTAN, Faisalabad, December 8, 9, 11, 12 (West Indies won by 156 runs)
b Mohammed Nazir   0   235   9   1   39 2 Mansoor Akhtar c C.H.Lloyd 176
c Javed Miandad   Majid Khan c D.A.Murray
  b Mohammed Nazir 1   242   9.4 0   25 4 Mansoor Akhtar c R.Nanan 145
                                            Zaheer Abbas lbw
                                            Sikandar Bakht c C.H.Lloyd
                                            Mohammed Nazir c R.Nanan
65. West Indians v Pakistan Combined XI, Bahawalpur, December 15, 16, 17 (Match drawn)
did not bat   - 380-5d 15   2   49 2 Iqbal Sikandar b   232
did not bat   - 144-3   Wasim Bari b
66. WEST INDIES v PAKISTAN, Karachi, December (22), 23, 24, 26, 27 (Match drawn)
b Mohammad Nazir   0   169   14   0   38 1 Ejaz Faqih b   128
                          17   1   54 2 Imran Khan c D.A.Murray 204-9
                                            Ejaz Faqih c D.A.Murray
67. WEST INDIES v PAKISTAN, Multan, December 30, 31 January 2, 3, 4 (Match drawn)
c Javed Miandad
  b Mohammad Nazir 3   249   12   1   45 1 Zaheer Abbas c D.A.Murray 166
did not bat   - 116-5

SEASON'S AVERAGES

Batting and Fielding

	M	I	NO	Runs	HS	Ave	100	50	Ct
Test matches	4	5	0	13	9	2.60	-	-	1
Other matches	3	3	0	57	24	19.00	-	-	1
Tour	7	8	0	70	24	8.75	-	-	2
Career	67	86	11	1128	72*	15.04	-	5	31

Bowling

	O	M	R	W	BB	Ave	5i	10m
Test matches	98.3	12	319	13	4-25	24.53	-	-
Other matches	52.5	8	146	12	5-9	12.16	1	-
Tour	151.2	20	465	25	5-9	18.60	1	-
Career	1752.4	449	4560	244	7-56	18.68	13	1

1980/81

Marshall's 17 wickets for Barbados were bettered only by Andy Roberts (Antigua) but he was unable to obtain a place in the Test side until the last match of the series. At the age of 23 he was now becoming the West Indies' fastest bowler and he opened their bowling for the first time at Kingston, Jamaica.

	Own Team Total	O	M	R	W		Opp Total	Ct

68. Barbados v Guyana, Bridgetown, January 17, 18, 19 (Barbados won by an innings and 260 runs)
run out   33 552-7d 13   3   39 2 M.R.Pydanna c T.R.O.Payne 184   2
                                            S.Shivnarine c D.A.Murray
                      14   4   24 3 R.Gomes c D.A.Murray   108
                                            S.Shivnarine b
                                            D.I.Kallicharran c A.E.Greenidge
69. President's Young West Indies XI v England XI, Pointe-a-Pierre, January 23, 24, 25, 26 (England XI won by 190 runs)
c C.M.Old b I.T.Botham 27 320   25   9   54 1 B.C.Rose b   483-6d
run out   31 181   18   4   48 3 B.C.Rose b   208-5d
                                            D.L.Bairstow lbw
                                            P.Willey c S.I.Williams

70. Barbados v Trinidad & Tobago, Port of Spain, January 30, 31 February 1, 2 (Trinidad & Tobago won by eight wickets)

c and b A.G.Burns	48	234	16	4	40	0	357
run out	1	169	-	-	-	-	48-2

71. Barbados v Jamaica, St Catherine's, February 7, 8, 9, 10 (Match drawn)

not out	49	196	27.1	8	75	6	R.A.Austin c A.L.Padmore	263
							C.W.Fletcher c C.G.Greenidge	
							E.H.Mattis c D.A.Murray	
							A.G.Barrett b	
							J.A.Williams lbw	
							M.A.Holding c T.F.Foster	
did not bat	-	176-4	17	2	49	1	L.G.Rowe	
							c sub (E.N.Trotman)	264-4d

72. Barbados v Combined Islands, Bridgetown, February 21, 22, 23 (Barbados won by an innings and 16 runs)

c and b N.R.Guishard	6	391	9	1	29	3	S.I.Williams c L.N.Reifer	139
							N.R.Guishard b	
							I.Cadette lbw	
			15.5	3	52	2	I.T.Shillingford c L.N.Reifer	236
							N.R.Guishard b	

73. Barbados v England XI, Bridgetown, March 7, 8, 9, 10 (Match drawn)

not out	29	334	19	6	42	1	M.W.Gatting c D.A.Murray	298
			18	7	25	3	M.W.Gatting b	219-6
							R.O.Butcher lbw	
							I.T.Botham c D.A.Murray	

74. WEST INDIES v ENGLAND, Kingston, April 10, 11, 12, 14, 15 (Match drawn)

b J.E.Embury	15	442	16	2	49	2	P.Willey c D.A.Murray	285
							I.T.Botham c C.G.Greenidge	
			5	0	15	1	G.A.Gooch c C.H.Lloyd	302-6d

SEASON'S AVERAGES

Batting and Fielding	M	I	NO	Runs	HS	Ave	100	50	Ct
Test matches	1	1	0	15	15	15.00	-	-	-
Shell Shield	4	5	1	137	49*	34.25	-	-	2
Other matches	2	3	1	87	31	43.50	-	-	-
Season	7	9	2	239	49*	34.14	-	-	2
Career	74	95	13	1367	72*	16.67	-	5	33

Bowling	O	M	R	W	BB	Ave	5i	10m
Test matches	21	2	64	3	2-49	21.33	-	-
Shell Shield	112	25	308	17	6-75	18.11	1	-
Other matches	80	26	169	8	3-25	21.12	-	-
Season	213	53	541	28	6-75	19.32	1	-
Career	1965.4	502	5101	272	7-56	18.75	14	1

1981

Marshall made a good start to his third county season punctuated by an untypical disaster at Basingstoke where he took 0-87 and recorded his first first-class 'pair'. Unusually, he missed seven matches and his bowling was consistent rather than spectacular but 68 wickets and 425 runs marked him as a good all-rounder in an improving side. Most notably he scored 75 and had match figures of 8-106 against Essex in August. He was awarded his county cap.

	Own Team Total	O	M	R	W		Opp Total	Ct
75. Hampshire v Somerset, Southampton, May 6, 7, 8 (Match drawn)								
c and b V.J.Marks	10 299-8d	29	9	62	3	B.C.Rose lbw	255	1
						I.T.Botham c R.J.Parks		
						V.J.Marks c C.G.Greenidge		
did not bat	- 7-0							

76. Hampshire v Leicestershire, Leicester, May 27, 28, 29 (Match drawn)

innings forfeit			19	10	57	6	B.F.Davison c R.J.Parks	224
							N.E.Briers c N.E.J.Pocock	
							R.W.Tolchard lbw	
							J.P.Agnew c R.J.Parks	
							A.M.E.Roberts b	
							L.B.Taylor b	
c D.I.Gower b L.B.Taylor	33	160-9	-	-	-	-		23-0

77. Hampshire v Middlesex, Basingstoke, June 3, 4, 5 (Match drawn)

b M.W.W.Selvey	0	211	31	9	87	0	322-6d
c J.D.Monteith b W.W.Daniel	0	261					

78. Hampshire v Glamorgan, Bournemouth, June 10, (11), 12 (Hampshire won by five wickets)

innings forfeit			26	8	64	1	A.Jones c C.G.Greenidge	281-7d	
did not bat	-	301-5	-	-	-	-		17-3d	1

79. Hampshire v Worcestershire, Worcester, June 13, 15, 16 (Hampshire won by an innings and 28 runs)

c E.J.O.Hemsley								
b H.L.Alleyne	40	337	19.3	6	46	4	P.A.Neale c C.G.Greenidge	115
							E.J.O.Hemsley c R.J.Parks	
							D.N.Patel c T.E.Jesty	
							A.P.Pridgeon b	
			25	11	53	1	H.R.Alleyne c T.E.Jesty	194

80. Hampshire v Gloucestershire, Southampton, June 20, 22, 23 (Match drawn)

did not bat	-	349-3d	6	0	19	0		277-5d
did not bat	-	249-3d	20.3	10	39	2	B.C.Broad b	270-6
							Zaheer Abbas c D.R.Turner	

81. Hampshire v Lancashire, Old Trafford, June 27, 29, 30 (Hampshire won by two wickets)

did not bat	-	260-3d	27	9	82	4	A.Kennedy lbw	349-6d
							D.Lloyd c R.J.Parks	
							C.H.Lloyd c N.E.J.Pocock	
							B.W.Reidy lbw	
b P.J.W.Allott	15	213-8	14	5	24	0		123

82. Hampshire v Nottinghamshire, Bournemouth, July 4, 6, 7 (Hampshire won by nine wickets)

b C.E.B.Rice	8	190	20	9	32	4	R.E.Dexter c R.J.Parks	143	1
							J.D.Birch c R.J.Parks		
							R.J.Hadlee c and b		
							C.W.Scott c M.J.Bailey		
did not bat	-	53-1	16.2	2	64	5	R.E.Dexter c C.L.Smith	99	
							C.E.B.Rice c M.C.J.Nicholas		
							K.E.Cooper b		
							C.W.Scott c D.R.Turner		
							M.K.Bore c N.E.J.Pocock		

83. Hampshire v Derbyshire, Portsmouth, July 15, 16, 17 (Hampshire won by an innings and 32 runs)

not out	40	345-8d	21	10	27	1	M.Hendrick c R.J.Parks	104
			30	14	59	3	J.G.Wright c R.J.Parks	209
							P.N.Kirsten c R.J.Parks	
							A.Hill c C.G.Greenidge	

84. Hampshire v Surrey, Portsmouth, July 18, 20, 21 (Surrey won by 130 runs)

c S.T.Clarke b I.R.Payne	7	164	22.4	4	68	3	R.D.V.Knight c R.J.Parks	204
							D.M.Smith b	
							P.I.Pocock c C.G.Greenidge	
c D.M.Smith b R.D.Jackman	0	91	15.5	4	60	5	A.R.Butcher	
							c sub (V.P.Terry)	181
							D.M.Smith c C.G.Greenidge	
							I.R.Payne c sub (S.J.Malone)	
							C.J.Richards b	
							R.D.Jackman c T.E.Jesty	

85. Hampshire v Kent, Canterbury, August 1, 3, 4 (Kent won by 181 runs)

b G.W.Johnson	0	217	23	5	60	2	C.J.Tavare lbw	315	1
							E.A.E.Baptiste c and b		
c L.Potter b G.W.Johnson	20	122	15	4	34	3	M.R.Benson c K.Stevenson	205-7d	
							L.Potter lbw		
							C.S.Cowdrey c R.J.Parks		

86. Hampshire v Yorkshire, Middlesbrough, August (8), 10, 13 (Match drawn)

did not bat	-	150-0d	19	4	49	1	K.Sharp b	205-6d	2
not out	28	130-7	7	4	5	1	K.Sharp c M.J.Bailey	208-3d	

87. Hampshire v Gloucestershire, Cheltenham, August 12, 13, 14 (Gloucestershire won by an innings and 86 runs)

st A.W.Stovold b D.A.Graveney	9	174	17	4	51	0		381-7d
c D.A.Graveney b Sadiq Mohammad	29	121						

88. Hampshire v Essex, Southampton, August 15, 17, 18 (Hampshire won by 136 runs)

not out	75	340-7d	24	4	67	4	K.W.R.Fletcher c J.M.Rice K.R.Pont b D.R.Pringle b D.E.East lbw	279
run out	10	180-7d	11	3	39	4	B.R.Hardie b A.W.Lilley c R.J.Parks K.W.R.Fletcher c R.E.Hayward D.E.East c K.Stevenson	105

89. Hampshire v Somerset, Taunton, August 22, 24 (Somerset won by nine wickets)

c J.Garner b I.T.Botham	41	184	25	8	68	5	J.W.Lloyds c T.E.Jesty I.V.A.Richards c T.E.Jesty D.J.S.Taylor c R.J.Parks P.M.Roebuck b N.F.M.Popplewell c M.C.J.Nicholas	287
b J.Garner	2	120	-	-	-	-		21-1

90. Hampshire v Sussex, Bournemouth, August 26, 27, 28 (Sussex won by eight wickets)

b I.A.Greig	1	148	154.4	1	62	6	G.D.Mendis c R.J.Parks I.A.Greig c C.G.Greenidge Imran Khan c R.J.Parks G.G.Arnold c T.M.Tremlett C.E.Waller c T.M.Tremlett G.S.le Roux c R.J.Parks	237
lbw b G.S.le Roux	38	223	6	3	13	0		135-2

91. Hampshire v Sussex, Hove, September 2, 3, 4 (Sussex won by nine wickets)

c C.P.Phillipson b I.A.Greig	18	241	16	6	30	0		416-7d
c I.A.Greig b G.S.le Roux	1	196	-	-	-	-		24-1

SEASON'S AVERAGES

Batting and Fielding	M	I	NO	Runs	HS	Ave	100	50	Ct
County Championship	17	23	3	425	75*	21.25	-	1	6
Career	91	118	16	1792	75*	17.56	-	6	39

Bowling	O	M	R	W	BB	Ave	5i	10m
County Championship	531.3	166	1321	68	6-57	19.42	5	-
Career	2497.1	668	6422	340	7-56	18.88	19	1

1981/82 – Young West Indies in Zimbabwe

Marshall was selected to tour with the "Young West Indies" side, the first Caribbean team to tour Africa. His main achievement was his maiden first-class century, batting at number seven.

	Own Team Total	O	M	R	W		Opp Total	Ct

92. Young West Indies v Zimbabwe, Salisbury, October 9, 10, 12 (Young West Indies won by seven wickets)

st D.L.Houghton b A.J.Traicos	34	302	13	2	46	2	J.G.Heron c P.J.L.Dujon A.J.Traicos c P.J.L.Dujon	163
did not bat	-	63-3	6	1	16	0		201

93. Young West Indies v Zimbabwe, Bulawayo, October 16, 17, 19 (Match drawn)

c R.H.Kaschula b D.A.G.Fletcher	19	215	22	7	46	1	D.L.Houghton lbw	279
c D.L.Houghton b A.J.Pycroft	109	318-9d						

94. Young West Indies v Zimbabwe, Salisbury, October 23, 24, 26 (Match drawn)

c and b V.R.Hogg	13	214	16.4	2	39	4	T.W.Dunk lbw	194
							K.M.Curran c A.L.Logie	
							V.R.Hogg c M.A.Tucker	
did not bat	-	116-2	23	8	45	0	R.H.Kaschula b	
								255-5d

SEASON'S AVERAGES

Batting and Fielding	M	I	NO	Runs	HS	Ave	100	50	Ct
Other matches	3	4	0	175	109	43.75	1	-	-
Career	94	122	16	1967	109	18.55	1	6	39

Bowling	O	M	R	W	BB	Ave	5i	10m
Other matches	80.4	20	192	7	4-39	27.42	-	-
Career	2577.5	688	6614	347	7-56	19.06	19	1

1981/82 – West Indies in Australia

Marshall travelled to Australia from Zimbabwe and in two matches took 11 wickets at less than ten each. However his tour was blighted by a serious back injury and he played in none of the Test matches.

	Own Team Total	O	M	R	W		Opp Total	Ct

95. West Indians v South Australia, Adelaide, November 13, 14, 15, 16 (West Indians won by 226 runs)

c W.B.Phillips b G.Winter	0	294	10	2	23	3	W.M.Darling c C.G.Greenidge 79	
							W.B.Phillips b	
							K.J.Wright lbw	
run out	66	236-5d	12	3	29	3	D.W.Hookes c D.A.Murray 225	
							S.Parkinson c sub (P.J.L.Dujon)	
							D.Sayers b	

96. West Indians v Queensland, Brisbane, December 11, 12, 13, 14 (West Indians won by an innings and 92 runs)

did not bat	-	539-7d	18	8	31	5	A.D.Parker c P.J.L.Dujon 165	
							T.V.Hohns c C.H.Lloyd	
							H.K.deJong lbw	
							G.Dymock c P.J.L.Dujon	
							D.J.Lillie b	
			6	1	22	0		282

SEASON'S AVERAGES

Batting and Fielding	M	I	NO	Runs	HS	Ave	100	50	Ct
Other matches	2	2	0	66	66	33.00	-	1	-
Career	96	124	16	2033	109	18.82	1	7	39

Bowling	O	M	R	W	BB	Ave	5i	10m
Other matches	46	14	105	11	5-31	9.54	1	-
Career	2623.5	702	6719	358	7-56	18.76	20	1

1982

Marshall's injury prevented him appearing in any Shell Shield matches but, after treatment, he resumed his county career somewhat tentatively. By his own account he bowled quickly for the first time only after an altercation with Younis Ahmed in August but he had been taking wickets all season, including five or more in an innings seven times by the occasion of his 8-71 against Worcestershire (Younis c Tremlett b Marshall). These were the best figures of his career and he added four more five-wicket hauls in his total of 134 wickets, the first Hampshire bowler to 100 wickets in a season since Sainsbury in 1971. Only Leicestershire's Nick Cook bowled more than his 822 overs during 1982 and only four Hampshire bowlers have ever taken more wickets for the county in one season: 'Lofty' Herman, Kennedy, Newman and Shackleton. He also scored his first century for the county in a ten-wicket win over Lancashire and was chosen as one of *Wisden*'s Cricketers of the Year (*Wisden* 1983). Hampshire finished in third place in the Championship.

	Own Team / Total	O	M	R	W		Opp / Total	Ct
97. Hampshire v Leicestershire, Southampton, May 5, 6, 7 (Match drawn)								
b L.B.Taylor	15 301-9d	20	6	56	2	J.C.Balderstone		
						c R.E.Hayward	281	
						N.E.Briers c R.J.Parks		
did not bat	- 81-1	21.4	6	44	0		214	1
98. Hampshire v Nottinghamshire, Trent Bridge, May 19, 20, 21 (Nottinghamshire won by 272 runs)								
lbw b R.J.Hadlee	9 70	23	6	53	3	R.T.Robinson c M.C.J.Nicholas	180	
						P.A.Todd c R.J.Parks		
						E.E.Hemmings c T.E.Jesty		
b M.Hendrick	17 56	24	5	52	1	M.A.Fell b	218-5d	
99. Hampshire v Kent, Bournemouth, June 2, 3, 4 (Kent won by six wickets)								
b E.A.E.Baptiste	14 158	31.2	10	84	5	R.A.Woolmer lbw	274	
						L.Potter b		
						S.G.Hinks c T.M.Tremlett		
						A.P.E.Knott c K.St.J.D.Emery		
						E.A.E.Baptiste lbw		
c N.R.Taylor								
b E.A.E.Baptiste	32 221	4	1	9	1	N.R.Taylor c R.J.Parks	106-4	
100. Hampshire v Surrey, Kennington Oval, June 5, 7, 8 (Hampshire won by 3 runs)								
c C.J.Richards								
b R.D.Jackman	25 148	20	7	38	3	G.S.Clinton lbw	214	
						R.D.V.Knight c N.G.Cowley		
						G.P.Howarth lbw		
c G.S.Clinton b D.J.Thomas	24 170	20.1	6	38	7	A.R.Butcher c T.M.Tremlett	101	
						G.S.Clinton c R.J.Parks		
						R.D.V.Knight lbw		
						G.P.Howarth lbw		
						G.R.J.Roope c R.J.Parks		
						D.J.Thomas c N.E.J.Pocock		
						S.T.Clarke c N.E.J.Pocock		
101. Hampshire v Lancashire, Southampton, June 9, 10, 11 (Hampshire won by ten wickets)								
not out	116 458-8d	18.1	7	48	5	G.Fowler c N.E.J.Pocock	210	
						C.H.Lloyd c J.W.Southern		
						D.Lloyd c J.M.Rice		
						J.Abrahams b		
						J.Simmons c J.M.Rice		
did not bat	- 115-0	32	9	108	3	G.Fowler c T.M.Tremlett	359	
						J.Abrahams b		
						C.H.Lloyd lbw		
102. Hampshire v Somerset, Bath, June 19, 21, 22 (Match drawn)								
c D.J.S.Taylor								
b I.V.A.Richards	14 259	25.1	8	71	3	P.M.Roebuck lbw	248	
						I.V.A.Richards lbw		
						N.F.M.Popplewell lbw		
did not bat	- 85-1							
103. Hampshire v Sussex, Basingstoke, June (23), 24, (25) (Match drawn)								
did not bat	- 202-2d	16	3	42	4	J.R.P.Heath lbw	106-6d	
						C.M.Wells lbw		
						P.W.G.Parker c M.C.J.Nicholas		
						G.S.le Roux c R.J.Parks		
did not bat	- 8-1							
104. Hampshire v Gloucestershire, Bristol, June 26, 28, 29 (Gloucestershire won by four wickets)								
innings forfeit							innings forfeit	
c P.Bainbridge								
b F.D.Stephenson	21 99	10	2	39	1	F.D.Stephenson lbw	101-6	

105. Hampshire v Kent, Maidstone, July 3, 5, 6 (Hampshire won by 45 runs)
c A.P.E.Knott b K.B.S.Jarvis 10   179   27.5   9   55   6   N.R.Taylor c J.M.Rice   181
                                                                C.J.Tavare c R.J.Parks
                                                                A.P.E.Knott c R.J.Parks
                                                                G.W.Johnson c R.J.Parks
                                                                G.R.Dilley c R.J.Parks
c A.P.E.Knott   K.B.S.Jarvis b
   b D.L.Underwood   22   283   21   5   54   4   C.J.Tavare c N.E.J.Pocock   236   1
                                                     C.S.Cowdrey c R.J.Parks
                                                     A.P.E.Knott lbw
                                                     G.W.Johnson lbw

106. Hampshire v Glamorgan, Cardiff, July 10, (12), 13 (Hampshire won by 116 runs)
b M.A.Nash   10   270   8   4   8   1   D.A.Francis b   54-2d
did not bat   -   70-0   19   6   46   2   R.C.Ontong c R.J.Parks   170
                                                     T.Davies lbw

107. Hampshire v Surrey, Portsmouth, July 17, 19, 20 (Surrey won by two wickets)
b D.J.Thomas   7   251-9d   23.2 9   66   1   D.M.Smith lbw   343-7d
b R.D.Jackman   20   221   16.3 1   64   4   A.R.Butcher c R.J.Parks   131-8
                                                      D.M.Smith b
                                                      C.J.Richards c R.J.Parks
                                                      D.J.Thomas c R.J.Parks

108. Hampshire v Glamorgan, Portsmouth, July 21, 22, 23 (Hampshire won by an innings and 78 runs)
did not bat   -   435-2d   19   2   41   1   D.A.Francis c R.J.Parks   164
                                    24   7   43   1   R.C.Ontong c J.M.Rice   193

109. Hampshire v Somerset, Bournemouth, July 31, August 2 (Hampshire won by 10 runs)
c C.H.Dredge b J.Garner 0   119   19   5   47   3   P.M.Roebuck
                                                      c M.C.J.Nicholas   194
                                                      N.A.Felton c R.J.Parks
                                                      M.R.Davis c C.G.Greenidge
b C.H.Dredge   25   157   16   3   37   5   P.M.Roebuck b   72
                                                      B.C.Rose c J.M.Rice
                                                      P.W.Denning lbw
                                                      D.J.S.Taylor c T.M.Tremlett
                                                      C.H.Dredge c R.J.Parks

110. Hampshire v Sussex, Eastbourne, August 7, 9, 10 (Match drawn)
b I.A.Greig   19   160   33   16   48   7   G.D.Mendis c C.G.Greenidge 230   1
                                                      C.M.Wells c R.J.Parks
                                                      P.W.G.Parker c C.G.Greenidge
                                                      J.R.T.Barclay lbw
                                                      C.P.Phillipson lbw
                                                      G.S.le Roux lbw
                                                      I.A.Greig c and b
b G.S.le Roux   42   240   19   5   59   4   G.D.Mendis lbw   122-8
                                                      A.M.Green b
                                                      P.W.G.Parker c N.E.J.Pocock
                                                      I.J.Gould b

111. Hampshire v Essex, Chelmsford, August 11, 12, 13 (Match drawn)
c J.K.Lever b N.Phillip 5   351   14   4   54   3   K.R.Pont c N.E.J.Pocock   230
                                                      S.Turner c C.G.Greenidge
                                                      R.E.East c T.M.Tremlett
did not bat   -   75-2   28   5   103 6   G.A.Gooch c R.J.Parks   261
                                                      K.R.Pont c R.J.Parks
                                                      S.Turner c C.G.Greenidge
                                                      D.E.East lbw
                                                      R.E.East c N.E.J.Pocock
                                                      J.K.Lever c T.E.Jesty

112. Hampshire v Worcestershire, Southampton, August 14, 16, 17 (Worcestershire won by one wicket)
c D.N.Patel b A.P.Pridgeon 44   259   22.5 7   71   8   M.J.Weston c R.J.Parks   167
                                                          J.A.Ormrod lbw
                                                          D.N.Patel c R.J.Parks
                                                          Younis Ahmed c T.M.Tremlett
                                                          T.S.Curtis c M.C.J.Nicholas
                                                          D.J.Humphries c R.J.Parks
                                                          A.P.Pridgeon b
                                                          S.P.Perryman c C.G.Greenidge

| did not bat | - | 191-3d | 24 | 8 | 57 | 3 | J.A.Ormrod lbw | 286-9 |

Younis Ahmed c N.E.J.Pocock
D.J.Humphries b

113. Hampshire v Northamptonshire, Northampton, August 21, 23, 24 (Match drawn)

| c R.J.Boyd-Moss b P.Willey | 1 | 268 | 28 | 4 | 84 | 2 | G.Cook lbw | 377-8d |

R.J.Boyd-Moss c M.C.J.Nicholas

| did not bat | - | 0-1 | | | | | | |

114. Hampshire v Gloucestershire, Bournemouth, August 25, 26, 27 (Hampshire won by eight wickets)

| b D.A.Graveney | 54 | 294 | 16 | 1 | 48 | 3 | B.Dudleston lbw | 272 |

J.N.Shepherd b
F.D.Stephenson lbw

| did not bat | - | 64-2 | 13 | 5 | 33 | 5 | B.Dudleston b | 84 | 1 |

A.J.Hignell lbw
A.J.Brassington b
A.J.Wright c N.E.J.Pocock
F.D.Stephenson c R.J.Parks

115. Hampshire v Yorkshire, Bournemouth, August 28, 30, 31 (Match drawn)

| st D.L.Bairstow b P.Carrick | 0 | 255 | 32 | 13 | 41 | 6 | C.W.J.Athey lbw | 196 |

S.N.Hartley c J.M.Rice
D.L.Bairstow lbw
P.Carrick b
A.Sidebottom lbw
C.M.Old b

| c A.Sidebottom b P.Carrick | 1 | 167-8d | 17 | 1 | 44 | 2 | G.Boycott lbw | 217-8 |

C.M.Old c N.E.J.Pocock

116. Hampshire v Derbyshire, Derby, September 1, 2, 3 (Match drawn)

| c R.W.Taylor b D.G.Moir | 6 | 225-9d | 29 | 9 | 60 | 6 | B.Wood b | 209 |

J.G.Wright lbw
J.H.Hampshire c T.E.Jesty
K.J.Barnett b
R.W.Taylor b
C.J.Tunnicliffe b

| not out | 0 | 179-5 | 10 | 2 | 21 | 0 | | 296-4d |

117. Hampshire v Middlesex, Uxbridge, September 8, 9, 10 (Middlesex won by 106 runs)

c J.M.Brearley

| b P.H.Edmonds | 29 | 178 | 20 | 3 | 67 | 4 | W.N.Slack c D.R.Turner | 207 |

R.G.P.Ellis b
M.W.Gatting c T.E.Jesty
J.E.Emburey lbw

c J.M.Brearley

| b P.H.Edmonds | 9 | 138 | 17 | 5 | 48 | 3 | W.N.Slack c J.M.Rice | 215 |

P.H.Edmonds lbw
N.G.Cowans b

118. Hampshire v Warwickshire, Southampton, September 11, 12, 14 (Hampshire won by 37 runs)

| c K.D.Smith b Asif Din | 14 | 306 | 26 | 8 | 74 | 5 | T.A.Lloyd b | 191 |

K.D.Smith c N.E.J.Pocock
D.L.Amiss lbw
Asif Din b
C.Lethbridge b

| not out | 28 | 261-4d | 17 | 2 | 53 | 1 | A.M.Ferreira b | 339 |

SEASON'S AVERAGES

Batting and Fielding	M	I	NO	Runs	HS	Ave	100	50	Ct
County Championship	22	31	3	633	116*	22.60	1	1	4
Career	118	155	19	2666	116*	19.60	2	8	43

Bowling	O	M	R	W	BB	Ave	5i	10m
County Championship	822	225	2108	134	8-71	15.73	12	4
Career	3445.5	927	8827	492	8-71	17.94	32	5

1982/83

Marshall appeared in the Test side for all five matches against India and took five wickets in an innings for the first time in the Trinidad Test. West Indies won the series 2-0 and Marshall took 42 wickets in the domestic season.

	Own Team Total	O	M	R	W		Opp Total	Ct

119. West Indies XI v Jamaican International XI, Kingston, September 25, 26, 27, (28) (Match drawn)
c sub (O.W.Peters)

b E.E.Hemmings	40 419	15	3	25	1	R.O.Butcher c P.J.L.Dujon	262	

120. Barbados v Leeward Islands, Bridgetown, January 21, 22, 23, 24 (Barbados won by 56 runs)

b E.A.E.Baptiste	3 242	16	2	57	1	A.L.Kelly lbw	253	2
b E.A.E.Baptiste	71 256	17	5	36	0		189	1

121. Barbados v Jamaica, Kingston, January 28, 29, 30, 31 (Barbados won by nine wickets)
st P.J.L.Dujon

b M.A.Tucker	35 435-8d	17.2	4	49	4	G.Powell c H.L.Alleyne	234	
						O.W.Peters c C.G.Greenidge		
						C.W.Fletcher lbw		
						C.A.Walsh b		
did not bat	- 55-1	18	4	46	3	C.W.Fletcher c R.L.Skeete	255	1
						O.W.Peters lbw		
						R.C.Haynes c W.W.Daniel		

122. Barbados v Guyana, Bridgetown, February 4, 5, 6, 7 (Match drawn)

c A.A.Lyght b L.A.Lambert	34 403	15	3	51	2	T.R.Etwaroo c L.N.Reifer	230	
						S.F.A.F.Bacchus c R.L.Skeete		
did not bat	- 132-4	26.4	5	86	2	L.A.Lambert lbw	420	
						R.F.Joseph c C.A.Best		

123. Barbados v Windward Islands, Kingstown, February 11, 12, 13, 14 (Windward Islands won by four wickets)

c L.D.John b N.F.Williams	2 243	30	9	68	1	A.D.Tesheira c T.R.O.Payne	307	
lbw b N.F.Williams	36 196	13	0	58	3	W.N.Slack c R.L.Skeete	134-6	
						L.D.John b		
						S.W.Julien c R.L.Skeete		

124. WEST INDIES v INDIA, Kingston, February 23, 24, 26, (27), 28 (West Indies won by four wickets)
c Yashpal Sharma

b Kapil Dev	23 254	16	4	35	2	S.M.Gavaskar c P.J.L.Dujon	251	1
						S.M.H.Kirmani c P.J.L.Dujon		
not out	0 173-6	24	6	56	3	A.D.Gaekwad		
						c C.G.Greenidge	174	
						M.Amarnath c J.Garner		
						D.B.Vengsarkar c J.Garner		

125. WEST INDIES v INDIA, Port of Spain, March 11, 12, 13, 15, 16 (Match drawn)

lbw b R.J.Shastri	14 394	19.1	6	37	5	D.B.Vengsarkar		
						c M.A.Holding	175	
						R.J.Shastri c H.A.Gomes		
						Kapil Dev c D.L.Haynes		
						B.S.Sandu c I.V.A.Richards		
						Maninder Singh c P.J.L.Dujon		
		27.1	8	72	0		469-7	

126. Barbados v Trinidad & Tobago, Port of Spain, March 19, 20, 21, 22 (Barbados won by 19 runs)

b G.Mahabir	0 212	13.2	4	22	2	D.Williams c C.A.Best	153	
						G.Mahabir c C.A.Best		
b G.Mahabir	28 204	30	10	52	2	D.Williams b	244	
						S.Jumadeen b		

127. WEST INDIES v INDIA, Georgetown, March 31, April (2), 3, (4), 5 (Match drawn)

lbw b Kapil Dev	27 470	13	2	39	1	M.Amarnath		
						c I.V.A.Richards	284-3	

128. WEST INDIES v INDIA, Bridgetown, April 15, 16, 17, 19, 20 (West Indies won by ten wickets)
c S.Venkataraghavan

b Kapil Dev	8 486	13	1	56	2	M.Amarnath c P.J.L.Dujon	209	2
						Kapil Dev c C.H.Lloyd		
did not bat	- 1-0	16	1	80	2	R.J.Shastri c C.H.Lloyd	277	
						Kapil Dev c C.H.Lloyd		

129. WEST INDIES v INDIA, St John's, April 28, 29, 30 May 1, 2 (Match drawn)

							Opp
b S.Venkataraghavan	2	550	27.5	5	87	4	S.M.Gavaskar c P.J.L.Dujon 457
							D.B.Vengsarkar c W.W.Davis
							L..Sivaramakrishnan c sub
							S.Venkataraghavan b
		18	7	33	2		A.D.Gaekwad lbw 247-5d
							D.B.Vengsarkar c P.J.L.Dujon

SEASON'S AVERAGES

Batting and Fielding	M	I	NO	Runs	HS	Ave	100	50	Ct
Test matches	5	6	1	74	27	14.80	-	-	3
Shell Shield	5	8	0	209	71	26.12	-	1	4
Other matches	1	1	0	40	40	40.00	-	-	-
Season	11	15	1	323	71	23.07	-	1	7
Career	129	170	20	2989	116*	19.92	2	9	50

Bowling	O	M	R	W	BB	Ave	5i	10m
Test matches	174.1	40	495	21	5-37	23.57	1	-
Shell Shield	196.2	46	525	20	4-49	26.25	-	-
Other matches	15	3	25	1	1-25	25.00	-	-
Season	385.3	89	1045	42	5-37	24.88	1	-
Career	3831.2	1016	9872	534	8-71	18.48	33	5

1983

Marshall resumed his Hampshire career in May but after three matches joined the West Indies party for the third World Cup. As expected they reached their third final but India surprised everyone by winning a low-scoring final. Marshall's disappointment did not affect his return to Hampshire where he added two centuries to an average of five wickets per match. Hampshire again finished third.

	Own Team Total	O	M	R	W		Opp Total	Ct
130. Hampshire v Warwickshire, Southampton, May (11), (12), 13 (Hampshire won by 9 runs)								
run out	79 216-6d	19	4	61	1	R.G.D.Willis c T.M.Tremlett	207	
131. Hampshire v Worcestershire, Southampton, May 25, 26, 27 (Hampshire won by seven wickets)								
c J.A.Ormrod						D.J.Humphries		
b J.D.Inchmore	39 235	21	6	39	3	c M.C.J.Nicholas	237	1
						R.K.Illingworth c R.J.Parks		
						A.E.Warner lbw		
did not bat	- 202-3	24	7	58	6	J.A.Ormrod c R.J.Parks	197	2
						P.A.Neale lbw		
						C.L.King c M.C.J.Nicholas		
						D.J.Humphries b		
						R.K.Illingworth c R.J.Parks		
						A.E.Warner c and b		
132. Hampshire v Kent, Canterbury, May (28), 30, 31 (Match drawn)							innings forfeit	
b G.W.Johnson	15 228						243-5	
did not bat	- 125-2d	14	8	16	0			
133. Hampshire v Lancashire, Liverpool, July 2, 4, 5 (Match drawn)						S.J.O'Shaughnessy b	305-7d	
not out	26 323-6d	21	4	60	2	J.Simmons lbw		
did not bat	- 246-1d	22	3	64	5	G.Fowler c J.W.Southern	138-8	
						D.P.Hughes c V.P.Terry		
						J.Abrahams c C.G.Greenidge		
						C.Maynard c N.E.J.Pocock		
						N.V.Radford c R.J.Parks		
134. Hampshire v Surrey, Southampton, July 9, 11, 12 (Match drawn)						D.B.Pauline b	339-6d	
not out	100 371-6d	11	4	20	2	D.M.Smith lbw		
did not bat	- 309-4d	10	4	25	1	D.B.Pauline lbw	177-5	1

135. Hampshire v Essex, Southend-on-Sea, July 13, 14, 15 (Hampshire won by four wickets)

c R.E.East b S.Turner   6   136   28.2   6   73   6   B.R.Hardie c M.C.J.Nicholas 202   1
K.S.McEwan c M.C.J.Nicholas
K.R.Pont c and b
N.Phillip c N.E.J.Pocock
R.E.East c N.E.J.Pocock
D.L.Acfield c V.P.Terry
not out   4   410-6   17   4   51   4   G.A.Gooch b   340-6d
B.R.Hardie c R.J.Parks
K.W.R.Fletcher b
K.R.Pont c C.G.Greenidge

136. Hampshire v Nottinghamshire, Bournemouth, July 16, 18, 19 (Hampshire won by eight wickets)

c M.K.Bore b M.Hendrick   15   404-6d   31   10   70   4   S.B.Hassan c C.G.Greenidge 233
E.E.Hemmings lbw
B.N.French c R.J.Parks
K.Saxelby c T.M.Tremlett
did not bat   -   68-2   20   4   46   3   S.B.Hassan c C.G.Greenidge 238   1
R.A.Pick b
M.K.Bore lbw

137. Hampshire v Derbyshire, Portsmouth, July 27, 28, 29 (Hampshire won by six wickets)

did not bat   -   250-4d   28   8   66   4   I.S.Anderson lbw   319
A.Hill c T.M.Tremlett
W.P.Fowler b
S.Oldham b
did not bat   -   260-4   14   2   47   1   C.J.Tunnicliffe
c C.G.Greenidge   188

138. Hampshire v Gloucestershire, Portsmouth, July 30, August 1, 2 (Match drawn)

did not bat   -   362-4d   12   4   29   3   B.C.Broad lbw   153
P.Bainbridge c T.M.Tremlett
S.Oldham b
32   10   107   2   B.C.Broad c C.G.Greenidge 306
P.Bainbridge b

139. Hampshire v Sussex, Eastbourne, August 10, 11, 12 (Hampshire won by three wickets)

not out   26   250-6d   26   5   58   4   G.D.Mendis b   263
R.S.Cowan c R.J.Parks
C.M.Wells c D.R.Turner
J.R.T.Barclay c C.G.Greenidge
c Imran Khan b C.E.Waller   13   285-7   9   2   23   0   269-7d

140. Hampshire v Nottinghamshire, Trent Bridge, August 13, 15, 16 (Match drawn)

c B.N.French b K.E.Cooper   17   194   25   5   55   2   D.W.Randall c R.J.Parks 239
B.N.French lbw
c M.Hendrick b K.E.Cooper   19   243-9d   4   0   9   0   28-0

141. Hampshire v Worcestershire, Worcester, August 20, 21, 22 (Hampshire won by an innings and 44 runs)

c J.A.Ormrod
b S.P.Perryman   37   365   13   3   34   1   J.A.Ormrod c R.J.Parks   175
19   10   24   3   J.A.Ormrod lbw   146
M.S.A.McEvoy lbw
D.N.Patel c T.M.Tremlett

142. Hampshire v Somerset, Bournemouth, August 24, 25 (Hampshire won by ten wickets)

c P.W.Denning
b J.W.Lloyds   50   211   13.3   4   29   7   J.W.Lloyds c T.E.Jesty   76
R.L.Ollis c R.J.Parks
P.W.Denning c R.J.Parks
P.A.Slocombe b
T.Gard c D.R.Turner
C.H.Dredge c R.J.Parks
S.C.Booth c N.E.J.Pocock
did not bat   -   39-0   17   4   49   2   R.L.Ollis c R.J.Parks   173
I.V.A.Richards c C.G.Greenidge

143. Hampshire v Kent, Bournemouth, August 27, 29, 30 (Hampshire won by eight wickets)

c D.G.Aslett
b D.L.Underwood   112   359   17   6   33   3   G.W.Johnson c V.P.Terry   162
D.L.Underwood hit wkt
K.D.Masters c C.G.Greenidge
did not bat   -   125-2   20   4   51   3   R.A.Woolmer lbw   319
A.P.E.Knott c V.P.Terry
G.W.Johnson lbw

144. Hampshire v Somerset, Taunton, August 31, September 1, 2 (Match drawn)

		O	M	R	W		Own/Opp Total
did not bat	- 253-3d	7	0	31	0		321-6d
did not bat	- 41-1	12	1	46	6	J.W.Lloyds c V.P.Terry	86
						J.G.Wyatt b	
						P.W.Denning c C.L.Smith	
						V.J.Marks c C.G.Greenidge	
						M.R.Davis b	
						S.C.Booth b	

145. Hampshire v Glamorgan, Southampton, September 10, 12, 13 (Match drawn)

		O	M	R	W		Total
lbw b M.W.W.Selvey	5 251-6d	18	7	44	1	M.W.W.Selvey c T.E.Jesty	252
		8	4	9	1	A.Jones b	76-2

SEASON'S AVERAGES

Batting and Fielding	M	I	NO	Runs	HS	Ave	100	50	Ct
County Championship	16	16	4	563	112	46.91	2	2	6
Career	145	186	24	3552	116*	21.92	4	11	56

Bowling	O	M	R	W	BB	Ave	5i	10m
County Championship	532.5	143	1327	80	7-29	16.58	5	1
Career	4364.1	1159	11199	614	8-71	18.23	38	6

1983/84 – West Indies in India

Marshall gave a masterful performance in the first Test at Kanpur. He made his highest Test score and at one stage had figures of 8-5-9-4 as India collapsed to an innings defeat. He also led the victory effort in the fifth Test as West Indies avenged the World Cup defeat. For the first time, Marshall opened the bowling throughout a series and justified the decision with 33 wickets.

	Own Team Total	O	M	R	W		Opp Total	Ct
146. West Indians v South Zone, Hyderabad, October 8, 9, 10 (Match drawn)								
did not bat	- 367-4d	13	5	20	1	M.Srinivaz Prasad b	175	
c C.S.Sureshkuma								
b N.S.Yadav	61 170-6							
147. WEST INDIES v INDIA, Kanpur, October 21, 22, 23, 25 (West Indies won by an innings and 83 runs)								
c and b Kapil Dev	92 454	15	7	19	4	S.M.Gavaskar c P.J.L.Dujon	207	
						A.D.Gaekwad c P.J.L.Dujon		
						M.Amarnath lbw		
						D.B.Vengsarkar b		
		17	7	47	4	S.M.Gavaskar c W.W.Davis	164	
						A.D.Gaekwad c I.V.A.Richards		
						R.M.H.Binny c P.J.L.Dujon		
						D.B.Vengsarkar c W.W.Davis		
148. WEST INDIES v INDIA, Delhi, October 29, 30 November 1, 2 (Match drawn)								
b Kapil Dev	17 384	24	1	105	1	Kapil Dev c C.H.Lloyd	464	
did not bat	- 120-2	18	4	52	3	D.B.Vengsarkar b	233	
						M.Amarnath c W.W.Davis		
						Kapil Dev c H.A.Gomes		
149. WEST INDIES v INDIA, Ahmedabad, November 12, 13, 14, 16 (West Indies won by 138 runs)								
b Maninder Singh	10 281	26	9	66	1	S.M.Patil c P.J.L.Dujon	241	
c sub b Kapil Dev	29 201	13	3	23	2	S.M.Patil c W.W.Daniel	103	
						Kirti Azad b		
150. WEST INDIES v INDIA, Bombay, November 24, 26, 27, 28, 29 (Match drawn)								
c S.M.Gavaskar b N.S.Yadav	4 393	32	6	88	3	S.M.Gavaskar lbw	463	
						R.M.H.Binny lbw		
						S.Madan Lal lbw		
did not bat	- 104-4	13	3	47	1	S.M.Gavaskar c W.W.Davis	173-5d	
151. WEST INDIES v INDIA, Calcutta, December 10, 11, 12, 14 (West Indies won by an innings and 46 runs)								
lbw b Maninder Singh	54 377	22	7	65	3	S.M.Gavaskar c P.J.L.Dujon	241	1
						A.D.Gaekwad b		
						M.Amarnath c and b		

```
        15    4    37    6    D.B.Vengsarkar  lbw              90
                             N.S.Yadav  b
                             A.Malhotra  c P.J.L.Dujon
                             R.J.Shastri  b
                             R.M.H.Binny  c R.A.Harper
                             Kapil Dev  c P.J.L.Dujon
152. WEST INDIES v INDIA, Madras, December (24), 26, 27, 28, 29 (Match drawn)
   b Kapil Dev       38  313   26   8   72   5   A.D.Gaekwad  c R.A.Harper    451-8d
                                                D.B.Vengsarkar  c R.A.Harper
                                                N.S.Yadav  c P.J.L.Dujon
                                                R.M.H.Binny
                                                      c sub (R.B.Richardson)
   did not bat            -   64-1               Kapil Dev  c sub (R.B.Richardson)
```

SEASON'S AVERAGES

Batting and Fielding	M	I	NO	Runs	HS	Ave	100	50	Ct
Test matches	6	7	0	244	92	34.85	-	2	1
Other matches	1	1	0	61	61	61.00	-	1	-
Tour	7	8	0	305	92	38.12	-	3	1
Career	152	194	24	3857	116*	22.68	4	14	57

Bowling	O	M	R	W	BB	Ave	5i	10m
Test matches	221	59	621	33	6-37	18.81	2	-
Other matches	13	5	20	1	1-20	20.00	-	-
Tour	234	64	641	34	6-37	18.85	2	-
Career	4598.1	1223	11840	648	8-71	18.27	40	6

1983/84

Marshall missed the first Test with an injured knee and unusually for the period the West Indies chose just three pace bowlers. The match was drawn but Marshall returned for the remaining four Tests which were dominated by the home side. Only Allan Border consistently resisted the efforts of Marshall (21 wickets) and Garner (31 wickets).

```
                      Own Team    O    M    R    W                           Opp     Ct
                        Total                                                 Total
153. WEST INDIES v AUSTRALIA, Port of Spain, March 16, 17, 18, 20, 21 (Match drawn)
   lbw b G.F.Lawson   10  468-8d  19   4   73   0                             255     1
                                  22   3   73   2   K.J.Hughes  lbw           299
                                                    G.F.Lawson  b

154. WEST INDIES v AUSTRALIA, Bridgetown, March 30, 31, April 1, 3, 4 (West Indies won by ten wickets)
   b R.M.Hogg         10  509     26   2   83   2   S.B.Smith  c P.J.L.Dujon  429
                                                    A.R.Border  c R.B.Richardson
   did not bat         -  21-0   15.5   1   42   5   S.B.Smith  b              97
                                                    G.M.Ritchie  c D.L.Haynes
                                                    W.B.Phillips  b
                                                    G.F.Lawson  c R.A.Harper
                                                    T.M.Alderman  b

155. WEST INDIES v AUSTRALIA, St John's, April 7, 8, 9, 11 (West Indies won by an innings and 36 runs)
   c D.W.Hookes b J.N.Maguire 6  498  18  2  70  1  G.M.Ritchie  c M.A.Holding  262   1
                                      17  5  51  3  K.J.Hughes  c I.V.A.Richards 200
                                                    R.D.Woolley  lbw
                                                    J.N.Maguire  b

156. WEST INDIES v AUSTRALIA, Kingston, April 28, 29, 30, May 2 (West Indies won by ten wickets)
   c D.W.Hookes
     b J.N.Maguire   19  305     18   4   37   3   S.B.Smith  c C.G.Greenidge  199
                                                   A.R.Border  c P.J.L.Dujon
                                                   G.M.Ritchie  c P.J.L.Dujon
```

did not bat   -   55-0   23   3   51   5   K.J.Hughes c C.G.Greenidge 160
D.W.Hookes c P.J.L.Dujon
T.G.Hogan b
G.F.Lawson b
R.M.Hogg b

SEASON'S AVERAGES

Batting and Fielding	M	I	NO	Runs	HS	Ave	100	50	Ct
Test matches	4	4	0	45	19	11.25	-	-	2
Career	156	198	24	3902	116*	22.42	4	14	59

Bowling	O	M	R	W	BB	Ave	5i	10m
Test matches	158.5	24	480	21	5-42	22.85	2	-
Career	4757	1247	12320	669	8-71	18.41	42	6

1984 – West Indies in England

Elvis Reifer replaced Marshall as Hampshire's overseas bowler while Marshall toured with West Indies. They demolished the home side by 5-0, known colloquially as the first 'Blackwash'. Marshall was magnificent throughout, not least at Leeds where he batted with a broken hand to enable Gomes to reach his century. Ignoring the injury he then recorded his best Test figures of 7-53 as England lost their last eight wickets for 49 runs.

	Own Team Total	O	M	R	W		Opp Total	Ct

157. West Indians v Somerset, Taunton, May 23, 24, 25 (West Indians won by an innings and 101 runs)
c N.F.M.Popplewell
b P.H.L.Wilson   34   342   11   4   13   2   P.M.Roebuck c M.A.Small   116
J.W.Lloyds c P.J.L.Dujon
19.2   7   31   5   J.G.Wyatt c R.B.Richardson   125
N.F.M.Popplewell c C.H.Lloyd
M.D.Crowe b
C.H.Dredge c P.J.L.Dujon
P.H.L.Wilson b

158. West Indians v Northamptonshire, Bletchley, June 9, 10, 11 (Match drawn)
c R.W.Hanley b D.S.Steele   15   268   17.4   4   36   4   R.G.Williams c C.H.Lloyd   220   1
D.Ripley b
R.W.Hanley lbw
B.J.Griffiths b
did not bat   -   50-0   15   4   36   0   220-5d

159. WEST INDIES v ENGLAND, Edgbaston, June 14, 15, 16, 18 (West Indies won by an innings and 180 runs)
lbw b D.R.Pringle   2   606   14   4   37   1   N.G.B.Cook c C.H.Lloyd   191
23   7   65   2   A.J.Lamb c I.V.A.Richards   235
G.Miller c R.A.Harper

160. WEST INDIES v ENGLAND, Lord's, June 28, 29, 30, July 2, 3 (West Indies won by nine wickets)
c D.R.Pringle
b R.G.D.Willis   29   245   36.5   10   85   6   B.C.Broad c P.J.L.Dujon   286
D.I.Gower lbw
A.J.Lamb lbw
M.W.Gatting lbw
N.A.Foster c R.A.Harper
R.G.D.Willis b
did not bat   -   344-1   22   6   85   2   A.J.Lamb c P.J.L.Dujon   300-9d
M.W.Gatting lbw

161. West Indians v Leicestershire, Leicester, July 7, 8, 9 (Match drawn)
did not bat   -   506-5d   10   3   28   2   J.J.Whitaker c and b   283
P.Willey b
-    -   -   -   136-5

162. WEST INDIES v ENGLAND, Headingley, July 12, 13, 14, 16 (West Indies won by eight wickets)
c I.T.Botham b P.J.W.Allott   4   302   6   4   6   0   270

did not bat   - 131-2   26   9   53   7   G.Fowler c and b   159   1
B.C.Broad c E.A.E.Baptiste
D.I.Gower lbw
P.R.Downton c P.J.L.Dujon
D.R.Pringle lbw
P.J.W.Allott lbw
N.G.B.Cook c C.H.Lloyd

163. West Indians v Middlesex, Lord's, August 4, 5, 6 (Match drawn)
    c R.O.Butcher b N.G.Cowans 7 211   9   2   34   1   K.P.Tomlins c D.L.Haynes   177-4d
    lbw b J.E.Emburey   0 224-6d 11   1   31   2   G.D.Barlow c R.A.Harper   87-2
                                     K.P.Tomlins b

164. WEST INDIES v ENGLAND, Kennington Oval, August 9, 10, 11, 13, 14 (West Indies won by 172 runs)
    c D.I.Gower b R.M.Ellison 0 190   17.5   5   35   5   P.I.Pocock c C.G.Greenidge 162
                                       A.J.Lamb lbw
                                       I.T.Botham c P.J.L.Dujon
                                       P.J.W.Allott b
                                       J.P.Agnew b
    c A.J.Lamb b I.T.Botham 12 346   22   5   71   1   G.Fowler c I.V.A.Richards 202   1

SEASON'S AVERAGES

Batting and Fielding	M	I	NO	Runs	HS	Ave	100	50	Ct
Test matches	4	5	0	47	29	9.40	-	-	2
Other matches	4	4	0	56	34	14.00	-	-	1
Tour	8	9	0	103	34	11.44	-	-	3
Career	164	207	24	4005	116*	21.88	4	14	62

Bowling	O	M	R	W	BB	Ave	5i	10m
Test matches	167.4	50	437	24	7-53	18.20	3	-
Other matches	93	25	209	16	5-31	13.06	1	-
Tour	260.4	75	646	40	7-53	16.15	4	-
Career	5017.4	1322	12966	709	8-71	18.28	46	6

1984/85 – West Indies in Australia

West Indies maintained their dominance over Australia until the final Test when, on a turning pitch, neither Marshall nor his team-mates performed to their usual standard. By then however the series was won conclusively and the West Indies' victories in the first three Tests gave them 11 consecutive victories. Marshall and Garner continued to form an incisive opening attack, sharing 47 wickets while Walsh made his West Indies debut. After the series Clive Lloyd retired as the captain of West Indies.

	Own Team Total	O	M	R	W		Opp Total	Ct
165. West Indians v Queensland, Brisbane, October (19), 20, 21, 22 (Match drawn)								
c J.R.Thomson b J.N.Maguire 1	177	17.1	5	37	3	R.B.Kerr c I.V.A.Richards	180	
						C.G.Rackemann c I.V.A.Richards		
						J.R.Thompson c C.H.Lloyd		
		3	2	7	1	K.C.Wessels c P.J.L.Dujon	10-1	
166. West Indies v South Australia, Adelaide, October 26, 27, 28, 29 (Match drawn)								
c A.M.J.Hilditch								
b T.B.A.May	35	242	21	5	75	4	A.M.J.Hilditch c P.J.L.Dujon 295	
						W.B.Phillips b		
						R.J.Inverarity b		
						T.B.A.May lbw		
not out	2	514-5d	11	2	26	0	200-6	
167. WEST INDIES v AUSTRALIA, Perth, November 9, 10, 11, 12 (West Indies won by an innings and 112 runs)								
c K.J.Hughes b R.M.Hogg	21	416	15	7	25	2	J.Dyson c C.H.Lloyd	76	2
						G.F.Lawson c P.J.L.Dujon		

```
                    21    4   68   4   J.Dyson b                        228
                                       A.R.Border c D.L.Haynes
                                       K.J.Hughes lbw
                                       R.M.Hogg b
```
168. WEST INDIES v AUSTRALIA, Brisbane, November 23, 24, 25, 26 (West Indies won by eight wickets)
```
b G.F.Lawson       57   424   14.4  5   39   2   A.R.Border c C.H.Lloyd       175   2
                                                 D.C.Boon c R.B.Richardson
did not bat         -   26-2   34   7   82   5   J.Dyson c P.J.L.Dujon        271
                                                 D.C.Boon c M.A.Holding
                                                 T.M.Alderman c R.B.Richardson
                                                 G.F.Lawson c I.V.A.Richards
                                                 R.G.Holland b
```
169. WEST INDIES v AUSTRALIA, Adelaide, December 7, 8, 9, 10, 11 (West Indies won by 191 runs)
```
c S.J.Rixon b G.F.Lawson  9   356    26   8   69   5   K.C.Wessels b            284
                                                       S.J.Rixon c I.V.A.Richards
                                                       A.R.Border c J.Garner
                                                       D.C.Boon c P.J.L.Dujon
                                                       T.M.Alderman c R.B.Richardson
did not bat        -   292-7d  15.5  4   38   5   J.Dyson lbw                   173
                                                       A.R.Border b
                                                       K.J.Hughes b
                                                       G.F.Lawson c P.J.L.Dujon
                                                       T.M.Alderman b
```
170. WEST INDIES v AUSTRALIA, Melbourne, December 22, 23, 24, 26, 27 (Match drawn)
```
c S.J.Rixon b R.M.Hogg  55   479   31.5  6   86   5   K.C.Wessels c P.J.L.Dujon  296
                                                      G.R.J.Matthews b
                                                      S.J.Rixon c R.B.Richardson
                                                      C.J.McDermott b
                                                      R.M.Hogg lbw
did not bat        -   186-5d   20   4   36   0                                  198-8
```
171. WEST INDIES v AUSTRALIA, Sydney, December 30, 31, January 1, 2 (Australia won by an innings and 55 runs)
```
st S.J.Rixon b R.G.Holland  0   163   37   2   111   0                           471-9d
not out             32   253
```

SEASON'S AVERAGES

Batting and Fielding	M	I	NO	Runs	HS	Ave	100	50	Ct
Test matches	5	6	1	174	57	34.80	-	2	4
Other matches	2	3	1	38	35	19.00	-	-	-
Tour	7	9	2	212	57	30.28	-	2	4
Career	171	216	26	4217	116*	22.19	4	16	66

Bowling	O	M	R	W	BB	Ave	5i	10m
Test matches	215.2	45	554	28	5-38	19.78	4	1
Other matches	52.1	14	145	8	4-75	18.12	-	-
Tour	267.3	59	699	36	5-38	19.41	4	1
Career	5285.1	1381	13665	745	8-71	18.34	50	7

1984/85

New Zealand toured and lost the four match series 2-0, Richards' first as captain. Marshall topped the bowling averages and had match figures of 11-120 in the third Test. Marshall did not appear in the Shell Shield season.

	Own Team Total	O	M	R	W		Opp Total	Ct

172. WEST INDIES v NEW ZEALAND, Port of Spain, March 29, 30, 31, April 2, 3 (Match drawn)
```
c sub (J.G.Bracewell)
b E.J.Chatfield   0   307   25   3   78   2   K.R.Rutherford            262
                                              c D.L.Haynes
                                              J.V.Coney lbw
```

c J.V.Coney b E.J.Chatfield 1 261-8d 26   4 65 4 J.J.Crowe c J.Garner   187-6

                                      M.D.Crowe c D.L.Haynes
                                      G.P.Howarth b
                                      J.V.Coney c P.J.L.Dujon

173. WEST INDIES v NEW ZEALAND, Georgetown, April 6, 7, 8, 10, 11 (Match drawn)

did not bat   - 511-6d 33   3 110 4 J.J.Crowe b   440

                                        G.P.Howarth c D.L.Haynes
                                      R.J.Hadlee c P.J.L.Dujon

did not bat   - 268-6   I.D.S.Smith lbw

174. WEST INDIES v NEW ZEALAND, Bridgetown, April 26, 27, 28, 30, May 1 (West Indies won by ten wickets)

c J.J.Crowe b E.J.Chatfield 63 336 15   3 40 4 J.G.Wright c P.J.L.Dujon   94

                                        K.R.Rutherford c I.V.A.Richards
                                        J.V.Coney c R.B.Richardson

did not bat   - 10-0 25.3 6 80 7 I.D.S.Smith c C.G.Greenidge

                                        G.P.Howarth c D.L.Haynes 248   1
                                        K.R.Rutherford c M.A.Holding
                                        M.D.Crowe c P.J.L.Dujon
                                        J.V.Coney c A.L.Logie
                                        I.D.S.Smith c and b
                                        D.A.Stirling b
                                        S.L.Boock c D.L.Haynes

175. WEST INDIES v NEW ZEALAND, Kingston, May 4, 5, 6, 8, 9 (West Indies won by ten wickets)

lbw b J.G.Bracewell   26 363 17   3 47 2 G.P.Howarth c H.A.Gomes 138   1

                                        K.R.Rutherford c P.J.L.Dujon

did not bat   - 59-0 28.4 8 66 4 K.R.Rutherford lbw   283   1

                                        I.D.S.Smith b
                                        R.J.Hadlee c C.A.Walsh
                                        J.G.Bracewell c H.A.Gomes

SEASON'S AVERAGES

Batting and Fielding	M	I	NO	Runs	HS	Ave	100	50	Ct
Test matches	4	4	0	90	63	22.50	-	1	3
Career	175	220	26	4307	116*	22.20	4	17	69

Bowling	O	M	R	W	BB	Ave	5i	10m
Test matches	170.1	30	486	27	7-80	18.00	1	1
Career	5455.2	1411	14151	772	8-71	18.33	51	8

1985

Marshall played under his second new captain of the year as Mark Nicholas took responsibility at Hampshire. They contested the Championship until the last afternoon before Middlesex clinched the title. Marshall contributed significantly with bat (five fifties) and ball and was unlucky to fall just five wickets short of 100 for the season – mainly because it was a very wet summer. The county match at Taunton was particularly dramatic. Somerset recovered from 108-6 to 298 and reduced Hampshire to 107-7 before a county record partnership by Tremlett and James gave Hampshire the lead. Somerset declared, setting Hampshire 323 which they reached with Marshall 49* and James scoring 39 in 3.3 overs. Marshall clinched the victory by hitting Joel Garner for 6.

	Own	Team Total	O	M	R	W		Opp Total	Ct

176. Hampshire v Somerset, Taunton, May 22, 23, 24 (Hampshire won by five wickets)

c sub (M.Booth) b J.Garner 24 334-8d 22   4 81 3 J.G.Wyatt c R.A.Smith   298

                                        N.F.M.Popplewell c K.D.James
                                        I.T.Botham b

not out   49 325-5 13   0 50 1 R.L.Ollis c V.P.Terry   358-5d

177. Hampshire v Glamorgan, Southampton, May 25, (27), 28 (Hampshire won by three wickets)
c Javed Miandad
    b S.J.Malone 12 115   21.2 4 57 4 Javed Miandad c R.J.Parks 197
    J.Derrick c M.C.J.Nicholas
    T.Davies c V.P.Terry
    S.J.Malone b
st T.Davies b R.C.Ontong 18 259-7 12 3 33 1 J.Derrick lbw 176-8d

178. Hampshire v Derbyshire, Basingstoke, May 29, 30, 31 (Hampshire won by four wickets)
c B.Roberts b A.E.Warner 64 218 19 5 57 2 K.J.Barnett lbw 246 1
    D.G.Moir lbw
c B.Roberts b G.Miller 8 380-6 16 5 39 3 K.J.Barnett c T.M.Tremlett 350-6d 1
    B.Roberts lbw
    W.P.Fowler c R.J.Parks

179. Hampshire v Yorkshire, Middlesbrough, June 1, 3, 4 (Match drawn)
c D.L.Bairstow b P.A.Booth 50 341-6d 20 8 48 5 G.Boycott lbw 283 1
    R.J.Blakey c R.J.Parks
    D.L.Bairstow lbw
    P.Carrick c R.J.Maru
    P.W.Jarvis b
c S.D.Fletcher b K.Sharp 60 223-6d 6 3 8 0 114-5

180. Hampshire v Warwickshire, Edgbaston, June 8, 10, 11 (Match drawn)
c G.W.Humpage
    b N.Gifford 10 433-8d 20 6 50 6 R.I.H.B.Dyer lbw 127 1
    K.D.Smith lbw
    A.I.Kallicharran lbw
    D.L.Amiss lbw
    D.S.Hoffman b
    N.Gifford c C.L.Smith
    24 7 68 3 R.I.H.B.Dyer lbw 198-7
    A.I.Kallicharran c V.P.Terry
    P.A.Smith c V.P.Terry

181. Hampshire v Middlesex, Bournemouth, June 12, 13, 14 (Match drawn)
c K.P.Tomlins
    b P.H.Edmonds 15 184 26 9 68 5 K.P.Tomlins c R.J.Parks 183
    R.O.Butcher c C.A.Connor
    C.T.Radley lbw
    K.R.Brown lbw
    P.H.Edmonds lbw
c N.F.Williams b J.F.Sykes 55 263-8d 24 7 59 3 R.O.Butcher lbw 166-8
    C.T.Radley c C.A.Connor
    P.H.Edmonds lbw

182. Hampshire v Sussex, Hove, June 15, 17, 18 (Match drawn)
lbw b Imran Khan 13 221-6d 15 7 28 0 257
c and b I.A.Greig 0 123-7 10 0 22 0 238-3d 1

183. Hampshire v Gloucestershire, Bristol, June 26, 27, 28 (Match drawn)
c R.C.Russell b C.A.Walsh 18 110 20 3 57 4 A.W.Stovold lbw 191 1
    P.Bainbridge c R.J.Parks
    B.F.Davison c C.L.Smith
    K.M.Curran c R.J.Parks
c D.V.Lawrence
    b C.W.J.Athey 8 312-7d 5 1 8 0 53-4

184. Hampshire v Essex, Southampton, June 29, July 1, 2 (Hampshire won by an innings and 57 runs)
c B.R.Hardie b D.R.Pringle 8 336-7d 16.5 5 42 6 B.R.Hardie b 96
    C.Gladwin c C.L.Smith
    P.J.Prichard b
    D.R.Pringle c V.P.Terry
    D.E.East c S.J.W.Andrew
    D.L.Acfield b
    21 7 54 3 P.J.Prichard lbw 183
    D.R.Pringle b
    K.R.Pont hit wkt

185. Hampshire v Lancashire, Liverpool, July 6, 8, 9 (Hampshire won by four wickets)
c and b I.Folley 15 331-5d 17 1 48 2 G.Fowler lbw 401-6d 1
    J.Abrahams b

c and b I.Folley   24 189-6   15   4   45   4 N.H.Fairbrother c R.J.Parks 115
                                            M.Watkinson lbw
                                            J.Simmons c V.P.Terry
                                            D.W.Varey lbw

186. Hampshire v Sussex, Portsmouth, July 10, 11, 12 (Match drawn)
c I.J.Gould b A.N.Jones   4 210   25   5   70   3 P.W.G.Parker c V.P.Terry 327-8d
                                            A.P.Wells b
c C.M.Wells b I.A.Greig   9 213-8   2   1   10   0 I.J.Gould c R.J.Parks
                                                              209-5d

187. Hampshire v Worcestershire, Portsmouth, July 13, 15, 16 (Match drawn)
c D.N.Patel b N.V.Radford 14 255   30.3 12   59   7 T.S.Curtis b   249
                                            D.B.D'Oliveira c M.C.J.Nicholas
                                            D.N.Patel lbw
                                            S.J.Rhodes c M.C.J.Nicholas
                                              P.J.Newport lbw
                                            N.V.Radford b
c S.J.Rhodes b P.J.Newport 0 211-6d 14   7   29   2 R.M.Ellcock lbw
                                            D.M.Smith c R.J.Parks 166-7
                                            P.A.Neale b

188. Hampshire v Surrey, Guildford, July 27, 29, (30) (Match drawn)
c A.Needham b P.I.Pocock 22 291   -   -   -   -
                                                              4-0

189. Hampshire v Somerset, Bournemouth, August 3, 5, 6 (Match drawn)
did not bat   - 346-2d 24   6   51   1 N.A.Felton b   232
                                   33   10   70   4 N.F.M.Popplewell
                                                c R.J.Parks 236-8
                                            P.M.Roebuck lbw
                                            V.J.Marks c R.J.Parks
                                            G.V.Palmer c R.J.Maru

190. Hampshire v Surrey, Southampton, August 10, 12, 13 (Match drawn)
c A.J.Stewart b A.H.Gray 8 303-9d   7   1   20   1 A.Needham c C.L.Smith 200-4d
c A.J.Stewart b A.R.Butcher 17 174-5d   7   0   23   1 A.Needham lbw   107-4

191. Hampshire v Glamorgan, Cardiff, August (14), 15, 16 (Glamorgan won by five wickets)
did not bat   - 270-3d
innings forfeit   innings forfeit
                                 20   6   36   1 A.L.Jones lbw   271-5

192. Hampshire v Leicestershire, Leicester, August 17, (19), (20) (Match drawn)
b P.Willey   36 162   4   1   11   0   106-5

193. Hampshire v Gloucestershire, Bournemouth, August 24, 26, 27 (Hampshire won by seven wickets)
b D.V.Lawrence   41 197   23   10   31   2 A.W.Stovold lbw   140
                                            R.C.Russell b
did not bat   - 102-3   20   6   38   4 A.W.Stovold b   157
                                            C.W.J.Athey lbw
                                            K.M.Curran lbw
                                            R.C.Russell c C.L.Smith

194. Hampshire v Leicestershire, Bournemouth, August 28, 29, 30 (Hampshire won by an innings and 56 runs)
b P.A.J.DeFreitas   43 371-5d 15.2 8   12   3 N.E.Briers b   100   1
                                            P.B.Clift c M.C.J.Nicholas
                                            N.G.B.Cook c T.M.Tremlett
                          23   11   53   1 J.C.Balderstone lbw   215

195. Hampshire v Kent, Folkestone, September 4, 5, 6 (Match drawn)
c C.S.Cowdrey b L.Potter 5 333-9d 24.3 5   46   3 S.G.Hinks b   259   1
                                            C.S.Cowdrey c V.P.Terry
                                            E.A.E.Baptiste c C.G.Greenidge
c C.J.Tavare
      b E.A.E.Baptiste 15 156-5d 14.4 3   31   1 G.R.Cowdrey c R.J.Parks 172-7   1

196. Hampshire v Northamptonshire, Southampton, September 11, 12, 13 (Northamptonshire won by one wicket)
c D.Ripley b R.A.Harper 14 300-8d 23   6   75   4 R.J.Boyd-Moss c V.P.Terry 304
                                            A.J.Lamb c R.J.Parks
                                            R.J.Bailey c V.P.Terry
                                              D.J.Wild b
not out   66 244-4d 11   2   31   1 A.J.Lamb c C.L.Smith 241-9

197. Hampshire v Nottinghamshire, Trent Bridge, September 14, 16, 17 (Match drawn)
did not bat   - 252-4d 24   4   62   1 D.W.Randall b   297
b R.A.Pick   23 268-9   -   -   -   -   234-6d

SEASON'S AVERAGES

Batting and Fielding	M	I	NO	Runs	HS	Ave	100	50	Ct
County Championship	22	33	2	768	66*	24.77	-	5	10
Career	197	253	28	5075	116*	22.55	4	22	79

Bowling	O	M	R	W	BB	Ave	5i	10m
County Championship	688.1	193	1680	95	7-59	17.68	5	-
Career	6143.3	1604	15831	867	8-71	18.25	56	8

1985/86

Marshall took 23 wickets in four matches for Barbados before the Test series with England in which West Indies won all five matches. None of the matches was even close with West Indies enjoying a first innings lead in excess of 100 in every match. Marshall scored two half centuries and he and Garner both took 27 wickets at less than 20, supported by Holding and Patrick Patterson. Despite their dominance, not one West Indies bowler took five wickets in an innings during the series.

	Own Team Total	O	M	R	W		Opp Total	Ct
198. Barbados v Trinidad & Tobago, Bridgetown, January 10, 11, 12 (Barbados won by an innings and 13 runs)								
c K.C.Williams b R.Nanan 13	350	16	1	51	3	H.A.Gomes c C.A.Best	177	1
						R.Nanan lbw		
						K.C.Williams lbw		
		11	3	27	2	R.S.Gabriel c T.Greenidge	160	
						A.H.Gray lbw		
199. Barbados v Windward Islands, Bridgetown, January 17, 18, 19, 20 (Barbados won by 118 runs)								
c S.A.E.Murphy b J.T.Etienne 2	175	13	5	39	4	L.C.Sebastien c N.D.Broomes	94	1
						L.A.Lewis c C.G.Greenidge		
						J.D.Charles lbw		
						I.Cadette b		
did not bat	- 338-5d	28	5	85	6	L.D.John b	301	
						I.Cadette c R.Holder		
						L.A.Lewis lbw		
						F.X.Maurice b		
						S.Mahon c T.R.O.Payne		
						D.J.Collymore c N.D.Broomes		
200. Barbados v Jamaica, Bridgetown, January 31, February 1, 2, 3 (Barbados won by 73 runs)								
c C.A.Davidson b M.A.Holding 11	224	16	2	35	4	O.W.Peters c T.R.O.Payne	142	1
						M.C.Neita c C.G.Greenidge		
						G.Heron c T.R.O.Payne		
						C.A.Davidson b		
b B.P.Patterson 17	172	24	4	73	3	C.A.Davidson lbw	181	
						M.A.Holding b		
						A.G.Daley c T.R.O.Payne		
201. Barbados v Guyana, Essequibo, February 6, 7, 8, 9 (Match drawn)								
c sub (Angus) b C.G.Butts 1	365	14	2	39	1	D.I.Kallicharran b	332	
not out 7	62-4	5	0	7	0		238-6d	1
202. WEST INDIES v ENGLAND, Kingston, February 21, 22, 23 (West Indies won by ten wickets)								
c sub (J.E.Emburey) b R.M.Ellison 6	307	11.	1	30	2	G.A.Gooch c J.Garner	159	
						I.T.Botham c B.P.Patterson		
did not bat	- 5-0	11	4	29	3	G.A.Gooch b	152	
						I.T.Botham b		
						D.M.Smith c H.A.Gomes		
203. WEST INDIES v ENGLAND, Port of Spain, March 7, 8, 9, 11, 12 (West Indies won by seven wickets)								
not out 62	399	15	3	38	4	G.A.Gooch c C.A.Best	176	2
						W.N.Slack c T.R.O.Payne		
						I.T.Botham c R.B.Richardson		
						R.M.Ellison lbw		

did not bat   -   95-3   32.2   9   94   4   P.Willey b   315
                                           I.T.Botham   c T.R.O.Payne
                                           P.R.Downton   lbw
                                           R.M.Ellison   lbw

204. WEST INDIES v ENGLAND, Bridgetown, March 21, 22, 23, 25 (West Indies won by an innings and 30 runs)

run out   4   418   14   1   42   4   R.T.Robinson c P.J.L.Dujon 189
                                           D.I.Gower c P.J.L.Dujon
                                           P.Willey c P.J.L.Dujon
                                           A.J.Lamb c R.B.Richardson
                           13   1   47   0   199   1

205. WEST INDIES v ENGLAND, Port of Spain, April 3, 4, 5 (West Indies won by ten wickets)

b J.E.Emburey   5   312   23   4   71   2   P.R.Downton c J.Garner   200   1
                                           J.E.Emburey c D.L.Haynes
did not bat   -   39-0   10   2   42   3   G.A.Gooch c P.J.L.Dujon   150
                                           I.T.Botham c H.A.Gomes
                                           P.Willey lbw

206. WEST INDIES v ENGLAND, St John's, April 11, 12, 13, 15, 16 (West Indies won by 240 runs)

c M.W.Gatting b G.A.Gooch 76   474   24   5   64   3   R.T.Robinson b   310
                                           D.I.Gower c P.J.L.Dujon
                                           R.M.Ellison c P.J.L.Dujon
did not bat   -   246-2d   16.1   6   25   2   A.J.Lamb b   170
                                           P.R.Downton lbw

SEASON'S AVERAGES

Batting and Fielding	M	I	NO	Runs	HS	Ave	100	50	Ct
Test matches	5	5	1	153	76	38.25	-	2	4
Shell Shield	4	6	1	51	17	10.20	-	-	4
Season	9	11	2	204	76	22.66	-	2	8
Career	206	264	30	5279	116*	22.55	4	24	87

Bowling	O	M	R	W	BB	Ave	5i	10m
Test matches	169.3	36	482	27	4-38	17.85	-	-
Shell Shield	127	22	353	23	6-85	15.34	1	1
Season	296.3	58	835	50	6-85	16.70	1	1
Career	6440	1662	16666	917	8-71	18.17	57	9

1986

Hampshire won the John Player Special League, clinching the title in the penultimate match at The Oval. They slipped to sixth in the Championship but Marshall took 100 wickets at 15 apiece, the lowest Hampshire average since Roberts in 1974. He was the last Hampshire bowler to take 100 wickets in a season although he enjoyed little success with the bat. During the season he passed 1000 first-class wickets by dismissing Martyn Moxon (Yorkshire).

                           Own Team   O   M   R   W   Opp   Ct
                           Total   Total

207. Hampshire v Nottinghamshire, Trent Bridge, April 26, 27, 28 (Hampshire won by nine wickets)

c and b C.E.B.Rice   35   241-8d   24   7   48   2   D.W.Randall b   265
                                           J.D.Birch b
did not bat   -   209-1   7   2   26   0   181-3d

208. Hampshire v Glamorgan, Southampton, April 30, May 2, 3 (Match drawn)

b G.C.Holmes   45   308-8d   20.5   5   46   2   H.Morris c R.J.Parks   201
                                           E.A.Moseley c C.L.Smith
                             15   5   42   0   342-7d

209. Hampshire v Lancashire, Old Trafford, May 7, (8), (9) (Match drawn)

did not bat   -   251-3

210. Hampshire v Gloucestershire, Bournemouth, May 24, 26, 27 (Gloucestershire won by 146 runs)

b I.R.Payne   23   190   20   4   42   1   A.W.Stovold
                                           c S.J.W.Andrew   296-7d   1

```
c A.W.Stovold b Payne      0  110    23    5    51    6    P.W.Romaines  c C.L.Smith  150-6d
                                                           A.W.Stovold   c R.J.Parks
                                                           A.J.Wright    b
                                                           P.Bainbridge  b
                                                           J.W.Lloyds    lbw
                                                           I.R.Payne     c R.J.Maru
```

211. Hampshire v Nottinghamshire, Southampton, May (31), June 2, (3) (Match drawn)
```
c R.T.Robinson b C.E.B.Rice  1  80-5d  13    3    38    5    R.T.Robinson  c R.J.Maru    162
                                                             B.C.Broad     c R.J.Parks
                                                             D.W.Randall   c R.J.Parks
                                                             C.E.B.Rice    c R.J.Parks
                                                             B.N.French    lbw
```

212. Hampshire v Somerset, Bournemouth, June 7, 8, 9 (Match drawn)
```
lbw b J.Garner       1  298     19    4    49    1    R.J.Harden  lbw    262-7d
did not bat          -  245-4d  8.5   5    11    2    R.J.Blitz   lbw    200-8
                                                      C.H.Dredge  b
```

213. Hampshire v Essex, Ilford, June 14, 16, 17 (Hampshire won by 12 runs)
```
lbw b D.R.Pringle    9  260     17    6    60    2    J.K.Lever   b      198
                                                      A.W.Lilley  lbw
lbw b N.A.Foster     0  135     21    7    26    4    J.K.Lever   c R.J.Parks    185
                                                      A.R.Border  c R.J.Parks
                                                      A.W.Lilley  c R.J.Maru
                                                      J.H.Childs  c M.C.J.Nicholas
```

214. Hampshire v Surrey, Basingstoke, June 18, 19 (Hampshire won by an innings and 193 runs)
```
not out             51  401-5d  17    7    26    4    G.S.Clinton  c M.C.J.Nicholas 144
                                                      T.E.Jesty    c C.G.Greenidge
                                                      M.P.Bicknell b
                                                      P.I.Pocock   b
                                 6    2    15    3    A.J.Stewart  c D.R.Turner    64
                                                      M.A.Lynch    c M.C.J.Nicholas
                                                      T.E.Jesty    c R.J.Parks
```

215. Hampshire v Kent, Southampton, June 21, 23, 24 (Kent won by five wickets)
```
c and b D.L.Underwood  1  214   17    4    38    2    T.R.Ward    c V.P.Terry    189
                                                      C.J.Tavare  c C.G.Greenidge
b D.L.Underwood      0  143     13    2    34    1    D.G.Aslett  lbw    172-5
```

216. Hampshire v Worcestershire, Worcester, June 28, 30, July 1 (Worcestershire won by six wickets)
```
b P.J.Newport        4  158     23    2    70    4    G.A.Hick    c M.C.J.Nicholas  204    1
                                                      D.M.Smith   c and b
                                                      P.A.Neale   c M.C.J.Nicholas
                                                      P.J.Newport lbw
b P.J.Newport       24  156     15    6    29    4    T.S.Curtis    c R.J.Parks    112-4
                                                      D.B.D'Oliveira lbw
                                                      G.A.Hick      b
                                                      P.A.Neale     c C.L.Smith
```

217. Hampshire v Leicestershire, Leicester, July 2, 3, 4 (Match drawn)
```
b L.B.Taylor         6  295-7d  15    5    32    0                        313-3d
did not bat          -  30-0    21    4    53    3    L.Potter  c R.J.Parks    251-8d
                                                      P.Willey  lbw
                                                      J.P.Agnew c R.J.Parks
```

218. Hampshire v Somerset, Taunton, July 5, 7, 8 (Match drawn)
```
did not bat          -  220-4d  21    7    40    5    P.M.Roebuck   c R.J.Parks    231
                                                      J.J.E.Hardy   c R.A.Smith
                                                      V.J.Marks     b
                                                      J.C.M.Atkinson lbw
                                                      C.H.Dredge    b
did not bat          -  41-2    11    0    29    0                          273-0d
```

219. Hampshire v Warwickshire, Portsmouth, July 19, 21 (Hampshire won by an innings and 43 runs)
```
did not bat          -  350-6d  16    6    22    5    P.A.Smith    lbw    110
                                                      B.M.McMillan c R.A.Smith
                                                      G.J.Parsons  c R.J.Parks
                                                      D.L.Amiss    c K.D.James
                                                      G.C.Small    b
                                19    4    51    2    B.M.McMillan c R.J.Parks    197    1
                                                      G.J.Parsons  c V.P.Terry
```

220. Hampshire v Derbyshire, Portsmouth, July 23, 24, 25 (Hampshire won by 5 runs)
```
b M.A.Holding        8  184     19    4    46    1    K.J.Barnett  c M.C.J.Nicholas  216
```

did not bat   - 254-2d   17   1   54   4   K.J.Barnett lbw   217
B.J.M.Maher b
B.Roberts c T.C.Middleton
I.S.Anderson c C.G.Greenidge

221. Hampshire v Gloucestershire, Cheltenham, August 2, 4, 5 (Gloucestershire won by 17 runs)
c C.A.Walsh b D.V.Lawrence 3   270   19   4   42   3   K.M.Curran c R.A.Smith   201
J.W.Lloyds c C.L.Smith
C.A.Walsh lbw
c C.W.J.Athey b C.A.Walsh 5   98   22   6   44   4   P.W.Romaines
     c T.C.Middleton   184
P.Bainbridge c R.A.Smith
C.A.Walsh b
D.V.Lawrence b

222. Hampshire v Kent, Canterbury, August 6, 7, 8 (Match drawn)
c S.A.Marsh b C.S.Cowdrey 0   234   26   8   34   2   S.G.Hinks b   431-8d   1
did not bat   - 181-5   D.G.Aslett lbw

223. Hampshire v Sussex, Southampton, August 9, 11, 12 (Match drawn)
not out   11   320-6d   16   3   43   0   302-4d
did not bat   - 242-2d   13.5   4   26   1   Imran Khan c R.J.Parks   209-8

224. Hampshire v Middlesex, Lord's, August 16, 18, 19 (Match drawn)
lbw b S.P.Hughes   13   158-7d   16   2   38   3   W.N.Slack c R.J.Parks   155
A.J.T.Miller b
R.O.Butcher lbw
did not bat   - 129-3   4.2   1   4   0   226-3d

225. Hampshire v Worcestershire, Bournemouth, August 20, 21, 22 (Match drawn)
c P.A.Neale b P.J.Newport 22   237   22   11   30   3   L.K.Smith c R.J.Parks   120
S.M.McEwan c V.P.Terry
G.A.Hick c R.J.Parks
c M.J.Weston b A.P.Pridgeon 0   91-4d   12   3   32   3   T.S.Curtis c C.G.Greenidge   160-5
D.B.D'Oliveira b
P.A.Neale lbw

226. Hampshire v Yorkshire, Bournemouth, August 23, (25), (26) (Match drawn)
did not bat   - 58-4   19   6   52   3   M.D.Moxon b   212   1
K.Sharp c T.C.Middleton
D.L.Bairstow c T.C.Middleton

227. Hampshire v Northamptonshire, Northampton, August (27), 28, 29 (Hampshire won by 169 runs)
did not bat   - 338-2d   innings forfeit
innings forfeit   17.4   3   41   4   W.Larkins lbw   169
R.A.Harper lbw
N.G.B.Cook c R.A.Smith
N.A.Mallender b

228. Hampshire v Derbyshire, Derby, August 30, September 1, 2 (Hampshire won by nine wickets)
did not bat   - 176-2d   21   5   49   5   B.J.M.Maher b   209
B.Roberts c R.A.Smith
G.Miller lbw
A.E.Warner lbw
O.H.Mortensen b
did not bat   - 257-1   7   4   12   2   K.J.Barnett c R.A.Smith   222-4d
B.J.M.Maher lbw

229. Hampshire v Sussex, Hove, September 10, 11, 12 (Match drawn)
b D.A.Reeve   1   385-7d   14   3   41   2   R.I.Alikhan c C.L.Smith   350-7d
P.W.G.Parker b
did not bat   - 245-2d   9   1   42   2   A.M.Green c R.A.Smith   243-8
P.W.G.Parker c R.A.Smith

SEASON'S AVERAGES

Batting and Fielding	M	I	NO	Runs	HS	Ave	100	50	Ct
County Championship	23	23	2	263	51*	12.52	-	1	5
Career	229	287	32	5542	116*	21.73	4	25	92

Bowling	O	M	R	W	BB	Ave	5i	10m
County Championship	656.3	171	1508	100	6-51	15.08	5	-
Career	7096.3	1833	18174	1017	8-71	17.87	62	9

1986/87 – West Indies in Pakistan

West Indies went down to a surprising defeat in the first Test, spun out by Abdul Qadir for a second innings total of 53. They squared the series immediately in a low-scoring match at Lahore where Marshall took five wickets in the first innings but the third match, and the series, were drawn.

	Own Team	Total	O	M	R	W		Opp Total	Ct
230. West Indians v President's XI, Rawalpindi, October 19, 20, 21 (Match drawn)									
not out	16	247	17	3	61	1	Shoaib Mohammad		
							c T.R.O.Payne	317	
did not bat	-	46-0							
231. WEST INDIES v PAKISTAN, Faisalabad, October 24, 26, 27, 28, 29 (Pakistan won by 186 runs)									
c Salim Yousuf									
b Wasim Akram	5	248	10	2	48	3	Mohsin Khan lbw	159	
							Mudassar Nazar c R.B.Richardson		
							Rameez Raja lbw		
c and b Abdul Qadir	10	53	36	3	83	2	Mudassar Nazar		
							c D.L.Haynes	328	
							Imran Khan c R.A.Harper		
232. WEST INDIES v PAKISTAN, Lahore, November 7, 8, 9 (West Indies won by an innings and 10 runs)									
not out	13	218	18	5	33	5	Mohsin Khan b	131	
							Rizwan-uz-Zaman c R.B.Richardson		
							Qasim Omar lbw		
							Asif Mujtaba b		
							Wasim Akram lbw		
			8	3	14	1	Rizwan-uz-Zaman b	77	
233. WEST INDIES v PAKISTAN, Karachi, November 20, 21, 22. 24, 25 (Match drawn)									
b Tauseef Ahmed	4	240	33	9	57	2	Mohsin Khan		
							c I.V.A.Richards 239		
							Asif Mujtaba c P.J.L.Dujon		
lbw b Imran Khan	0	211	19	5	31	3	Mohsin Khan		
							c C.G.Greenidge	125-7	
							Salim Yousuf c D.L.Haynes		
							Javed Miandad b		

SEASON'S AVERAGES

Batting and Fielding	M	I	NO	Runs	HS	Ave	100	50	Ct
Test matches	3	5	1	32	13*	8.00	-	-	-
Other matches	1	1	1	16	16*	-	-	-	-
Tour	4	6	2	48	16*	12.00	-	-	-
Career	233	293	34	5590	116*	21.58	4	25	92

Bowling	O	M	R	W	BB	Ave	5i	10m
Test matches	114	27	266	16	5-33	16.62	1	-
Other matches	17	3	61	1	1-61	61.00	-	-
Tour	131	30	327	17	5-23	19.23	1	-
Career	7227.3	1863	18501	1034	8-71	17.89	63	9

1986/87 – West Indies in New Zealand

With players of the quality of Richard Hadlee, Martin Crowe and John Wright, New Zealand contested an interesting series. Marshall led an unfamiliar attack of Butts, Gray and Walsh in the victorious Second Test but Hadlee, Chatfield and Snedden bowled New Zealand to victory and a shared series at Christchurch. Marshall did not bowl as New Zealand lost 5 wickets in struggling to their victory target of 33.

	Own Team Total	O	M	R	W		Opp Total	Ct

234. WEST INDIES v NEW ZEALAND, Wellington, February 20, 21, 22, 23, 24 (Match drawn)

	Own Team Total	O	M	R	W		Opp Total	Ct
c and b S.L.Boock	30	345	22	3	57	2	J.V.Coney c A.L.Logie	228
did not bat	-	50-2	20	6	43	0	S.L.Boock c J.Garner	386-5d

235. WEST INDIES v NEW ZEALAND, Auckland, February 27, 28, March 1, 2, 3 (West Indies won by ten wickets)

	Own Team Total	O	M	R	W		Opp Total	Ct
c J.J.Crowe b S.L.Boock	6	418-9d	17	3	43	4	J.G.Wright c R.B.Richardson	157
							K.R.Rutherford b	
							M.D.Crowe c P.J.L.Dujon	
did not bat	-	13-0	33	7	71	2	E.J.Chatfield c A.L.Logie	
							K.R.Rutherford	
							c R.B.Richardson	273
							D.N.Patel lbw	

236. WEST INDIES v NEW ZEALAND, Christchurch, March (12), 13, 14, 15 (New Zealand won by five wickets)

	Own Team Total	O	M	R	W		Opp Total	Ct
c M.C.Snedden b E.J.Chatfield	2	100	27	2	75	1	M.D.Crowe b	332-9d
b R.J.Hadlee	45	264	-	-	-	-		33-5

SEASON'S AVERAGES

Batting and Fielding	M	I	NO	Runs	HS	Ave	100	50	Ct
Test matches	3	4	0	83	45	20.75	-	-	-
Career	236	297	34	5673	116*	21.57	4	25	92

Bowling	O	M	R	W	BB	Ave	5i	10m
Test matches	119	21	289	9	4-43	32.11	-	-
Career	7346.3	1884	18790	1043	8-71	18.01	63	9

1986/87

Marshall's busy 'winter' ended with a single appearance for his home island before he returned to Hampshire.

237. Barbados v Trinidad & Tobago, Bridgetown, April 11, 12, 13 (Barbados won by an innings and 203 runs)

	Own Team Total	O	M	R	W		Opp Total	Ct
did not bat	-	469-3d	12	3	19	3	P.V.Simmons b	143
							K.C.Williams c C.A.Best	
							R.Nanan lbw	
			14	6	35	4	D.Deyal c W.E.Reid	123
							A.L.Logie b	
							A.Rajah c W.E.Reid	
							K.C.Williams lbw	

SEASON'S AVERAGES

Batting and Fielding	M	I	NO	Runs	HS	Ave	100	50	Ct
Shell Shield	1	-	-	-	-	-	-	-	-
Career	237	297	34	5673	116*	21.57	4	25	92

Bowling	O	M	R	W	BB	Ave	5i	10m
Shell Shield	26	9	54	7	4-35	7.71	-	-
Career	7372.3	1893	18844	1050	8-71	17.94	63	9

1987

Hampshire finished fifth in the Championship but neither Marshall nor the side enjoyed as much success as in the previous season. His batting made an increasing impression in another wet season.

He began the season with 90* in a declared total against Northamptonshire but it was July before he managed five wickets, in an innings victory at Gloucester, a feat he was unable to repeat. In the last match of the season he rescued Hampshire from 93-6 but played-on needing one run for his century. He received the bowling award playing for the MCC in their Bicentenary match against the Rest of the World at Lord's in August.

	Own Team Total	O	M	R	W		Opp Total	Ct

238. Hampshire v Northamptonshire, Southampton, April 25, 26, 27 (Northamptonshire won by five wickets)

	Own Team Total	O	M	R	W		Opp Total	Ct
not out	90 303-7d	14.3	3	46	1	A.Walker c R.J.Parks	275	
b N.G.B.Cook	2 240-7d	18	1	66	1	W.Larkins c R.J.Parks	269-5	

239. Hampshire v Yorkshire, Headingley, May 6, 7, 8 (Yorkshire won by 15 runs)

	Own Team Total	O	M	R	W		Opp Total	Ct
b P.W.Jarvis	22 148	20	5	48	3	R.J.Blakey b	286-8d	
						K.Sharp c R.J.Maru		
						S.N.Hartley c C.G.Greenidge		
c P.Carrick b A.Sidebottom 44	247	16	5	37	4	A.A.Metcalfe c C.L.Smith	124	
						S.N.Hartley lbw		
						P.Carrick lbw		
						A.Sidebottom c R.J.Parks		

240. Hampshire v Nottinghamshire, Bournemouth, May 20, 21, 22 (Match drawn)

	Own Team Total	O	M	R	W		Opp Total	Ct
c P.Johnson b R.J.Hadlee 16	331-7d	13	3	42	1	D.W.Randall lbw	198	
		26	4	71	4	M.Newell c R.J.Parks	249	
						R.T.Robinson c T.M.Tremlett		
						P.Johnson c R.J.Maru		
						E.E.Hemmings c D.R.Turner		

241. Hampshire v Gloucestershire, Southampton, May 30, June 1, (2) (Match drawn)

	Own Team Total	O	M	R	W		Opp Total	Ct
run out	1 314-6d	22	9	50	2	K.P.Tomlins c V.P.Terry	284	1
						D.A.Graveney b		
did not bat	- 62-1							

242. Hampshire v Glamorgan, Swansea, June 3, 4, 5 (Match drawn)

	Own Team Total	O	M	R	W		Opp Total	Ct
c J.A.Hopkins b J.Derrick 16	237-8d	19	6	42	3	H.Morris c R.J.Maru	127	2
						R.C.Ontong lbw		
						M.P.Maynard c V.P.Terry		
		5	1	22	0		51-4	1

243. Hampshire v Sussex, Horsham, June 6, 8, (9) (Match drawn)

	Own Team Total	O	M	R	W		Opp Total	Ct
not out	0 307-5d	10	6	9	1	A.M.Green b	79-4	

244. Hampshire v Surrey, Kennington Oval, June 13, 15, 16 (Match drawn)

	Own Team Total	O	M	R	W		Opp Total	Ct
c C.J.Richards b M.P.Bicknell 46	201	14	3	51	0		383-6d	
did not bat	- 171-2							

245. Hampshire v Yorkshire, Basingstoke, June (17), 18, (19) (Match drawn)

	Own Team Total	O	M	R	W		Opp Total	Ct
did not bat	- 139-0							

246. Hampshire v Middlesex, Southampton, June 20, (22), 23 (Hampshire won by eight wickets)

	Own Team Total	O	M	R	W		Opp Total	Ct
did not bat	- 50-4d	18	3	44	3	P.R.Downton c R.J.Parks	219	1
						N.F.Williams lbw		
						S.P.Hughes b		
did not bat	- 270-2	-	-	-	-		100-2d	

247. Hampshire v Warwickshire, Edgbaston, June 27, 29, 30 (Hampshire won by nine wickets)

	Own Team Total	O	M	R	W		Opp Total	Ct
did not bat	- 396-2d	19	12	22	1	Asif Din c C.L.Smith	168	
did not bat	- 44-1	22.5	5	66	3	D.L.Amiss lbw	271	
						A.C.Storie b		
						A.A.Donald c R.J.Maru		

248. Hampshire v Gloucestershire, Gloucester, July 1, 2, 3 (Hampshire won by an innings and 107 runs)

	Own Team Total	O	M	R	W		Opp Total	Ct
not out	61 462-4d	11	1	35	2	P.W.Romaines		
						c C.G.Greenidge	136	
						D.A.Graveney c C.G.Greenidge		
		15	3	49	5	R.C.Russell b	219	
						K.M.Curran b		
						M.W.Alleyne c C.L.Smith		
						C.A.Walsh b		
						D.A.Graveney lbw		

249. Hampshire v Derbyshire, Heanor, July 4, 5, 6 (Derbyshire won by four wickets)

	Own Team Total	O	M	R	W		Opp Total	Ct
did not bat	- 349-2d	18	4	38	1	B.Roberts c V.P.Terry	314-7d	
c R.J.Finney b P.G.Newman 26	261-6d	14	2	52	1	B.J.M.Maher lbw	298-6	

250. Hampshire v Warwickshire, Bournemouth, July 18, 19, 20 (Match drawn)

c D.A.Thorne b G.J.Parsons 12　224-9d　17　7　32　4　T.A.Lloyd c R.J.Parks　110-6d
　　　　　　　　　　　　　　　　　　　　　　　　　　　　P.A.Smith c C.G.Greenidge
　　　　　　　　　　　　　　　　　　　　　　　　　　　　G.W.Humpage c C.G.Greenidge
innings forfeit　　　　　　　　8　5　9　2　G.A.Tedstone c C.L.Smith
　　　　　　　　　　　　　　　　　　　　　　T.A.Lloyd c M.C.J.Nicholas　58-3
　　　　　　　　　　　　　　　　　　　　　　A.J.Moles c C.L.Smith

251. Hampshire v Sussex, Portsmouth, July 22, 23, 24 (Match drawn)

did not bat　　　　　-　128-3d　18　6　37　2　R.I.Alikhan c C.L.Smith　165
　　　　　　　　　　　　　　　　　　　　　　　　　A.P.Wells c R.J.Maru
　　　　　　　　　　　　5　2　10　0　　　　　　　　　　　　　147-5d

252. Hampshire v Essex, Portsmouth, July 25, 27, 28 (Match drawn)

b J.K.Lever　　　　24　205　25　6　51　4　A.W.Lilley c R.J.Parks　184
　　　　　　　　　　　　　　　　　　　　　　　D.R.Pringle c R.J.Maru
　　　　　　　　　　　　　　　　　　　　　　　D.E.East c C.G.Greenidge
　　　　　　　　　　　　　　　　　　　　　　　J.K.Lever c R.A.Smith
not out　　　　　45　200-8d　10　4　7　0　　　　　　　　　　123-4

253. Hampshire v Somerset, Weston-super-Mare, August 5, 6, 7 (Match drawn)

lbw b A.N.Jones　38　193　18　4　46　1　N.D.Burns c and b　300　1
not out　　　　　1　225-5　15　2　44　1　P.M.Roebuck c R.A.Smith　225-8d

254. Hampshire v Lancashire, Southampton, August 8, 10, 11 (Match drawn)

c M.Watkinson
b B.P.Patterson 21　256-7d　23　5　56　2　G.Fowler lbw　315
　　　　　　　　　　　　　　　　　　　　　　　P.J.W.Allott c R.J.Maru
　　　　　　　　　　　5　2　6　0　　　　　　　　　　　　　147-3

255. M.C.C. v Rest of the World, Lord's, August 20, 21, 22, 24, (25) (Match drawn)

did not bat　　　-　455-5d　20　3　53　3　D.L.Haynes c C.E.B.Rice　421-7d　1
　　　　　　　　　　　　　　　　　　　　　　　D.B.Vengsarkar c G.A.Gooch
　　　　　　　　　　　　　　　　　　　　　　　P.J.L.Dujon c G.A.Gooch
did not bat　　　-　318-6d　2.3　0　10　1　S.M.Gavaskar b　13-1

256. Hampshire v Worcestershire, Worcester, August 26, 27, 28 (Hampshire won by 31 runs)

run out　　　24　238　9　2　27　0　　　　　　　　　　152-2d
did not bat　-　186-3d　9　1　23　4　G.J.Lord c C.L.Smith　241
　　　　　　　　　　　　　　　　　　　　　P.A.Neale b
　　　　　　　　　　　　　　　　　　　　　N.V.Radford lbw
　　　　　　　　　　　　　　　　　　　　　S.M.McEwan c R.J.Maru

257. Hampshire v Kent, Maidstone, August 29, 31, September 1 (Hampshire won by seven wickets)

c S.A.Marsh b C.Penn　5　159　19.1　6　50　3　S.A.Marsh lbw　189
　　　　　　　　　　　　　　　　　　　　　　　　C.Penn c R.A.Smith
　　　　　　　　　　　　　　　　　　　　　　　　D.L.Underwood b
did not bat　　　-　224-3　28　3　58　4　C.J.Tavare c C.L.Smith　190
　　　　　　　　　　　　　　　　　　　　　E.A.E.Baptiste c V.P.Terry
　　　　　　　　　　　　　　　　　　　　　S.A.Marsh lbw
　　　　　　　　　　　　　　　　　　　　　C.Penn c R.A.Smith

258. Hampshire v Leicestershire, Southampton, September 2, 3, 4 (Match drawn)

c P.Whitticase b J.P.Agnew　5　304-8d　21.1　6　57　4　P.Willey c V.P.Terry　286
　　　　　　　　　　　　　　　　　　　　　　　　　　　P.B.Clift c R.J.Maru
　　　　　　　　　　　　　　　　　　　　　　　　　　　G.J.F.Ferris b
　　　　　　　　　　　　　　　　　　　　　　　　　　　P.M.Such c R.J.Parks
did not bat　　　-　92-2　8　2　33　1　N.E.Briers c V.P.Terry　246-6d

259. Hampshire v Middlesex, Lord's, September 9, 10, 11 (Match drawn)

b A.R.C.Fraser　99　250　15　4　49　2　M.R.Ramprakash lbw　128
　　　　　　　　　　　　　　　　　　　　　P.R.Downton c R.A.Smith
c M.W.Gatting
b P.C.R.Tufnell　12　214　23　6　60　2　J.D.Carr c R.J.Parks　296-6
　　　　　　　　　　　　　　　　　　　　　J.E.Emburey b

SEASON'S AVERAGES

Batting and Fielding	M	I	NO	Runs	HS	Ave	100	50	Ct
County Championship	21	22	5	610	99	35.88	-	3	10
Other matches	1	-	-	-	-	-	-	-	1
Season	22	22	5	610	99	35.88	-	3	7
Career	259	319	39	6283	116*	22.43	4	28	99

Bowling	O	M	R	W	BB	Ave	5i	10m
County Championship	571.4	149	1445	72	5-54	20.06	1	-
Other matches	22.3	3	63	4	3-53	15.75	-	-
Season	594.1	152	1508	76	5-49	19.84	1	-
Career	7966.4	2045	20352	1126	8-71	18.07	64	9

1987/88

Marshall appeared with unusual regularity for Barbados and contributed with bat and ball. He missed the first Test which Pakistan won by 9 wickets and then opened the bowling with Ambrose in a drawn match in Trinidad. With match figures of 9-144 and an innings of 48, he led West Indies to victory and a drawn series on his home ground. Despite missing one match he was the West Indies leading wicket taker and headed their averages.

	Own Team Total	O	M	R	W		Opp Total	Ct
260. Barbados v Trinidad & Tobago, Port of Spain, January 29, 30, 31, February 1 (Match drawn)								
c A.Rajah b R.Nanan	71 250	24	2	60	2	A.H.Gray lbw I.R.Bishop c and b	292	2
b A.H.Gray	2 205							
261. Barbados v Windward Islands, St George's, February 4, 5, 6, 7 (Barbados won by 144 runs)								
lbw b W.W.Davis	16 279	19	5	55	5	L.D.John c T.R.O.Payne D.Joseph lbw J.D.Charles c T.R.O.Payne W.W.Davis lbw J.T.Etienne b	154	
not out	55 241-7d	24	7	54	4	D.Joseph lbw J.D.Charles c H.Springer S.L.Mahon c V.S.Greene J.T.Murray c H.Springer	222	1
262. Barbados v Guyana, Bridgetown, February 13, 14, 15 (Barbados won by ten wickets)								
c R.Seeram b S.Matthews	77 474-8d	17	2	67	3	G.E.Charles c V.S.Greene M.R.Pydanna c J.Garner B.St.A.Browne lbw	233	1
did not bat	- 71-0	20.1	1	67	3	R.Seeram lbw G.E.Charles b C.G.Butts c sub	309	
263. Barbados v Jamaica, Kingston, February 20, 21, 22, 23 (Jamaica won by 53 runs)								
c C.A.Walsh b M.A.Tucker	1 181	18	8	59	1	R.C.Haynes lbw	263	
b C.A.Walsh	8 227	15.4	6	24	5	W.W.Lewis b P.J.L.Dujon c sub (V.S.Greene) M.A.Tucker lbw C.A.Walsh b B.P.Patterson b	198	1
264. Barbados v Leeward Islands, Bridgetown, February 26, 27, 28, 29 (Leeward Islands won by ten wickets)								
c sub b N.C.Guishard	56 243	21	1	80	4	A.L.Kelly lbw I.V.A.Richards c T.R.O.Payne R.M.Otto c T.R.O.Payne L.Harris c H.Springer	406	
b W.K.M.Benjamin	12 208	-	-	-	-		47-0	
265. WEST INDIES v PAKISTAN, Port of Spain, April 14, 15, 16, 17, 19 (Match drawn)								
not out	10 174	20	4	55	4	Mudassar Nazar c D.L.Haynes Ramiz Raja c R.B.Richardson Imran Khan c A.L.Logie Salim Yousuf c P.J.L.Dujon	194	
b Abdul Qadir	2 391	30	4	85	2	Ramiz Raja c I.V.A.Richards Wasim Akram c R.B.Richardson	341-9	

266. WEST INDIES v PAKISTAN, Bridgetown, April 22, 23, 24, 26, 27 (West Indies won by two wickets)

				O	M	R	W	
c Aamer Malik								
b Imran Khan	48	306		18.4	3	79	4	Javed Miandad
								c R.B.Richardson 309
								Salim Malik b
								Wasim Akram c W.K.M.Benjamin
								Abdul Qadir c C.A.Walsh
lbw b Wasim Akram	15	268-8		23	3	65	5	Ramiz Raja c A.L.Logie 262
								Javed Miandad c P.J.L.Dujon
								Aamer Malik c A.L.Logie
								Wasim Akram lbw
								Abdul Qadir c C.G.Greenidge

SEASON'S AVERAGES

Batting and Fielding	M	I	NO	Runs	HS	Ave	100	50	Ct
Test matches	2	4	1	75	48	25.00	-	-	-
Red Stripe	5	9	1	298	77	37.25	-	4	5
Season	7	13	2	373	77	33.90	-	4	5
Career	266	332	41	6656	116*	22.87	4	32	104

Bowling	O	M	R	W	BB	Ave	5i	10m
Test matches	91.4	14	284	15	5-65	18.93	1	-
Red Stripe	159.5	35	466	27	5-24	17.25	2	-
Season	251.3	49	750	42	5-24	17.85	3	-
Career	8218.1	2094	21102	1168	8-71	18.06	67	9

1988 – West Indies in England

England made a fine start to the series when Gooch and Broad put on 125 for the first wicket at Nottingham but their ten wickets only added a further 120 as Marshall took 6-69. He then scored 72 as West Indies took a big lead but Gooch's marvellous century saved the match. Six wickets again (ten in the match) helped West Indies to victory at Lord's but Marshall's astonishing performance was in the third Test at Old Trafford. England, trailing by 249, were dismissed for 93 with Marshall taking 7-22. These were his best figures in a Test career which was fast approaching 300 wickets. Marshall's team-mate Robin Smith made his debut in the fourth Test but England lost again and the series ended 4-0 at The Oval. Marshall finished 13 wickets ahead of the nearest bowler on either side although, surprisingly, was only third in the averages on 12.65 – a measure of West Indies' superiority. Marshall's Hampshire colleagues appeared in their first Lord's final, where his replacement Jefferies bowled them to victory over Derbyshire.

	Own Team	Total	O	M	R	W		Opp Total	Ct
267. West Indians v Somerset, Taunton, May 14, 15 (West Indians won by ten wickets)									
b D.J.Foster	9	251	8.4	3	23	2	G.D.Rose c W.K.M.Benjamin	113	
							C.H.Dredge c R.B.Richardson		
did not bat	-	12-0	13	0	31	1	M.D.Crowe c P.J.L.Dujon	146	
268. West Indians v Gloucestershire, Bristol, May 26, 27, 28 (Match drawn)									
st R.C.Russell b J.W.Lloyds	46	257	4.5	1	14	4	A.J.Wright c sub	140	2
							D.J.Thomas b		
							V.S.Greene c A.L.Logie		
							D.V.Lawrence b		
b V.S.Greene	23	233	3	0	5	0		98-1	
269. WEST INDIES v ENGLAND, Trent Bridge, June 2, 3, 4, 6, 7 (Match drawn)									
b J.E.Emburey	72	448-9d	30	4	69	6	G.A.Gooch b	245	
							B.C.Broad b		
							M.W.Gatting c A.L.Logie		
							A.J.Lamb lbw		
							D.R.Pringle b		
							J.E.Emburey c P.J.L.Dujon		
				13	4	23	1	M.W.Gatting b	301-3	

270. WEST INDIES v ENGLAND, Lord's, June 16, 17, 18, 20, 21 (West Indies won by 134 runs)
c G.A.Gooch b G.R.Dilley 11 209 18 5 32 6 G.A.Gooch b 165
                                              B.C.Broad lbw
                                              A.J.Lamb lbw
                                              P.R.Downton lbw
                                              P.W.Jarvis c D.L.Haynes
                                              G.R.Dilley b
b P.W.Jarvis 6 397 25 5 60 4 G.A.Gooch lbw 307
                                              B.C.Broad c P.J.L.Dujon
                                              P.R.Downton lbw
                                              G.C.Small c I.V.A.Richards

271. WEST INDIES v ENGLAND, Old Trafford, June 30, July 1, 2, 4, 5 (West Indies won by an innings and 156
runs)
not out 43 384-7d 12 5 19 2 M.D.Moxon b 135
                                              M.W.Gatting lbw
                       15.4 5 22 7 G.A.Gooch lbw 93
                                              M.W.Gatting c R.B.Richardson
                                              D.I.Gower c R.B.Richardson
                                              D.J.Capel c sub (K.L.T.Arthurton)
                                              P.R.Downton c R.A.Harper
                                              P.A.J.DeFreitas c R.A.Harper
                                              G.R.Dilley b

272. West Indians v Glamorgan, Swansea, July (14), 15, 16 (Match drawn)
did not bat - 302-3d 6 3 15 0 180-5d
did not bat - 67-1

273. WEST INDIES v ENGLAND, Headingley, July 21, 22, 23, 25, 26 (West Indies won by ten wickets)
c G.A.Gooch b D.R.Pringle 3 275 23 8 55 3 G.A.Gooch c P.J.L.Dujon 201
                                              C.S.Cowdrey lbw
                                              D.R.Pringle c P.J.L.Dujon
did not bat - 67-0 17 4 47 2 D.I.Gower c P.J.L.Dujon 138
                                              R.A.Smith lbw

274. West Indians v Essex, Chelmsford, July 30, 31, August 1 (Match drawn)
st D.E.East b G.Miller 76 378 7 0 22 0 250-9d
did not bat - 280-3d - - - - 113-5

275. WEST INDIES v ENGLAND, Kennington Oval, August 4, 5, 6, 8 (West Indies won by eight wickets)
c and b J.H.Childs 0 183 24.3 3 64 3 R.A.Smith c R.A.Harper 205 1
                                              D.R.Pringle c P.J.L.Dujon
                                              N.A.Foster c sub (K.L.T.Arthurton)
did not bat - 226-2 25 6 52 1 T.S.Curtis lbw 202

SEASON'S AVERAGES

Batting and Fielding	M	I	NO	Runs	HS	Ave	100	50	Ct
Test matches	5	6	1	135	72	27.00	-	1	1
Other matches	4	4	0	154	76	38.50	-	1	2
Tour	9	10	1	289	76	32.11	-	2	3
Career	275	342	42	6945	116*	23.15	4	34	107

Bowling	O	M	R	W	BB	Ave	5i	10m
Test matches	203.1	49	443	35	7-22	12.65	3	1
Other matches	42.3	7	110	7	4-14	15.71	-	-
Tour	245.4	56	553	42	7-22	13.16	3	1
Career	8463.5	2150	21655	1210	8-71	17.89	70	10

1988/89 – West Indies in Australia

Marshall made a low-key start to the tour but took ten wickets in the first three Tests which West Indies won to clinch the series. Australia were building the side that would perform so impressively in the following decade and they had much the better of the final two matches. For the West Indies, Ambrose was the most successful strike bowler with Walsh also prominent.

	Own Team Total	O	M	R	W		Opp Total	Ct

276. West Indians v Western Australia, Perth, October 28, 29, 30, 31 (Western Australia won by seven wickets)

	Own Team Total	O	M	R	W		Opp Total	Ct
b T.G.Hogan	31	213	19	5	54	0		
c K.H.Macleay							247	
b T.M.Alderman	1	236	10	1	36	0		
							206-3	

277. West Indians v South Australia, Adelaide, November 4, 5, 6, 7 (West Indians won by an innings and 20 runs)

	Own Team Total	O	M	R	W		Opp Total	Ct
not out	21	593-8d	13	2	31	1	A.M.J.Hilditch	
							c R.B.Richardson 163	
			9	2	42	0		410

278. WEST INDIES v AUSTRALIA, Brisbane, November 18, 19, 20, 21 (West Indies won by nine wickets)

c A.R.Border

	Own Team Total	O	M	R	W		Opp Total	Ct
b C.J.McDermott	11	394	18	3	39	2	D.C.Boon lbw	167
did not bat	-	63-1	26	2	92	4	S.R.Waugh lbw	
							D.C.Boon c P.J.L.Dujon	289
							S.R.Waugh c D.L.Haynes	
							I.A.Healy c C.E.L.Ambrose	
							A.I.C.Dodemaide c I.V.A.Richards	

279. WEST INDIES v AUSTRALIA, Perth, December 2, 3, 4, 5, 6 (West Indies won by 169 runs)

c M.R.J.Veletta

	Own Team Total	O	M	R	W		Opp Total	Ct
b M.G.Hughes	4	449	23	3	84	1	I.A.Healy lbw	395-8d
c I.A.Healy								
b A.I.C.Dodemaide	23	349-9d	12	0	50	2	G.R.Marsh c A.L.Logie	234
							M.R.J.Veletta c P.J.L.Dujon	

280. WEST INDIES v AUSTRALIA, Melbourne, December 24, 26, 27, 28, 29 (West Indies won by 285 runs)

	Own Team Total	O	M	R	W		Opp Total	Ct
c D.M.Jones b S.R.Waugh	7	280	30	8	68	0			
c T.M.Alderman							242	1
b S.R.Waugh	19	361-9d	9	3	12	1	D.C.Boon lbw	114

281. WEST INDIES v AUSTRALIA, Sydney, January 26, 27, 28, 29, 30 (Australia won by seven wickets)

	Own Team Total	O	M	R	W		Opp Total	Ct
c G.R.Marsh b A.R.Border	9	224	31	16	29	5	G.R.Marsh c P.J.L.Dujon	401
							A.R.Border b	
							I.A.Healy c A.L.Logie	
							P.L.Taylor lbw	
							T.V.Hohns b	
c P.L.Taylor b A.R.Border	3	256	8	2	17	1	D.C.Boon c R.A.Harper	82-3

282. WEST INDIES v AUSTRALIA, Adelaide, February 3, 4, 5, 6, 7 (Match drawn)

	Own Team Total	O	M	R	W		Opp Total	Ct
c G.R.Marsh b M.R.Whitney	0	369	23	3	67	1	A.R.Border b	515
did not bat	-	233-4	12	2	30	0		224-4d

SEASON'S AVERAGES

Batting and Fielding	M	I	NO	Runs	HS	Ave	100	50	Ct
Test matches	5	8	0	76	23	9.50	-	-	1
Other matches	2	3	1	53	31	26.50	-	-	-
Tour	7	11	1	129	31	12.90	-	-	1
Career	282	353	43	7074	116*	22.81	4	34	108

Bowling	O	M	R	W	BB	Ave	5i	10m
Test matches	192	42	488	17	5-29	28.70	1	-
Other matches	51	10	163	1	1-31	163.00	-	-
Tour	243	52	651	18	5-29	36.16	1	-
Career	8706.5	2202	22306	1228	8-71	18.16	71	10

1988/89

Marshall missed the first Test of the series with India which was ruined by rain. Ian Bishop made his debut and retained his place alongside Walsh and Ambrose as Marshall returned. Now the West Indies senior fast bowler, he dominated the final three Tests, all of which were won by the West Indies.

	Own Team Total	O	M	R	W		Opp Total	Ct

283. Barbados v Jamaica, Bridgetown, February 24, 25, 26, 27 (Match drawn)
b C.A.Walsh | 89 314 | 18 | 3 | 59 | 1 | W.W.Lewis b | 287 |
| | | 1 | 0 | 1 | 0 | | 331-8 | |

284. WEST INDIES v INDIA, Bridgetown, April 7, 8, 9, 11, 12 (West Indies won by eight wickets)
not out | 40 377 | 22 | 0 | 56 | 1 | K.S.More c P.J.L.Dujon | 321 |
did not bat | - 196-2 | 26 | 6 | 60 | 5 | N.S.Sidhu c A.L.Logie | 251 |
						M.Azharuddin c P.J.L.Dujon		
						Kapil Dev c P.J.L.Dujon		
						K.S.More b		
						Arshad Ayub b		

285. WEST INDIES v INDIA, Port of Spain, April 15, 16, 17, 19, 20 (West Indies won by 217 runs)
st K.S.More b Arshad Ayub 18 314 | 17 | 7 | 34 | 5 | Arun Lal c I.V.A.Richards | 150 |
						N.S.Sidhu b		
						R.J.Shastri c A.L.Logie		
						S.V.Manjrekar lbw		
						Kapil Dev c P.J.L.Dujon		
lbw b Kapil Dev	26 266	19.5	2	55	6	Arun Lal c P.J.L.Dujon	213
						W.V.Raman lbw		
						D.B.Vengsarkar c A.L.Logie		
						S.V.Manjrekar lbw		
						K.S.More lbw		
						C.Sharma b		

286. WEST INDIES v INDIA, Kingston, April 28, 29, 30, May 2, 3 (West Indies won by seven wickets)
b Kapil Dev | 0 384 | 19 | 4 | 56 | 1 | Arun Lal c I.V.A.Richards | 289 |
did not bat | - 60-3 | . 7.3 | 0 | 29 | 1 | C.Sharma b | 152 |

SEASON'S AVERAGES

Batting and Fielding	M	I	NO	Runs	HS	Ave	100	50	Ct
Test matches	3	4	1	84	40*	28.00	-	-	-
Red Stripe	1	1	0	89	89	89.00	-	1	-
Season	4	5	1	173	89	43.25	-	1	-
Career	286	358	44	7247	116*	23.07	4	35	108

Bowling	O	M	R	W	BB	Ave	5i	10m
Test matches	111.2	18	290	19	6-55	15.26	3	1
Red Stripe	19	3	60	1	1-59	60.00	-	-
Season	130.2	21	350	20	6-55	17.50	3	1
Career	8837.1	2223	22656	1248	8-71	18.15	74	11

1989

Marshall missed the first month of county cricket with a hand injury but then enjoyed a successful all-round season. Hampshire challenged for the Championship and NatWest Trophy but fell away in late season and were disappointed in both competitions.

	Own Team Total	O	M	R	W		Opp Total	Ct

287. Hampshire v Leicestershire, Bournemouth, May 27, 29, 30 (Hampshire won by 119 runs)
c N.E.Briers b C.C.Lewis | 25 288 | 16.3 | 7 | 38 | 1 | G.J.F.Ferris b | 293 |
did not bat | - 239-4d | 11.1 | 4 | 33 | 4 | T.J.Boon c R.J.Parks | 115 | 1
						L.Potter c R.J.Parks		
						G.J.Parsons c.R.J.Parks		
						J.P.Agnew b		

288. Hampshire v Kent, Tunbridge Wells, June 3, 5, 6 (Match drawn)
c A.P.Igglesden
b C.S.Cowdrey | 61 213 | 21 | 3 | 64 | 2 | M.R.Benson c R.J.Parks | 276-3 |
| | | | | | | R.F.Pienaar c M.C.J.Nicholas | | |

289. Hampshire v Surrey, Basingstoke, June 7, 8, 9 (Hampshire won by eight wickets)
did not bat | - 251-4d | 20 | 4 | 67 | 2 | C.K.Bullen lbw | 291 |
| | | | | | | M.Frost b | | |

did not bat — 157-2   13.2   1   39   5   D.J.Bicknell c C.L.Smith   116
G.P.Thorpe b
D.M.Ward c V.P.Terry
I.A.Greig b
M.Frost c V.P.Terry

290. Hampshire v Essex, Ilford, June 21, 22, 23 (Essex won by 102 runs)

c P.J.Prichard b J.H.Childs   0   244   21   8   49   1   M.E.Waugh c R.J.Parks   277
c A.W.Lilley b N.Shahid   6   165   15   3   39   3   B.R.Hardie c M.C.J.Nicholas 234-9d
A.W.Lilley lbw
P.J.Prichard c V.P.Terry

291. Hampshire v Sussex, Southampton, June 24, 26, 27 (Match drawn)

c A.C.S.Pigott
b A.M.Babington   0   356-8d   15   3   53   2   C.M.Wells c R.J.Parks   287
I.J.Gould b
did not bat — 171-3d   6   1   23   0   116-5

292. Hampshire v Yorkshire, Southampton, July 1, 3 (Yorkshire won by three wickets)

c D.Byas b A.Sidebottom   2   144   9   2   16   2   P.Carrick b   107
A.Sidebottom lbw
b M.D.Moxon   0   153   17   1   45   1   R.J.Blakey c R.J.Parks   191-7

293. Hampshire v Northamptonshire, Northampton, July 8, 10, 11 (Hampshire won by nine wickets)

not out   10   366-6d   14.2   6   20   4   W.Larkins lbw   166
N.A.Felton c J.R.Wood
N.G.B.Cook c C.L.Smith
M.A.Robinson lbw
did not bat — 57-1   25   11   36   5   R.J.Bailey c R.J.Parks   253
D.J.Capel lbw
A.Fordham c R.J.Parks
J.G.Thomas c R.J.Parks
W.W.Davis c V.P.Terry

294. Hampshire v Lancashire, Portsmouth, July 22, 24, 25 (Hampshire won by three wickets)

not out   41   336-4d   18   1   63   2   G.Fowler c R.J.Parks   475-4d
M.A.Atherton c R.J.Maru
c D.P.Hughes b I.D.Austin   48   287-7   9   3   18   1   M.A.Atherton c C.L.Smith   147-6d

295. Hampshire v Gloucestershire, Portsmouth, July 26, 27, 28 (Hampshire won by an innings and 118 runs)

c and b K.B.S.Jarvis   21   406-9d   28   7   64   3   C.W.J.Athey b   240
K.M.Curran c R.J.Maru
G.A.Tedstone c V.P.Terry
12   3   14   3   A.J.Wright c R.J.Maru   48
M.C.J.Ball c T.C.Middleton
C.W.J.Athey c M.C.J.Nicholas

296. Hampshire v Derbyshire, Derby, August 5, 7, 8 (Match drawn)

not out   27   472-6d   10   1   41   1   P.G.Newman c V.P.Terry   178
30   9   69   6   K.J.Barnett b   326-9
P.D.Bowler c M.C.J.Nicholas
J.E.Morris b
R.Sharma c R.J.Parks
A.E.Warner c M.C.J.Nicholas
M.A.Holding lbw

297. Hampshire v Warwickshire, Bournemouth, August 9, 10, 11 (Warwickshire won by 60 runs)

not out   8   103-5d   17   8   26   2   Asif Din c V.P.Terry   229
R.G.Twose c V.P.Terry
c A.A.Donald
b N.M.K.Smith   46   176   3   3   0   0   110-2d

298. Hampshire v Worcestershire, Bournemouth, August 12, 14, 15 (Worcestershire won by an innings and 91 runs)

c S.M.McEwan
b S.R.Lampitt   11   137   29   7   67   2   C.M.Tolley lbw   325
D.B.D'Oliveira c V.P.Terry
c P.Bent b R.K.Illingworth   23   97

299. Hampshire v Somerset, Taunton, August 19, 21, 22 (Somerset won by eight wickets)

run out   2   257   18   5   60   2   P.M.Roebuck c J.R.Wood   303-8d
C.J.Tavare b
c N.A.Mallender b A.N.Jones 0   138   9   3   33   2   S.J.Cook b   93-2
R.J.Harden c R.A.Smith

300. Hampshire v Glamorgan, Southampton, September 8, 9, 10, 11 (Glamorgan won by 30 runs)

lbw b S.L.Watkin	13	201	25.2	6	68	5	M.P.Maynard b I.Smith lbw S.J.Dennis c R.A.Smith S.L.Watkin b S.R.Barwick b	247
lbw b S.L.Watkin	0	149	15.5	5	22	3	S.P.James b S.L.Watkin c K.D.James S.R.Barwick c K.D.James	133

301. Hampshire v Gloucestershire, Bristol, September 13, 14, (15), (16) (Match drawn)

not out   68   287-7

SEASON'S AVERAGES

Batting and Fielding	M	I	NO	Runs	HS	Ave	100	50	Ct
County Championship	15	21	5	412	68*	25.75	-	2	2
Career	301	379	49	7659	116*	23.20	4	37	110

Bowling	O	M	R	W	BB	Ave	5i	10m
County Championship	428.3	115	1067	64	6-69	16.67	4	-
Career	9265.4	2338	23723	1312	8-71	18.08	78	11

1989/90

England gave Test debuts to Hussain and Stewart and surprised many people with an emphatic victory in the first Test. Bishop and Ambrose formed the West Indies opening attack and Marshall appeared in just two matches with little success.

	Own Team Total	O	M	R	W		Opp Total	Ct
302. Barbados v Guyana, Bridgetown, January 19, 20, 21, 22 (Barbados won by seven wickets)								
c R.Seeram b L.A.Joseph	59 452-8d	16	2	64	2	S.Dhaniram c C.A.Best A.F.D.Jackman lbw	231	
did not bat	- 43-3	19	9	23	1	A.F.Sattaur c R.L.Hoyte	260	
303. Barbados v Trinidad & Tobago, Pointe-a-Pierre, January 26, 27, 28, 29 (Barbados won by an innings and 87 runs)								
c R.J.Bishop b R.Dhanraj	3 441-8d	14	5	27	2	R.J.Bishop b D.I.Mohammed lbw	182	1
		4	0	20	1	P.V.Simmons c H.Springer	172	
304. WEST INDIES v ENGLAND, Kingston, February 24, 25, 26, 28, 29 (England won by nine wickets)								
b A.R.C.Fraser	0 164	18	3	46	1	G.C.Small lbw	364	
not out	8 240	-	-	-	-		41-1	
305. Barbados v England XI, Bridgetown, March 30, 31, April 1 (Match drawn)								
c C.C.Lewis b E.E.Hemmings	24 367	16	3	57	3	A.J.Stewart c C.A.Best D.J.Capel c C.G.Greenidge R.A.Smith lbw	158	
c sub (D.L.Bairstow) b C.C.Lewis	31 225-5d	5	0	16	0		126-1	
306. WEST INDIES v ENGLAND, Bridgetown, April 5, 6, 7, 8, 10 (West Indies won by 164 runs)								
c A.J.Lamb b G.C.Small	4 446	23	6	55	2	N.Hussain lbw D.J.Capel c C.G.Greenidge	358	
c R.A.Smith b G.C.Small	7 267	18	8	31	0		191	

SEASON'S AVERAGES

Batting and Fielding	M	I	NO	Runs	HS	Ave	100	50	Ct
Test matches	2	4	1	19	8*	6.33	-	-	-
Red Stripe	2	2	0	62	59	31.00	-	1	1
Other matches	1	2	0	55	31	27.50	-	-	-
Season	5	8	1	136	59	19.42	-	1	1
Career	306	387	50	7795	116*	23.13	4	38	111

Bowling	O	M	R	W	BB	Ave	5i	10m
Test matches	59	17	132	3	2-55	44.00	-	-
Red Stripe	53	16	134	6	2-27	22.33	-	-
Other matches	21	3	73	3	3-57	24.33	-	-
Season	133	36	339	12	3-57	28.25	-	-
Career	9398.4	2374	24062	1324	8-71	18.17	78	11

1990

Hampshire finished 3rd in the Championship. Excluding his debut season (1979) Hampshire had never finished below 7th in seasons when Marshall played and never above 15th in the years he toured with West Indies. The season was dominated by batsmen but only Ian Bishop enjoyed a lower average for the season. The two met in a match at Portsmouth when Marshall gave a remarkable all-round performance. Batting at five he scored 32 and 60 and took 3-60 in Derbyshire's first innings. They were set a target of 235 to win and raced to 140 before the second wicket fell but Marshall took seven wickets in 51 balls and Hampshire won by 48 runs. Marshall took 19 wickets in the Portsmouth 'Week' and scored two centuries in consecutive matches earlier in the season. He finished just 38 runs short of 1000 for the season.

	Own Team Total	O	M	R	W		Opp Total	Ct

307. Hampshire v Sussex, Southampton, May 15, 16, 17, 18 (Hampshire won by an innings and 157 runs)

	Own Team Total	O	M	R	W		Opp Total	Ct
c I.J.Gould b A.R.Hansford 85	600-8d	15	3	26	2	N.J.Lenham c D.I.Gower / I.J.Gould c C.L.Smith	152	
		24	10	66	0		291	2

308. Hampshire v Surrey, Kennington Oval, May 19, 21, 22 (Match drawn)

	Own Team Total	O	M	R	W		Opp Total	Ct
not out 47	250-4d	20	4	65	3	M.A.Lynch c D.I.Gower / G.P.Thorpe c R.J.Parks / I.A.Greig c V.P.Terry	374-5d	
not out 51	238-5	7	1	14	0		204-5d	

309. Hampshire v Essex, Southampton, May 23, 24, 25 (Match drawn)

	Own Team Total	O	M	R	W		Opp Total	Ct
did not bat -	260-2d	21	3	49	1	M.E.Waugh c R.J.Parks	315-4d	
b N.A.Foster 9	102-4	15	5	18	2	N.Shahid b / A.C.H.Seymour c R.J.Parks	210	

310. Hampshire v Yorkshire, Headingley, May 26, 28, 29 (Hampshire won by five wickets)

	Own Team Total	O	M	R	W		Opp Total	Ct
c R.J.Blakey b P.Carrick 117	337-7d	22	7	44	1	P.Carrick c R.J.Maru	300-8d	
b D.Gough 28	215-5	22	5	51	3	D.L.Bairstow lbw / P.Carrick c D.I.Gower / D.Gough c K.J.Shine	251	

311. Hampshire v Leicestershire, Leicester, June 2, 4, (5) (Match drawn)

	Own Team Total	O	M	R	W		Opp Total	Ct
b A.D.Mullally 112	349-7d	13	2	44	2	T.J.Boon c C.A.Connor / P.Willey c C.A.Connor	178	1
		15	4	44	3	J.J.Whitaker b / P.Willey c V.P.Terry / L.Potter b	189-5	

312. Hampshire v Glamorgan, Southampton, June 16, 18, 19 (Glamorgan won by four wickets)

	Own Team Total	O	M	R	W		Opp Total	Ct
c C.P.Metson b S.J.Dennis 4	363-8d	3	1	9	0		71-1d	
did not bat -	71-0d	22.4	7	63	2	C.G.Holmes c V.P.Terry / I.Smith c R.J.Parks	367-6	

313. Hampshire v Gloucestershire, Gloucester, June 20, (21), (22) (Match drawn)

	Own Team Total	O	M	R	W		Opp Total	Ct
		6	0	20	1	A.J.Wright c C.A.Connor	54-2	

314. Hampshire v Lancashire, Old Trafford, June 23, 25, 26 (Match drawn)

	Own Team Total	O	M	R	W		Opp Total	Ct
c G.Fowler b M.Watkinson 86	300-5d	5	0	28	0		58-0	
did not bat -	87-1d	14	2	42	2	G.D.Mendis c R.J.Parks / N.J.Speak b	131-4	

315. Hampshire v Nottinghamshire, Portsmouth, July 18, 19, 20 (Hampshire won by eight wickets)

	Own Team Total	O	M	R	W		Opp Total	Ct
c M.Newell b J.A.Afford 5	301-9d	16.1	4	30	4	K.P.Evans c V.P.Terry / F.D.Stephenson lbw / B.N.French lbw / K.E.Cooper b	110	

not out	23	84-2	21.1	4	64	5	M.Newell c R.J.Parks	274	l

B.N.French lbw
K.P.Evans c R.J.Parks
K.E.Cooper c R.J.Maru
J.A.Afford c R.J.Parks

316. Hampshire v Derbyshire, Portsmouth, July 21, 23, 24 (Hampshire won by 48 runs)
c C.J.Adams b I.R.Bishop   32   307   21   7   60   3   B.Roberts c R.J.Parks   300-6d
C.J.Adams c R.J.Parks
K.J.Barnett b

c K.J.Barnett
b O.H.Mortensen   60   227   15   4   47   7   P.D.Bowler b   186   l
J.E.Morris c and b
B.Roberts c R.J.Parks
C.J.Adams c R.J.Parks
K.M.Krikken lbw
A.E.Warner c R.J.Parks
D.E.Malcolm b

317. Hampshire v Sussex, Arundel, July 25, 26, 27 (Match drawn)
c A.I.C.Dodemaide
b I.D.K.Salisbury   11   254-5d   16   4   35   3   J.W.Hall lbw   383-9d
P.W.G.Parker b
A.I.C.Dodemaide lbw

c B.T.P.Donelan
b I.D.K.Salisbury   34   220-6   9   4   18   0   144-7d

318. Hampshire v Warwickshire, Edgbaston, July 28, 30, 31 (Warwickshire won by six wickets)
c D.A.Reeve
b A.R.K.Pierson   26   307-8d   8   3   17   0   253-3d
c T.M.Moody
b A.R.K.Pierson   10   216-4d   8   1   27   0   274-4

319. Hampshire v Northamptonshire, Bournemouth, August 4, 6 (Hampshire won by an innings and 22 runs)
did not bat   -   360-3d   17   4   37   4   A.Fordham c R.J.Parks   141
D.Ripley c V.P.Terry
J.G.Hughes c R.J.Maru
M.A.Robinson b

10   4   24   3   A.Fordham c R.J.Parks   197
W.Larkins lbw
R.J.Bailey lbw

320. Hampshire v Middlesex, Bournemouth, August 8, 9, 10 (Match drawn)
lbw b P.C.R.Tufnell   9   296   25   5   54   2   M.A.Roseberry c R.J.Maru   430-7d
M.R.Ramprakash c R.J.Parks

11   2   28   2   M.R.Ramprakash lbw   151
K.R.Brown lbw

321. Hampshire v Somerset, Taunton, August 18, 19, 20, 21 (Somerset won by five wickets)
lbw b I.G.Swallow   58   401-9d   16   3   43   3   R.J.Harden lbw   301-9d
G.D.Rose c C.L.Smith
N.A.Mallender b

did not bat   -   201-3d   11   2   34   1   S.J.Cook lbw   304-5

322. Hampshire v Surrey, Southampton, August 23, 24, 25, 27 (Surrey won by nine wickets)
lbw b M.A.Feltham   6   197   32   12   64   0   517   l
c A.J.Stewart
b K.T.Medlycott   31   393   -   -   -   -   75-1

323. Hampshire v Glamorgan, Pontypridd, September 7, 8, 9 (Hampshire won by eight wickets)
c R.D.B.Croft b M.Frost   51   313   22.4   6   45   5   M.P.Maynard c R.J.Maru   210
C.P.Metson b
S.L.Watkin c R.A.Smith
S.Bastien c R.J.Maru
M.Frost c A.N.Aymes

did not bat   -   72-2   22.4   8   47   6   M.P.Maynard c V.P.Terry   172
P.A.Cottey c A.N.Aymes
A.Dale c A.N.Aymes
R.D.B.Croft c V.P.Terry
C.P.Metson c R.A.Smith
S.Bastien c D.I.Gower

324. Hampshire v Gloucestershire, Southampton, September 18, 19, 20, 21 (Hampshire won by two wickets)
c R.C.Russell
b D.V.Lawrence   21   169   21   4   54   2   A.J.Wright c V.P.Terry   263
D.V.Lawrence b

c C.A.Walsh

b D.A.Graveney   46   446-8   27   7   70 0   350-8d   1

SEASON'S AVERAGES

Batting and Fielding	M	I	NO	Runs	HS	Ave	100	50	Ct
County Championship	18	24	3	962	117	45.80	2	6	7
Career	324	411	53	8757	117	24.46	6	44	118

Bowling		O	M	R	W	BB	Ave	5i	10m
County Championship		554.2	141	1381	72	7-47	19.18	4	2
Career	(6-ball)	9953	2515	25443	1396	8-71	18.22	82	13

1990/91 – West Indies in Pakistan

The three match series was drawn. Marshall's best performance was in the second innings at Faisalabad when he took four wickets in 26 balls and West Indies won. Desmond Haynes captained the touring side in the absence of Richards.

		Own Team Total	O	M	R	W		Opp Total	Ct
325. WEST INDIES v PAKISTAN, Karachi, November 15, 16, 17, 19, 20 (Pakistan won by eight wickets)									
b Waqar Younis		13 261	24	5	48	2	Shoaib Mohammad	345	
							c R.B.Richardson		
b Wasim Akram		21 181	5	1	8	0	Salim Malik c P.J.L.Dujon	98-2	
326. WEST INDIES v PAKISTAN, Faisalabad, November 23, 24, 25 (West Indies won by seven wickets)									
b Wasim Akram		20 195	8	1	30	0		170	
did not bat		- 130-3	4.2	0	24	4	Salim Malik b	154	
							Imran Khan c P.J.L.Dujon		
							Akram Raza b		
							Waqar Younis c P.J.L.Dujon		
327. WEST INDIES v PAKISTAN, Lahore, December 6, 7, 8, 10, 11 (Match drawn)									
b Wasim Akram		27 294	5	2	8	0		122	
b Wasim Akram		11 173	19	5	48	0		242-6	

SEASON'S AVERAGES

Batting and Fielding	M	I	NO	Runs	HS	Ave	100	50	Ct
Test matches	3	5	0	92	27	18.40	-	-	-
Career	327	416	53	8849	117	24.37	6	44	118

Bowling	O	M	R	W	BB	Ave	5i	10m
Test matches	65.2	14	166	6	4-24	27.66	-	-
Career	10018.2	2529	25609	1402	8-71	18.26	82	13

1990/91

Marshall remained a dominant force in domestic cricket and Barbados won three of the four matches in which he appeared. He played in all five Tests as West Indies took the series 2-1. Marshall's best figures were 3-31 but he was very consistent and topped the bowling averages with most wickets. Ambrose and Patterson opened the bowling and Richards returned as captain. Marshall had now easily exceeded Lance Gibbs' 309 Test wickets, the only other West Indian to take 300.

	Own Team Total	O	M	R	W		Opp Total	Ct

328. Barbados v Guyana, Bridgetown, January 11, 12, 13, 14 (Barbados won by eight wickets)

	Own Team Total	O	M	R	W		Opp Total	Ct
c G.E.Charles b B.St.A.Browne	89 319	13.5	1	27	4	S.Dhaniram c S.L.Campbell	182	
						C.L.Hooper c S.L.Campbell		
						M.A.Harper c S.L.Campbell		
						S.N.Mohammed lbw		
did not bat	- 106-2	12.5	1	49	2	C.G.Butts b	242	
						S.N.Mohammed c D.L.Haynes		

329. Barbados v Leeward Islands, St John's, January 18, 19, 20, 21 (Barbados won by 258 runs)

	Own Team Total	O	M	R	W		Opp Total	Ct
c I.V.A.Richards b K.C.G.Benjamin	48 333	12	2	23	2	D.Joseph c C.O.Browne	216	1
						E.A.E.Baptiste lbw		
c and b I.V.A.Richards	15 252	15	8	20	2	A.C.H.Walsh lbw	111	
						D.Joseph c R.I.C.Holder		

330. Barbados v Trinidad & Tobago, Bridgetown, January 25, 26, 27, 28 (Barbados won by nine wickets)

	Own Team Total	O	M	R	W		Opp Total	Ct
c B.C.Lara b R.Nanan	3 199	21.4	4	76	4	D.I.Mohammed c C.A.Best	267	
						A.L.Logie c S.M.Skeete		
						A.H.Gray c C.O.Browne		
						R.Sieuchan c A.C.Cummins		
did not bat	- 282-1	14	1	54	3	D.I.Mohammed b	212	
						N.Bidhesi lbw		
						D.Williams c C.O.Browne		

331. Barbados v Windward Islands, Bridgetown, February 1, 2, 3, 4 (Match drawn)

	Own Team Total	O	M	R	W		Opp Total	Ct
not out	5 420-5d	14	2	35	2	L.D.John c C.O.Browne	317	
						I.B.A.Allen c C.A.Best		
		17	5	51	3	J.Eugene c D.L.Haynes	229-8	
						J.D.Charles lbw		
						J.R.Murray lbw		

332. WEST INDIES v AUSTRALIA, Kingston, March 1, 2, 3, 5, 6 (Match drawn)

	Own Team Total	O	M	R	W		Opp Total	Ct
lbw b C.J.McDermott	0 264	22	3	57	1	M.E.Waugh lbw	371	
did not bat	- 334-3							

333. WEST INDIES v AUSTRALIA, Georgetown, March 23, 24, 25, 27, 28 (West Indies won by ten wickets)

	Own Team Total	O	M	R	W		Opp Total	Ct
not out	22 569	23	3	67	3	D.C.Boon c P.J.L.Dujon	348	
						A.R.Border b		
						D.M.Jones b		
did not bat	- 31-0	15	2	31	3	D.C.Boon c P.J.L.Dujon	248	
						A.R.Border c P.J.L.Dujon		
						G.R.J.Matthews c P.J.L.Dujon		

334. WEST INDIES v AUSTRALIA, Port of Spain, April 5, 6, 8, 9, 10 (Match drawn)

	Own Team Total	O	M	R	W		Opp Total	Ct
c C.J.McDermott b A.R.Border	12 227	18.1	3	55	3	M.A.Taylor c C.A.Walsh	294	
						M.E.Waugh lbw		
						I.A.Healy c P.J.L.Dujon		
		10	3	24	1	G.R.Marsh lbw	123-3d	

335. WEST INDIES v AUSTRALIA, Bridgetown, April 19, 20, 21, 23, 24 (West Indies won by 343 runs)

	Own Team Total	O	M	R	W		Opp Total	Ct
c G.R.Marsh b B.A.Reid	17 149	16	1	60	3	D.C.Boon c C.L.Hooper	134	
						A.R.Border b		
						D.M.Jones lbw		
c I.A.Healy b C.J.McDermott	15 536-9d	17	6	35	3	M.A.Taylor lbw	208	
						M.G.Hughes c P.J.L.Dujon		
						I.A.Healy lbw		

336. WEST INDIES v AUSTRALIA, St John's, April 27, 28, 29, May 1 (Australia won by 157 runs)

	Own Team Total	O	M	R	W		Opp Total	Ct
c I.A.Healy b M.E.Waugh	28 214	22	1	72	2	D.M.Jones lbw	403	
						I.A.Healy c P.J.L.Dujon		
lbw b M.G.Hughes	51 297	13.1	3	36	2	P.L.Taylor lbw	265	
						C.J.McDermott c P.J.L.Dujon		

SEASON'S AVERAGES

Batting and Fielding	M	I	NO	Runs	HS	Ave	100	50	Ct
Test matches	5	7	1	145	51	24.16	-	1	-
Red Stripe	4	5	1	160	89	40.00	-	1	2
Season	9	12	2	305	89	30.50	-	2	2
Career	336	428	55	9154	117	24.54	6	46	120

Bowling	O	M	R	W	BB	Ave	5i	10m
Test matches	156.2	25	437	21	3-31	20.80	-	-
Red Stripe	120.2	24	335	22	4-27	15.22	-	-
Season	276.4	49	772	43	4-27	17.95	-	-
Career	10295	2578	26381	1445	8-71	18.25	82	13

1991 – West Indies in England

Marshall toured England for the last time as his Test career came to a close. England won the first Test at Leeds and the series was contested keenly, ending 2-2. Marshall's best performance was in the fourth Test at Birmingham which West Indies won. His Test career finished with 376 wickets in 81 matches at an average only just over 20. Just over one third of those wickets were Englishmen. His batting average, under 20, was disappointing for a player who had the potential to be a genuine all-rounder.

	Own	Team Total	O	M	R	W		Opp Total	Ct
337. West Indians v Middlesex, Lord's, May 18, 19, 20 (West Indians won by six wickets)									
c sub b S.P.Hughes	19	384-9d	11	1	31	0		275	
did not bat	-	72-4	6	1	17	0		177	
338. West Indians v Somerset, Taunton, May 29, 30, 31 (Match drawn)									
c R.J.Harden									
b A.N.Hayhurst	14	342-7d	15	4	35	2	A.N.Hayhurst lbw	270-7d	
							R.J.Harden c D.Williams		
did not bat	-	261-2d	8	0	35	1	R.J.Harden c D.Williams	198	
339. WEST INDIES v ENGLAND, Headingley, June 6, 7, 8, 9, 10 (England won by 115 runs)									
c G.A.Hick b D.R.Pringle	0	173	13	4	46	3	G.A.Gooch c P.J.L.Dujon	198	
							A.J.Lamb c C.L.Hooper		
							M.R.Ramprakash c C.L.Hooper		
lbw b D.R.Pringle	1	162	25	4	58	3	D.R.Pringle c P.J.L.Dujon	252	
							S.L.Watkin c C.L.Hooper		
							D.E.Malcolm b		
340. West Indians v Derbyshire, Derby, June 12, 13, 14 (Match drawn)									
did not bat	-	261-5d	8	1	27	1	P.D.Bowler c C.B.Lambert	204-8d	
did not bat	-	199-4	9	2	22	1	I.Folley b	185-9	
341. WEST INDIES v ENGLAND, Lord's, June 20, 21, 22, (23), 24 (Match drawn)									
lbw b D.R.Pringle	25	419	30	4	78	2	A.J.Lamb c D.L.Haynes	354	
did not bat	-	12-2							
342. WEST INDIES v ENGLAND, Trent Bridge, July 4, 5, 6, 8, 9 (West Indies won by nine wickets)									
c R.K.Illingworth									
b P.A.J.DeFreitas	67	397	21.5	6	54	2	G.A.Gooch lbw	300	
							D.V.Lawrence c I.B.A.Allen		
did not bat	-	115-1	21	6	49	2	M.A.Atherton b	211	
							A.J.Lamb lbw		
343. West Indians v Glamorgan, Swansea, July 16, 17, 18 (Match drawn)									
not out	46	416-7d	10	2	34	2	M.P.Maynard c D.Williams	252	
							P.A.Cottey c R.B.Richardson		
	-	-	-	-				102-3	
344. WEST INDIES v ENGLAND, Edgbaston, July 25, 26, 27, 28 (West Indies won by seven wickets)									
not out	6	292	12.4	1	33	4	G.A.Gooch b	188	
							A.J.Lamb lbw		
							P.A.J.DeFreitas c R.B.Richardson		
							C.C.Lewis lbw		

did not bat — 157-3   19.4   3   53   2   M.R.Ramprakash
                                                    c P.J.L.Dujon   255
                               D.R.Pringle   c A.L.Logie

345. West Indians v Gloucestershire, Bristol, July 31, August 1,2 (Match drawn)
did not bat — 368-4d   16   2   57   1   R.J.Scott   c D.Williams   271-6d
c T.H.C.Hancock
       b A.M.Smith   1   261-5d   6   2   6   0   132-4

346. WEST INDIES v ENGLAND, Kennington Oval, August 8, 9, 10, 11, 12 (England won by five wickets)
c I.T.Botham b P.C.R.Tufnell 0   176   24   5   62   1   R.A.Smith   lbw   419
b P.A.J.DeFreitas   17   385   5   3   9   1   G.A.Gooch   lbw   146-5

347. West Indies XI v World XI, Scarborough. August 28, 29, 30 (Match drawn)
did not bat — 423-6d   21   6   76   2   Mudassar Nazar
                                        c C.L.Hooper   375
                          Kapil Dev   c C.B.Lambert
did not bat — 362-7d   -   -   -   -   255-5

SEASON'S AVERAGES

Batting and Fielding	M	I	NO	Runs	HS	Ave	100	50	Ct
Test matches	5	7	1	116	67	19.33	-	1	-
Other tour matches	5	4	1	80	46*	26.66	-	-	-
Tour	10	11	2	186	67	20.66	-	1	-
Other matches	1	-	-	-	-	-	-	-	-
Season	11	11	2	196	67	21.77	-	1	-
Career	347	439	57	9350	117	24.47	6	47	120

Bowling	O	M	R	W	BB	Ave	5i	10m
Test matches	172.1	36	442	20	4-33	22.10	-	-
Other tour matches	89	15	264	8	2-34	33.00	-	-
Tour	261.1	51	706	28	4-33	25.21	-	-
Other matches	21	6	76	2	2-76	38.00	-	-
Season	282.1	57	782	30	4-33	26.06	-	-
Career	10577.1	2635	27163	1475	8-71	18.41	82	13

1992

For the first time since his career began, Marshall played no first-class cricket during the English winter. He returned to Hampshire who, strengthened by the acquisition of Gower, were reigning NatWest Champions. They started the season in impressive form but a disastrous performance against Essex at Bournemouth saw their Championship hopes disappear and they finished 15th. There was compensation for Marshall when he appeared in his first Lord's final for the county and obtained a winners' medal with the best bowling in the match. He failed to take 50 Championship wickets for the first time in a full season, but passed 1500 career wickets. He was a member of the Hampshire side which played the first Championship match at Arundel Castle.

	Own Team Total	O	M	R	W		Opp Total	Ct
348. Hampshire v Sussex, Southampton, April 25, 27, (28), 29 (Hampshire won by 150 runs)								
did not bat	- 468-2d	5	0	16	0		169-2d	
innings forfeit		10	1	44	1	P.Moores c M.C.J.Nicholas	149	2
349. Hampshire v Yorkshire, Headingley, May 7, 8, 9, 10 (Match drawn)								
not out	46 397-8d	22.5	7	29	3	A.P.Grayson c V.P.Terry	250	
						C.S.Pickles c A.N.Aymes		
						M.A.Robinson b		
		2	0	8	0		74-1	

350. Hampshire v Surrey, Southampton, May 19, 20, 21, 22 (Hampshire won by ten wickets)
c and b N.M.Kendrick   10   552-9d   19.3   6   58   6   D.J.Bicknell c A.N.Aymes   184
                                                                    G.P.Thorpe c R.J.Maru
                                                                    D.M.Ward c J.R.Wood
                                                                    J.D.Robinson c V.P.Terry
                                                                    N.F.Sargeant b
did not bat   -   2-0   26   9   72   2   M.P.Bicknell lbw
                                                                    G.P.Thorpe c R.J.Maru   369
                                                                    N.F.Sargeant b

351. Hampshire v Lancashire, Old Trafford, May 23, 25, 26 (Hampshire won by 172 runs)
not out   13   349-5d   10   1   48   0
did not bat   -   316-4d   5.1   2   8   1   R.C.Irani c A.N.Aymes   322-6d
                                                                                                  171

352. Hampshire v Warwickshire, Edgbaston, June 12, 13, 15 (Match drawn)
c G.C.Small b P.A.Smith   0   290   23   4   59   3   D.P.Ostler b   216
                                                                    D.A.Reeve c A.N.Aymes
                                                                    R.G.Twose c D.I.Gower
did not bat   -   182-3d   17   3   42   1   P.A.Smith lbw   198-8   1

353. Hampshire v Leicestershire, Leicester, June 16, 17, 18 (Match drawn)
did not bat   -   282-3d   23   9   48   2   N.E.Briers b   450-7d
                                                                    B.F.Smith lbw
lbw b G.J.Parsons   8   394-9   -   -   -   -   140-5d

354. Hampshire v Essex, Bournemouth, June 19, 20, 22 (Essex won by 79 runs)
b J.P.Stephenson   36   300-8d   14.1   6   32   2   P.J.Prichard lbw   149   1
                                                                    N.Hussain c T.C.Middleton
c M.A.Garnham b M.C.Ilott   2   80   32   7   68   1   P.J.Prichard c R.J.Parks   310

355. Hampshire v Sussex, Arundel, June 30, July 1, 2 (Hampshire won by 130 runs)
c P.Moores b A.C.S.Pigott   12   271-9d
innings forfeit   innings forfeit
                                             16   3   44   3   D.M.Smith c R.J.Parks   141
                                                                    J.A.North lbw
                                                                    B.T.P.Donelan c T.C.Middleton

356. Hampshire v Nottinghamshire, Southampton, July (3), 4, 6 (Nottinghamshire won by five wickets)
not out   37   261-6d
innings forfeit   innings forfeit
                                             13   1   55   2   B.C.Broad c R.J.Parks   262-5
                                                                    R.T.Robinson c R.J.Parks

357. Hampshire v Derbyshire, Portsmouth, July 14, 15, 16 (Derbyshire won by an innings and 135 runs)
c P.D.Bowler
       b O.H.Mortensen   1   158   21   1   77   1   J.E.Morris c V.P.Terry   475-4d
c C.J.Adams b I.R.Bishop   0   182

358. Hampshire v Glamorgan, Portsmouth, July 17, 18, 20 (Match drawn)
c I.V.A.Richards b M.Frost   70   338-9d   19   6   37   1   I.V.A.Richards c D.I.Gower 208   3
lbw b S.L.Watkin   1   167-9d   18   5   54   1   H.Morris lbw   284-6   1

359. Hampshire v Gloucestershire, Cheltenham, July 21, 22, 23 (Match drawn)
c M.W.Alleyne b C.A.Walsh   5   167   26   11   47   1   G.D.Hodgson c J.R.Ayling   339-8d   1
c M.J.Scott b C.A.Walsh   39   274   2.5   0   20   0   95-7

360. Hampshire v Worcestershire, Worcester, August 4, 5, 6 (Match drawn)
c and b C.M.Tolley   58   261-8d   25   6   51   1   C.M.Tolley c A.N.Aymes   335-9d
not out   4   251-6   6   2   18   0   179-3d

361. Hampshire v Kent. Canterbury, August 7, 8, 10 (Kent won by nine wickets)
c G.J.Kersey b M.A.Ealham   17   288   19   4   47   1   T.R.Ward lbw   252-6d
c and b M.J.McCague   6   70   4   1   18   0   109-1

362. Hampshire v Northamptonshire, Bournemouth, August 14, 15, 17 (Northamptonshire won by ten wickets)
c R.J.Bailey b K.M.Curran   30   260   23.3   8   49   4   N.A.Felton c A.N.Aymes   338-8d
                                                                    R.J.Bailey c D.I.Gower
                                                                    D.J.Capel c A.N.Aymes
                                                                    A.R.Roberts c S.D.Udal
c D.Ripley b J.P.Taylor   3   100   -   -   -   -   23-0

363. Hampshire v Middlesex, Bournemouth, August 18, 19, 20 (Match drawn)
lbw b C.W.Taylor   37   386-9d   20   6   45   3   M.A.Roseberry c and b   115   1
                                                                    P.N.Weekes c A.N.Aymes
                                                                    K.R.Brown c A.N.Aymes
                                             21   5   50   0   346-9   1

364. Hampshire v Somerset, Weston-super-Mare, August 21, 22, 24 (Match drawn)
did not bat   -   47-1d   22   6   47   3   M.N.Lathwell b   370-8d
                                                                    N.D.Burns c A.N.Aymes
                                                                    G.D.Rose lbw

did not bat   -   62-1d   innings forfeit

365. Hampshire v Essex, Chelmsford, August 31, September 1, 2, 3 (Essex won by eight wickets)
lbw b P.M.Such   39   233   24   7   40   1   J.P.Stephenson   c A.N.Aymes   298
c P.J.Prichard b J.H.Childs   12   229   11   3   33   0   165-2

366. Hampshire v Worcestershire, Southampton, September 12, 13, 14, 15 (Match drawn)
retired hurt   27   231   15   3   33   3   W.P.C.Weston   c A.N.Aymes   228-8d
                                            R.K.Illingworth   b
                                            D.A.Leatherdale   lbw
did not bat   -   261-5d   13   1   51   2   T.S.Curtis   lbw   254-7
                                            S.J.Rhodes   c K.D.James

SEASON'S AVERAGES

Batting and Fielding	M	I	NO	Runs	HS	Ave	100	50	Ct
County Championship	19	25	5	513	70	25.65	-	2	11
Career	366	464	62	9863	117	24.53	6	49	131

Bowling	O	M	R	W	BB	Ave	5i	10m
County Championship	529	134	1348	49	6-58	27.51	1	-
Career	11106.1	2769	28511	1524	8-71	18.70	83	13

1992/93

Marshall had coached in South Africa a decade earlier and returned to play for Natal where he contributed to the development of a number of young cricketers including Pollock and Klusener. He enjoyed significant success in the Castle Cup.

	Own Team Total	O	M	R	W		Opp Total	Ct

367. Natal v Eastern Province, Port Elizabeth, October 23, 24, 25 (Natal won by ten wickets)
c and b E.A.E.Baptiste   2   418   10   0   23   1   M.C.Venter   b   119
did not bat   -   14-0   312

368. Natal v Border, Pietermaritzburg, November 6, 7, 8, 9 (Natal won by seven wickets)
c B.M.Osborne
     b R.J.McCurdy   3   210   17   3   36   4   P.C.Strydom   lbw   199
                                            D.O.Nosworthy   c sub
                                            I.L.Howell   c A.C..Hudson
                                            S.J.Palframan   c N.E.Wright
did not bat   -   272-3   25.4   8   61   4   B.M.Osborne   b   281   1
                                            P.N.Kirsten   c U.H.Goedeke
                                            M.R.Hobson   c I.B.Hobson
                                            R.J.McCurdy   b

369. Natal v Western Province, CapeTown, November (20), 21, 22, 23 (Western Province won by five wickets)
c A.J.Lamb b B.M.McMillan   0   102   22   2   56   3   M.F.Voss   c E.L.R.Stewart   219   1
                                            L.F.Bleekers   c E.L.R.Stewart
                                            E.O.Simons   lbw
c R.J.Ryall b M.W.Pringle   35   294   16   6   39   1   M.F.Voss   c E.L.R.Stewart   178-5

370. Natal v Northern Transvaal, Durban, January 1, 2, 3, 4 (Northern Transvaal won by 124 runs)
c R.V.Jennings
    b C.van Noordwyk   3   137   17   3   59   1   M.D.Haysman
                                            c E.L.R.Stewart   209
c R.V.Jennings b S.Elworthy   31   285   24   8   47   2   M.J.R.Rindel   c M.B.Logan   337-8d
                                            G.C.Abbott   c E.L.R.Stewart

371. Natal v Transvaal, Johannesburg, January 9, 10, 11, 12 (Natal won by 49 runs)
b S.D.Jack   12   279   21   6   45   6   M.Yashad   b   154   1
                                            B.M.White   c and b
                                            L.Seeff   lbw
                                            R.P.Snell   b
                                            J.A.Teeger   b
                                            C.E.Eksteen   b

c D.J.Cullinan b C.E.Eksteen 1   71   23   9   30   3   L.Seeff lbw   147
                                       S.J.Cook lbw
                                       C.E.Eksteen lbw

SEASON'S AVERAGES

Batting and Fielding	M	I	NO	Runs	HS	Ave	100	50	Ct
Castle Cup	5	8	0	87	35	10.87	-	-	4
Career	371	472	62	9950	117	24.26	6	49	135

Bowling	O	M	R	W	BB	Ave	5i	10m
Castle Cup	202.4	49	451	28	6-45	16.10	1	-
Career	11308.5	2818	20962	1552	8-71	18.66	84	13

1993

Marshall was no longer a major force in county cricket but he did complete 10,000 first-class runs. His finest performance was at Swansea in August when he scored 75 in his one innings and had match figures of 8-93 but this was a brief glimpse of the old Marshall and constitued more than 25% of his season's total with bat and ball. At the end of the season he retired from county cricket with 826 wickets. For Hampshire, only Derek Shackleton has a better career average than Marshall's 18.64 and he bowled on uncovered pitches. Marshall played in 210 matches for the county and also scored 5847 runs at an average over 25 per innings.

	Own Team Total	O	M	R	W		Opp Total	Ct
372. Hampshire v Somerset, Southampton, April 29, 30, May 1, 2 (Somerset won by an innings and 148 runs)								
lbw b A.R.Caddick	0 156	30	8	67	1	R.J.Harden b	500-6d	
c N.A.Folland b G.D.Rose	8 196							
373. Hampshire v Durham, Stockton-on-Tees, May 13, (14), 15, (17) (Match drawn)								
did not bat	- 289-3							
374. Hampshire v Yorkshire, Southampton, May (20), 21, 22, 24 (Yorkshire won by six wickets)								
c R.D.Stemp b M.J.Foster	4 307-8d	18	8	35	2	R.B.Richardson c sub (R.J.Maru) b	248	
c R.J.Blakey b R.D.Stemp	34 162-9d	10	1	44	1	D.Byas b R.J.Blakey c A.N.Aymes	224-4	
375. Hampshire v Derbyshire, Derby, May (27), 28, 29, 31 (Match drawn)								
lbw b A.E.Warner	5 243	17	2	69	1	K.J.Barnett b		
did not bat	- 290-4d						389-7d	1
376. Hampshire v Kent, Basingstoke, June 10, 11, (12), (13) (Match drawn)								
lbw b M.V.Fleming	0 232-7	21.3	5	67	3	T.R.Ward b M.R.Benson b M.M.Patel lbw	275	1
377. Hampshire v Northamptonshire, Northampton June 17, 18, 19, 21 (Hampshire won by seven wickets)								
lbw b J.P.Taylor	8 247	13	5	29	3	M.B.Loye c K.D.James K.M.Curran b	125	
did not bat	- 182-3	30	12	53	2	J.P.Taylor c R.S.M.Morris D.Ripley b N.G.B.Cook b	303	
378. Hampshire v Gloucestershire, Bristol, July, 1, 2, 3, 5 (Hampshire won by one wicket)								
did not bat	- 393-6d	33	10	81	0			
c M.J.Gerrard b M.Davies	16 213-9	8	3	19	1	B.C.Broad c V.P.Terry	501-7d 102	
379. Hampshire v Worcestershire, Portsmouth, July 15, 16, 17, (19) (Match drawn)								
c G.A.Hick b K.C.G.Benjamin	0 355-9d	21	8	37	3	T.S.Curtis c A.N.Aymes W.P.C.Weston c A.N.Aymes D.B.D'Oliveira c R.S.M.Morris	206-6	
380. Hampshire v Warwickshire, Southampton, July 29, 30, 31, August 2 (Warwickshire won by 80 runs)								
c K.J.Piper b M.A.V.Bell	12 294	19	4	57	1	T.L.Penney b	190	
c T.L.Penney b P.A.Booth	32 208	25	7	50	0		392	

381. Hampshire v Lancashire, Southampton, August 12, 13, 14, 15 (Match drawn)

lbw b M.Watkinson	6	384	14	2	44	0		386
did not bat	-	258-6d	6	2	10	0		138-3

382. Hampshire v Glamorgan, Swansea, August 19, 20, 21, 23 (Hampshire won by 98 runs)

not out	75	417	23	8	62	5	A.Dale lbw	288	1
							D.L.Hemp c A.N.Aymes		
							R.D.B.Croft c S.D.Udal		
							C.P.Metson lbw		
							R.P.Lefebvre c and b		
did not bat	-	196-4d	15	6	31	3	I.V.A.Richards c A.N.Aymes	227	
							C.P.Metson lbw		
							R.P.Lefebvre c and b		

383. Hampshire v Sussex, Portsmouth, August 26, 27, 28, 30 (Sussex won by 57 runs)

retired hurt	11	349	33	10	73	1	C.W.J.Athey c A.N.Aymes	439
c A.P.Wells								318-7d
b I.D.K.Salisbury	35	351	-	-	-	-		

384. Hampshire v Leicestershire, Southampton, September 9, 10, (11), (13) (Match drawn)

c V.J.Wells b D.J.Millns	4	115	9	1	31	1	P.N.Hepworth lbw	85-1

SEASON'S AVERAGES

Batting and Fielding	M	I	NO	Runs	HS	Ave	100	50	Ct
County Championship	13	16	2	250	75*	17.85	-	1	3
Career	384	488	64	10200	117	24.05	6	50	138

Bowling	O	M	R	W	BB	Ave	5i	10m
County Championship	345.3	102	859	28	5-62	30.67	1	-
Career	11654.2	2920	29821	1580	8-71	18.87	85	13

1993/94

Marshall returned to Natal and enjoyed some success including his last first-class century. His side lost their second successive limited-overs final.

	Own Team Total	O	M	R	W		Opp Total	Ct

385. Natal v Eastern Province, Durban, October 22, 23, 24, 25 (Match drawn)

not out	39	359	31.4	8	63	2	K.C.Wessels lbw	422
							B.N.Schultz b	
did not bat	-	170-5						

386. Natal v Orange Free State, Bloemfontein, October 29, 30, 31, November 1 (Orange Free State won by 151 runs)

not out	59	435	27	6	104	1	G.F.J.Liebenberg	
							c E.L.R.Stewart	450-8d
c W.J.Cronje b B.T.Player	18	181	9	1	31	0		317-4d

387. Natal v Border, East London, November 25, 26, 27, 28 (Match drawn)

c P.J.Botha b O.D.Gibson	10	443	24	7	61	1	F.J.C.Cronje c U.H.Goedeke	392
			27	6	54	0		152-1

388. Natal v Western Province, Pietermaritzburg, December 10, 11, 12, 13 (Match drawn)

not out	120	429	28	8	62	3	S.G.Koenig lbw	300
							D.Jordaan lbw	
							A.P.Kuiper c D.N.Crookes	
			24	11	32	1	E.O.Simons lbw	173-6

389. Natal v Northern Transvaal, Durban, December 26, 27, 28, 29 (Natal won by 136 runs)

run out	16	346	19.2	8	35	3	C.B.Lambert lbw	103-4d
							V.F.duPreez c D.J.Watson	
							R.F.Pienaar c U.H.Goedeke	
did not bat	-	91-2d	22	7	47	2	M.J.R.Rindel lbw	198	1
							R.E.Bryson b	

390. Natal v England 'A', Durban, January 1, 2, 3, 4 (Natal won by an innings and 57 runs)

not out	14	458-9d	7	4	4	0	116
			28	9	53	0	285

391. Natal v Boland, Stellenbosch, February 11, 12, 13, 14 (Boland won by 134 runs)
```
   lbw b M.Erasmus          73   306   16    9   24   1   M.Erasmus  c N.E.Wright         351
   b C.W.Henderson           8   187   27   10   57   2   W.S.Truter  c M.L.Bruyns       276-8d
                                                          L.Germishuys  b
```
392. Natal v Transvaal, Durban, February 26, 27, 28, March 1 (Match drawn)
```
   c M.Yachad b R.P.Snell   16   464   30   11   61   3   B.M.White  c N.C.Johnson        296
                                                          M.W.Rushmere  b
                                                          S.D.Jack  lbw
   b S.D.Jack               47   144   11    5   10   0                                   123-3
```

SEASON'S AVERAGES

Batting and Fielding	M	I	NO	Runs	HS	Ave	100	50	Ct
Castle Cup	7	10	3	406	120*	50.00	1	2	1
Other matches	1	1	1	14*	-	-	-	-	-
Season	8	11	4	420	120*	60.00	1	2	1
Career	392	499	68	10620	120*	24.64	7	52	139

Bowling	O	M	R	W	BB	Ave	5i	10m
Castle Cup	296	97	641	19	3-35	33.73	-	-
Other matches	35	13	57	0	-	-	-	-
Season	331	110	698	19	3-35	36.73	-	-
Career	11985.2	3030	30519	1599	8-71	19.08	85	13

1994

Marshall played one match in the Scarborough Festival and, in this final first-class match on English soil, took 3-60 against the South Africans.

	Own Team Total	O	M	R	W		Opp Total	Ct

393. Scarborough President's XI v South Africans, Scarborough, August 31, September 1, 2 (Match drawn)
```
   did not bat            -  343-6d                                             innings forfeit
   innings forfeit                   16    2   60   3   A.C.Hudson  c C.W.Scott       270-6
                                                       G.F.J.Liebenberg  b
                                                       D.J.Cullinan  lbw
```

SEASON'S AVERAGES

Batting and Fielding	M	I	NO	Runs	HS	Ave	100	50	Ct
Other matches	1	-	-	-	-	-	-	-	-
Career	393	499	68	10620	120*	24.64	7	52	139

Bowling	O	M	R	W	BB	Ave	5i	10m
Other matches	16	2	60	3	3-60	20.00	-	-
Career	12001.2	3032	30579	1602	8-71	19.08	85	13

1994/95

He returned to their country to play for Natal and was delighted to be a member of the side which won the Castle Cup. He made a significant all-round contribution with a batting average of almost 30 and 35 wickets at 16 apiece.

	Own Team Total	O	M	R	W		Opp Total	Ct

394. Natal v Orange Free State, Durban, November 5, 6, 7 (Natal won by nine wickets)
```
   c G.F.J.Liebenberg
     b F.D.Stephenson    28   236   15    7   32   1   J.M.Arthur  c N.C.Johnson        126
```

did not bat   -   141-1   25.3 13   42   4   G.F.J.Liebenberg
                                                     c E.L.R.Stewart   250
                                                 W.J.Cronje c E.L.R.Stewart
                                                 F.D.Stephenson c E.L.R.Stewart
                                                 B.T.Player c E.L.R.Stewart

395. Natal v Border, Durban, November 11, 12, 13, 14 (Natal won by 12 runs)
c P.N.Kirsten b O.D.Gibson   0   179   22   9   47   4   A.G.Lawson c N.C.Johnson 115
                                                         D.J.Cullinan b
                                                         P.J.Botha c A.C.Hudson
                                                         I.L.Howell lbw
c I.L.Howell b O.D.Gibson 21   183   27   11   51   3   P.C.Strydom c N.E.Wright   235
                                                         S.L.Palframan c N.C.Johnson
                                                         J.A.Ehrke b

396. Natal v Western Province, CapeTown, December 10, 11, 12, 13 (Match drawn)
lbw b A.C.Dawson   19   390   28   9   58   3   S.G.Koenig b   303   1
                                                H.H.Gibbs lbw
                                                J.H.Kallis lbw
did not bat   -   246-5d 10   3   18   1   H.D.Ackerman c M.L.Bruyns 193-6

397. Natal v Transvaal, Johannesburg, December 17, 18, 19, 20 (Natal won by 244 runs)
not out   82   339   10   1   28   2   N.Pothias c M.L.Bruyns   162
                                                S.J.Cook lbw
c and b M.J.Vandrau 16   244   18   7   47   1   B.M.White c M.L.Bruyns   177

398. Natal v Boland, Durban, January 13, 14, 15, 16 (Natal won by 111 runs)
not out   16   450-8d 22   9   77   2   K.M.Curran st M.L.Bruyns   250
                                                C.W.Henderson c N.E.Wright
did not bat   -   40-1d 10   4   17   3   M.S.Nackerdien b   129
                                                W.S.Truter c D.J.Watson
                                                L.M.Germishuys c D.J.Watson

399. Natal v Northrn Transvaal, Durban, January 26, 27, 28, 29 (Natal won by five wickets)
c C.B.Lambert b S.Elworthy 10   208   25   7   48   3   C.B.Lambert lbw   270
                                                       M.J.G.Davis c M.L.Bruyns
                                                       L.P.Vorster c D.N.Crookes
did not bat   -   223-5   22   11   40   4   C.B.Lambert lbw   159
                                                M.J.G.Davis lbw
                                                R.F.Pienaar c M.L.Bruyns
                                                P.S.deVilliers lbw

400. Natal v Eastern Province, Port Elizabeth, February 3, 4, 5 (Natal won by ten wickets)
lbw b T.G.Shaw   13   377   13   7   21   1   A.G.Huckle b   218
did not bat   -   19-0   16   0   40   3   G.Morgan c M.L.Bruyns   175
                                                D.J.Callaghan b
                                                L.J.Koen c M.L.Bruyns

401. Natal v Border, East London, February 17, 18, 19, 20 (Match drawn)
not out   4   303   -   -   -   -   202

SEASON'S AVERAGES

Batting and Fielding	M	I	NO	Runs	HS	Ave	100	50	Ct
Castle Cup	8	10	3	209	82*	29.85	-	1	1
Career	401	509	71	10829	120*	24.72	7	53	140

Bowling	O	M	R	W	BB	Ave	5i	10m
Castle Cup	263.3	98	566	35	4-40	16.17	-	-
Career	12264.5	3130	31145	1637	8-71	19.02	85	13

1995/96

Marshall's career came to a close with a couple of successful lbw appeals at a rainy Centurion Park. His bowling was less incisive in this final season but he was desperately unlucky not to add one more century at Bloemfontein as he battled to save Natal from a heavy defeat.

	Own Team Total	O	M	R	W		Opp Total	Ct

402. Natal v Border, East London, October 27, 28, 29, 30 (Natal won by an innings and 80 runs)

	Own Team Total	O	M	R	W		Opp Total	Ct
lbw b I.L.Howell	18 448	7	1	21	1	P.N.Kirsten b	91	1
		26.3	10	48	4	S.C.Pope c M.L.Bruyns	277	
						P.N.Kirsten lbw		
						D.J.Cullinan b		
						B.C.Fourie lbw		

403. Natal v Transvaal, Durban, November 3, 4, 5, 6 (Natal won by 167 runs)

	Own Team Total	O	M	R	W		Opp Total	Ct
b R.P.Snell	4 297	5.5	2	12	1	A.M.Bacher lbw	259	
not out	5 253	11	1	29	1	N.Pothias c N.C.Johnson	124	1

404. Natal v Eastern Province, Durban, November 24, 25, 26, 27 (Natal won by an innings and 159 runs)

	Own Team Total	O	M	R	W		Opp Total	Ct
did not bat	- 449-5d	8	3	12	1	P.G.Amm lbw	71	
		12	6	21	0		219	

405. Natal v Free State, Bloemfontein, December 8, 9, 10, 11 (Free State won by eight wickets)

	Own Team Total	O	M	R	W		Opp Total	Ct
c L.J.Wilkinson b H.C.Bakkes	7 167	28	10	72	0			
not out	99 474	4	0	10	0		532-7d	1
							113-2	

406. Natal v Northern Transvaal, Durban, January 1, 2, 3 (Natal won by an innings and 17 runs)

	Own Team Total	O	M	R	W		Opp Total	Ct
c I.Pistorius b M.J.R.Rindel	38 369	11	1	41	2	I.Pistorius lbw	161	2
						C.van Noordwyk c E.L.R.Stewart		
		15	5	19	0		191	

407. Natal v Western Province, Durban, January 26, 27, 28, 29 (Match drawn)

	Own Team Total	O	M	R	W		Opp Total	Ct
c D.L.Haynes b B.M.McMillan	4 277	9	2	14	1	G.Kirsten c T.Bosch	85	
		16	4	53	1	J.H.Kallis c R.E.Veenstra	273-7	

408. Natal v Northern Transvaal, Centurion, February 9, 10, 11, 12 (Match drawn)

	Own Team Total	O	M	R	W		Opp Total	Ct
did not bat	- 167-6	23.1	5	51	2	A.J.Seymore lbw	213	
						M.J.G.Davis lbw		

SEASON'S AVERAGES

Batting and Fielding	M	I	NO	Runs	HS	Ave	100	50	Ct
Castle Cup	7	7	2	175	99*	35.00	-	1	5
Career	408	516	73	11004	120*	24.83	7	54	145

Bowling	O	M	R	W	BB	Ave	5i	10m
Castle Cup	176.3	50	403	14	4-48	28.78	-	-
Career	12441.2	3180	31548	1651	8-71	19.10	85	13

Season by Season (Batting & Fielding)

Season		M	I	NO	R	HS	Ave	100	50	Ct
1977/78	WI	1	1	0	0	0	0.00	-	-	-
1978/79	WI in Ind/SL	11	15	2	160	59	12.30	-	1	6
1978/79	WI	4	5	1	38	17	9.50	-	-	2
1979	Hampshire	19	25	2	197	38	8.56	-	-	12
1979/80	WI in Aus/NZ	4	6	2	59	23*	14.75	-	-	2
1979/80	WI	4	4	1	142	55	47.33	-	1	1
1980	WI in Eng	12	12	2	211	52	21.10	-	1	2
1980	Hampshire	5	10	1	251	72*	27.88	-	2	4
1980/81	WI in Pak	7	8	0	70	24	8.75	-	-	2
1980/81	WI	7	9	2	239	49*	34.14	-	-	2
1981	Hampshire	17	23	3	425	75*	21.25	-	1	6
1981/82	YWI in Zim	3	4	0	175	109	43.75	1	-	-
1981/82	WI in Aus	2	2	0	66	66	33.00	-	1	-
1982	Hampshire	22	31	3	633	116*	22.60	1	1	4
1982/83	WI	11	15	1	323	71	23.07	-	1	7
1983	Hampshire	16	16	4	563	112	46.91	2	2	6
1983/84	WI in Ind	7	8	0	305	92	38.12	-	3	1
1983/84	WI	4	4	0	45	19	11.25	-	-	2
1984	WI in Eng	8	9	0	103	34	11.44	-	-	3
1984/85	WI in Aus	7	9	2	212	57	30.28	-	2	4
1984/85	WI	4	4	0	90	63	22.50	-	1	3
1985	Hampshire	22	33	2	768	66*	24.77	-	5	10
1985/86	WI	9	11	2	204	76	22.66	-	2	8
1986	Hampshire	23	23	2	263	51*	12.52	-	1	5
1986/87	WI in Pak	4	6	2	48	16*	12.00	-	-	-
1986/87	WI in NZ	3	4	0	83	45	20.75	-	-	-
1986/87	WI	1	-	-	-	-	-	-	-	-
1987	Hants/MCC	22	22	5	610	99	35.88	-	3	7
1987/88	WI	7	13	2	373	77	33.90	-	4	5
1988	WI in Eng	9	10	1	289	76	32.11	-	2	3
1988/89	WI in Aus	7	11	1	129	31	12.90	-	-	1
1988/89	WI	4	5	1	173	89	43.25	-	1	-
1989	Hampshire	15	21	5	412	68*	25.75	-	2	2
1989/90	WI	5	8	1	136	59	19.42	-	1	1
1990	Hampshire	18	24	3	962	117	45.80	2	6	7
1990/91	WI in Pak	3	5	0	92	27	18.40	-	-	-
1990/91	WI	9	12	2	305	89	30.50	-	2	2
1991	WI in Eng	11	11	2	196	67	21.77	-	1	-
1992	Hampshire	19	25	5	513	70	25.65	-	2	11
1992/93	RSA	5	8	0	87	35	10.87	-	-	4
1993	Hampshire	13	16	2	250	75*	17.85	-	1	3
1993/94	WI	8	11	4	420	120*	60.00	1	2	1
1994	Pres XI	1	-	-	-	-	-	-	-	-
1994/95	RSA	8	10	3	209	82*	29.85	-	1	1
1995/96	RSA	7	7	2	175	99*	35.00	-	1	5
Total		**408**	**516**	**73**	**11004**	**120***	**24.83**	**7**	**54**	**145**

Season by Season (Bowling)

Season		O	M	R	W	BB	Ave	5i	10m
1977/78	WI	33.4	7	97	7	6-77	13.85	1	-
1977/78	WI in Ind/SL	286.3	70	810	42	6-42	19.28	3	1
1978/79	WI	124.3	22	401	25	6-82	16.04	2	-
1979	Hampshire	467	146	1051	47	5-56	22.36	1	-
1979/80	WI in Aus/NZ	107	27	293	14	5-43	20.92	1	-
1979/80	WI	105.1	29	273	18	6-38	15.16	1	-
1980	WI in Eng	336.3	86	864	49	7-56	17.63	2	-
1980	Hampshire	141	42	306	17	5-39	18.00	1	-
1980/81	WI in Pak	151.2	20	465	25	5-9	18.60	1	-
1980/81	WI	213	53	541	28	6-75	19.32	1	-
1981	Hampshire	531.3	166	1321	68	6-57	19.42	5	-
1981/82	YWI in Zim	80.4	20	192	7	4-39	27.42	-	-
1981/82	WI in Aus	46	14	105	11	5-31	9.54	1	-
1982	Hampshire	822	225	2108	134	8-71	15.73	12	4
1982/83	WI	385.3	89	1045	42	5-37	24.88	1	-
1983	Hampshire	532.5	143	1327	80	7-29	16.58	5	1
1983/84	WI in Ind	234	64	641	34	6-37	18.85	2	-
1983/84	WI	158.5	24	480	21	5-42	22.85	2	-
1984	WI in Eng	260.4	75	646	40	7-53	16.15	4	-
1984/85	WI in Aus	267.3	59	699	36	5-38	19.41	4	1
1984/85	WI	170.1	30	486	27	7-80	18.00	1	1
1985	Hampshire	688.1	193	1680	95	7-59	17.68	5	-
1985/86	WI	296.3	58	835	50	6-85	16.70	1	1
1986	Hampshire	656.3	171	1508	100	6-51	15.08	5	-
1986/87	WI in Pak	131	30	327	17	5-23	19.23	1	-
1986/87	WI in NZ	119	21	289	9	4-43	32.11	-	-
1986/87	WI	26	9	54	7	4-35	7.71	-	-
1987	Hants/MCC	594.1	152	1508	76	5-49	19.84	1	-
1987/88	WI	251.3	49	750	42	5-24	17.85	3	-
1988	WI in Eng	245.4	56	553	42	7-22	13.16	3	1
1988/89	WI in Aus	243	52	651	18	5-29	36.16	1	-
1988/89	WI	130.2	21	350	20	6-55	17.50	3	1
1989	Hampshire	428.3	115	1067	64	6-69	16.67	4	-
1989/90	WI	133	36	339	12	3-57	28.25	-	-
1990	Hampshire	554.2	141	1381	72	7-47	19.18	4	2
1990/91	WI in Pak	65.2	14	166	6	4-24	27.66	-	-
1990/91	WI	276.4	49	772	43	4-27	17.95	-	-
1991	WI in Eng	282.1	57	782	30	4-33	26.06	-	-
1992	Hampshire	529	134	1348	49	6-58	27.51	1	-
1992/93	RSA	202.4	49	451	28	6-45	16.10	1	-
1993	Hampshire	345.3	102	859	28	5-62	30.67	1	-
1993/94	WI	331	110	698	19	3-35	36.73	-	-
1994	Pres XI	16	2	60	3	3-60	20.00	-	-
1994/95	RSA	263.3	98	566	35	4-40	16.17	-	-
1995/96	RSA	176.3	50	403	14	4-48	28.78	-	-
Total		**12441.2**	**3180**	**31548**	**1651**	**8-71**	**19.10**	**85**	**13**

Test Record Season by Season (Batting and Fielding)

Season		M	I	NO	R	HS	Ave	100	50	Ct
1978/79	v India	3	5	1	8	5	2.00	-	-	1
1980	v England	4	5	0	90	45	18.00	-	-	2
1980/81	v Pakistan	4	5	0	13	9	2.60	-	-	1
1980/81	v England	1	1	0	15	15	15.00	-	-	-
1982/83	v India	5	6	1	74	27	14.80	-	-	3
1983/84	v India	6	7	0	244	92	34.85	-	2	1
1983/84	v Australia	4	4	0	45	19	11.25	-	-	2
1984	v England	4	5	0	47	29	9.40	-	-	2
1984/85	v Australia	5	6	1	174	57	34.80	-	2	4
1984/85	v New Zealand	4	4	0	90	63	22.50	-	1	3
1985/86	v England	5	5	1	153	76	38.25	-	2	4
1986/87	v Pakistan	3	5	1	32	13*	8.00	-	-	-
1986/87	v New Zealand	3	4	0	83	45	20.75	-	-	-
1987/88	v Pakistan	2	4	1	75	48	25.00	-	-	-
1988	v England	5	6	1	135	72	27.00	-	1	1
1988/89	v Australia	5	8	0	76	23	9.50	-	-	1
1988/89	v India	3	4	1	84	40*	28.00	-	-	-
1989/90	v England	2	4	1	19	8*	6.33	-	-	-
1990/91	v Pakistan	3	5	0	92	27	18.40	-	-	-
1990/91	v Australia	5	7	1	145	51	24.16	-	1	-
1991	v England	5	7	1	116	67	19.33	-	1	-
Total		**81**	**107**	**11**	**1810**	**92**	**18.85**	**-**	**10**	**25**

Test Record Season by Season (Bowling)

Season		O	M	R	W	BB	Ave	5i	10m
1978/79	v India	78	11	265	3	1-44	88.33	-	-
1980	v England	172.3	42	436	15	3-36	29.06	-	-
1980/81	v Pakistan	98.3	12	319	13	4-25	24.53	-	-
1980/81	v England	21	2	64	3	2-49	21.33	-	-
1982/83	v India	174.1	40	495	21	5-37	23.57	1	-
1983/84	v India	221	59	621	33	6-37	18.81	2	-
1983/84	v Australia	158.5	24	480	21	5-42	22.85	2	-
1984	v England	167.4	50	437	24	7-53	18.20	3	-
1984/85	v Australia	215.2	45	554	28	5-38	19.78	4	1
1984/85	v New Zealand	170.1	30	486	27	7-80	18.00	1	1
1985/86	v England	169.3	36	482	27	4-38	17.85	-	-
1986/87	v Pakistan	114	27	266	16	5-33	16.62	1	-
1986/87	v New Zealand	119	21	289	9	4-43	32.11	-	-
1987/88	v Pakistan	91.4	14	284	15	5-65	18.93	1	-
1988	v England	203.1	49	443	35	7-22	12.65	3	1
1988/89	v Australia	192	42	488	17	5-29	28.70	1	-
1988/89	v India	111.2	18	290	19	6-55	15.26	3	1
1989/90	v England	59	17	132	3	2-55	44.00	-	-
1990/91	v Pakistan	65.2	14	166	6	4-24	27.66	-	-
1990/91	v Australia	156.2	25	437	21	3-31	20.80	-	-
Total		**2930.4**	**614**	**7876**	**376**	**7-22**	**20.94**	**22**	**4**

Record Against Each Test Country (Batting and Fielding)

Opponent	M	I	NO	R	HS	Ave	100	50	Ct
England	26	33	4	575	76	19.82	-	4	9
Australia	19	25	2	440	57	19.13	-	3	7
India	17	22	3	410	92	21.57	-	2	5
New Zealand	7	8	0	173	63	21.62	-	1	3
Pakistan	12	19	2	212	48	12.47	-	-	1
Totals	**81**	**107**	**11**	**1810**	**92**	**18.85**	**-**	**10**	**25**

Record Against Each Test Country (Bowling)

Opponent	O	M	R	W	BB	Ave	5i	10m
England	965	232	2436	127	7-22	19.18	6	1
Australia	722.3	136	1959	87	5-29	22.51	7	1
New Zealand	289.1	51	775	36	7-80	21.52	1	1
India	584.3	128	1671	76	6-37	21.98	6	1
Pakistan	369.3	67	1035	50	5-33	20.70	2	-
Total	**2930.4**	**614**	**7876**	**376**	**7-22**	**20.94**	**22**	**4**

Test Record at Each Venue (Batting and Fielding)

WEST INDIES	M	I	NO	R	HS	Ave	100	50	Ct
Bridgetown	8	11	1	231	63	23.10	-	1	4
Georgetown	3	2	1	49	27	49.00	-	-	-
Kingston	8	10	2	97	26	12.12	-	-	3
Port of Spain	8	11	2	160	62*	17.77	-	1	4
St John's	4	5	0	163	76	32.60	-	2	1
Total	**31**	**39**	**6**	**700**	**76**	**21.21**	**-**	**4**	**12**

ENGLAND	M	I	NO	R	HS	Ave	100	50	Ct
Edgbaston	2	2	1	8	6*	8.00	-	-	-
Headingley	4	5	0	8	4	1.60	-	-	3
Kennington Oval	4	6	0	74	45	12.33	-	-	2
Lord's	3	4	0	71	29	17.75	-	-	-
Old Trafford	2	2	1	61	43*	61.00	-	-	-
Trent Bridge	3	4	0	166	72	41.50	-	2	-
Total	**18**	**23**	**2**	**388**	**72**	**18.47**	**-**	**2**	**5**

AUSTRALIA	M	I	NO	R	HS	Ave	100	50	Ct
Adelaide	2	2	0	9	9	4.50	-	-	-
Brisbane	2	2	0	68	57	34.00	-	1	2
Melbourne	2	3	0	81	55	27.00	-	1	1
Perth	2	3	0	48	23	16.00	-	-	2
Sydney	2	4	1	44	32*	14.66	-	-	-
Total	**10**	**14**	**1**	**250**	**57**	**19.23**	**-**	**2**	**5**

INDIA	M	I	NO	R	HS	Ave	100	50	Ct
Ahmedabad	1	2	0	39	29	19.50	-	-	-
Bangalore	1	2	0	5	5	2.50	-	-	-
Bombay	1	1	0	4	4	4.00	-	-	-
Calcutta	2	3	0	56	54	18.66	-	1	2
Delhi	1	1	0	17	17	17.00	-	-	-
Kanpur	2	2	1	93	92	93.00	-	1	-
Madras	1	1	0	38	38	38.00	-	-	-
Total	**9**	**12**	**1**	**252**	**92**	**22.90**	**-**	**2**	**2**

NEW ZEALAND	M	I	NO	R	HS	Ave	100	50	Ct
Auckland	1	1	0	6	6	6.00	-	-	-
Christchurch	1	2	0	47	45	23.50	-	-	-
Wellington	1	1	0	30	30	30.00	-	-	-
Total	**3**	**4**	**0**	**83**	**45**	**20.75**	**-**	**-**	**-**

PAKISTAN	M	I	NO	R	HS	Ave	100	50	Ct
Faisalabad	3	5	0	36	20	7.20	-	-	-
Karachi	3	5	0	38	21	7.60	-	-	-
Lahore	3	4	1	60	27	20.00	-	-	1
Multan	1	1	0	3	3	3.00	-	-	-
Total	**10**	**15**	**1**	**137**	**27**	**9.78**	**-**	**-**	**1**

Test Record at Each Venue (Bowling)

WEST INDIES	O	M	R	W	BB	Ave	5i	10m
Bridgetown	302	48	911	49	7-80	18.59	4	1
Georgetown	84	10	247	11	4-110	22.45	-	-
Kingston	236.1	45	603	31	5-51	19.45	1	-
Port of Spain	333.4	69	951	47	6-55	20.23	3	1
St John's	156.1	34	438	19	4-87	23.05	-	-
Total	**1112**	**206**	**3150**	**157**	**7.80**	**20.08**	**8**	**2**

ENGLAND	O	M	R	W	BB	Ave	5i	10m
Edgbaston	69.2	15	188	9	4-33	20.88	-	-
Headingley	140	41	329	23	7-53	14.30	1	-
Kennington Oval	170.5	40	417	14	5-35	29.78	1	-
Lord's	131.5	30	340	20	6-32	17.00	2	1
Old Trafford	74.4	20	193	14	7-22	13.78	1	-
Trent Bridge	128.5	31	291	14	6-69	20.78	1	-
Total	**715.3**	**177**	**1758**	**94**	**7-22**	**18.70**	**6**	**1**

AUSTRALIA	O	M	R	W	BB	Ave	5i	10m
Adelaide	76.5	17	204	11	5-38	18.54	2	1
Brisbane	92.4	17	252	13	5-82	19.38	1	-
Melbourne	90.5	21	202	6	5-88	33.66	1	-
Perth	71	12	227	9	4-68	25.22	-	-
Sydney	76	20	157	6	5-29	26.16	1	-
Total	**407.2**	**87**	**1042**	**45**	**5-29**	**23.15**	**. 5**	**1**

INDIA	O	M	R	W	BB	Ave	5i	10m
Ahmedabad	39	12	89	3	2-23	29.66	-	-
Bangalore	18	2	53	1	1-53	53.00	-	-
Bombay	45	9	135	4	3-88	33.75	-	-
Calcutta	63	17	191	10	6-37	19.10	1	-
Delhi	42	5	157	4	3-52	39.25	-	-
Kanpur	66	17	189	9	4-19	21.00	-	-
Madras	26	8	72	5	5-72	14.40	1	-
Total	**299**	**70**	**886**	**36**	**6-27**	**24.61**	**2**	**-**

NEW ZEALAND	O	M	R	W	BB	Ave	5i	10m
Auckland	50	10	114	6	4-43	19.00	-	-
Christchurch	27	2	75	1	1-75	75.00	-	-
Wellington	42	9	100	2	2-57	50.00	-	-
Total	**119**	**21**	**289**	**9**	**4-43**	**32.11**	**-**	**-**

PAKISTAN	O	M	R	W	BB	Ave	5i	10m
Faisalabad	67	7	249	15	4-24	16.60	-	-
Karachi	112	21	236	10	3-31	23.60	-	-
Lahore	86.5	24	221	9	5-33	24.55	-	-
Multan	12	1	45	1	1-45	45.00	-	-
Total	**277.5**	**53**	**751**	**35**	**5-33**	**21.45**	**1**	**-**

Hundred Partnerships in Tests

7th Wicket

139	(55)	with I.V.A.Richards	v Australia	Melbourne	1984/85
130	(92)	with C.G.Greenidge	v India	Kanpur	1983/84

Record against Each Opponent (Batting and Fielding)

Opponent	M	I	NO	R	HS	Ave	100	50	Ct
Australia	19	25	2	440	57	19.13	-	3	7
Boland	2	3	1	97	73	48.50	-	1	-
Border	5	6	1	56	21	11.20	-	-	2
Combined Islands	3	4	1	69	55	23.00	-	1	-
Combined XI	1	0	0	0	0	-	-	-	-
Derbyshire	14	15	3	288	64	24.00	-	2	6
Durham	1	0	0	0	0	-	-	-	-
Eastern Province	4	3	1	54	39*	27.00	-	-	1
East Zone	1	0	0	0	0	-	-	-	2
England	29	38	5	717	76	21.72	-	4	9
England A	1	1	1	14	14*	-	-	-	-
Essex	12	20	3	387	76	22.76	-	2	3
Glamorgan	18	16	2	370	75*	26.42	-	3	11
Gloucestershire	20	25	2	568	68*	24.69	-	3	9
Governor's XI	2	3	0	57	24	19.00	-	-	1
Guyana	8	9	1	322	89	40.25	-	3	6
India	18	24	4	414	92	20.70	-	2	7
Indian Colts	1	1	0	12	12	12.00	-	-	-
International XI	1	1	0	40	40	40.00	-	-	-
Invitation XI	1	1	0	1	1	1.00	-	-	-
Jamaica	8	10	1	260	89	28.88	-	1	3
Karnataka	1	2	0	11	9	5.50	-	-	1
Kent	14	20	0	352	112	17.60	1	1	8
Lancashire	11	13	5	457	116*	57.12	1	1	2
Leeward Islands	3	6	0	205	71	34.16	-	2	4
Leicestershire	12	12	0	303	112	25.25	1	-	5
Middlesex	11	15	0	314	99	20.93	-	2	3
New Zealand	7	8	0	173	63	21.62	-	1	3
Northamptonshire	11	14	4	359	90*	35.90	-	3	1
Northern Districts	1	1	0	7	7	7.00	-	-	-
Northern Transvaal	5	5	0	98	38	19.60	-	-	3
North Zone	1	2	1	38	26*	38.00	-	-	-
Nottinghamshire	11	15	2	247	37*	19.00	-	-	-
Orange Free State	3	5	2	211	99*	70.33	-	2	3
Oxford University	1	1	0	25	25	25.00	-	-	1
Pakistan	12	19	2	212	48	12.47	-	-	1
President's XI	1	1	1	16	16*	-	-	-	-
Queensland	2	1	0	1	1	1.00	-	-	-
Rest of the World	1	0	0	0	0	-	-	-	1
Somerset	22	25	3	482	67	21.90	-	3	3
South Africa	1	-	-	-	-	-	-	-	-
South Australia	3	5	2	124	66	41.33	-	1	-
South Zone	2	2	0	81	61	40.50	-	1	1
Sri Lanka	2	3	0	12	9	4.00	-	-	-
Surrey	14	21	4	524	100*	30.82	1	2	3
Sussex	19	25	4	390	85	18.57	-	1	6
Transvaal	4	8	2	183	82*	30.50	-	1	2
Trinidad & Tobago	9	11	1	214	71	21.40	-	1	5
Warwickshire	12	14	3	311	79	28.27	-	1	3
Wellington	1	2	1	13	13*	13.00	-	-	2
Western Australia	2	4	1	70	31	23.33	-	-	-
Western Province	4	5	1	178	120*	44.50	1	-	2
West Zone	1	1	0	59	59	59.00	-	1	1
Windward Islands	4	6	2	116	55*	29.00	-	1	3
Worcestershire	15	20	2	437	58	24.27	-	2	7
World XI	1	-	-	-	-	-	-	-	-
Yorkshire	12	15	2	440	117	33.84	1	2	4
Zimbabwe	3	4	0	175	109	43.75	1	-	-
Total	408	516	73	11004	120*	24.83	7	54	145

Record against Each Opponent (Bowling)

Opponent	O	M	R	W	BB	Ave	5i	10m
Australia	722.3	136	1959	87	5-29	22.51	7	1
Boland	75	32	175	8	3-17	21.87	-	-
Border	176.1	55	379	21	4-36	18.04	-	-
Combined Islands	71.2	12	258	14	4-54	18.42	-	-
Combined XI	15	2	49	2	2-49	24.50	-	-
Derbyshire	452.5	123	1171	63	7-47	18.58	4	1
East Zone	35.3	10	125	11	6-71	11.36	2	-
Eastern Province	115.4	28	235	11	3-40	21.36	-	-
England A	35	13	57	0	-	-	-	-
England	1066	261	2678	138	7-22	19.40	6	1
Essex	423.2	111	1070	61	6-42	17.54	3	1
Glamorgan	519.5	159	1189	68	6-47	17.48	5	1
Gloucestershire	558.1	145	1392	71	6-51	19.60	4	-
Governor's XI	37.5	6	97	10	5-9	9.70	1	-
Guyana	237.5	46	664	37	5-39	17.94	1	-
India	605.3	130	1753	77	6-37	22.76	6	1
Indian Colts	29	12	50	4	4-50	12.50	-	-
International XI	15	3	25	1	1-25	25.00	-	-
Invitation XI	25	7	57	3	2-32	19.00	-	-
Jamaica	266.5	60	774	46	6-75	16.82	4	-
Karnataka	30	8	74	8	6-42	9.25	1	-
Kent	420	109	960	52	6-55	18.46	2	1
Lancashire	316.5	78	882	38	5-48	23.21	2	-
Leeward Islands	81	21	216	9	4-80	24.00	-	-
Leicestershire	293.5	97	724	35	6-57	20.68	1	-
Middlesex	330.2	82	858	39	5-68	22.00	1	-
New Zealand	289.1	51	775	36	7-80	21.52	1	1
Northern Districts	22	4	66	0	-	-	-	-
North Zone	14	4	41	2	2-41	20.50	-	-
Northamptonshire	325.4	88	780	50	5-36	15.60	1	-
Northern Transvaal	178.3	55	387	19	4-40	20.36	-	-
Nottinghamshire	341.4	78	866	49	5-38	17.67	3	-
Orange Free State	108.3	37	291	6	4-42	48.50	-	-
Oxford University	6	2	12	0	-	-	-	-
Pakistan	369.3	67·	1035	50	5-33	20.70	2	-
President's XI	17	3	61	1	1-61	61.00	-	-
Queensland	44.1	16	97	9	5-31	10.77	1	-
Rest of the World	22.3	3	63	4	3-53	15.75	-	-
Somerset	611.3	150	1548	82	7-29	18.87	6	-
South Africa	16	2	60	3	3-60	20.00	-	-
South Australia	76	16	226	11	4-75	20.54	-	-
South Zone	52	14	136	9	4-45	15.11	-	-
Sri Lanka	42	16	93	5	4-32	18.60	-	-
Surrey	369.2	102	986	56	7-38	17.60	4	1
Sussex	468.3	129	1169	52	7-48	22.48	2	1
Transvaal	129.5	42	262	17	6-45	15.41	1	-
Trinidad & Tobago	261.5	61	649	39	6-38	16.64	1	-
Warwickshire	376.5	122	856	46	6-50	18.60	3	-
Wellington	33	9	83	7	5-43	11.85	1	-
West Zone	19	0	46	1	1-46	46.00	-	-
Western Australia	56	13	177	4	3-66	44.25	-	-
Western Province	155	45	332	14	3-56	23.71	-	-
Windward Islands	158	38	445	28	6-85	15.89	2	1
Worcestershire	515	153	1199	86	8-71	13.94	5	1
World XI	21	6	76	2	2-76	38.00	-	-
Yorkshire	305.5	88	668	42	6-41	15.90	2	-
Zimbabwe	80.4	20	192	7	4-39	27.42	-	-
Total	12441.2	3180	31548	1651	8-71	19.10	85	13

Record at Each Venue (Batting and Fielding)

WEST INDIES	M	I	NO	R	HS	Ave	100	50	Ct
Bridgetown	30	36	3	1012	89	30.66	-	8	16
Essequibo	1	2	1	8	7*	8.00	-	-	1
Georgetown	4	3	1	54	27	27.00	-	-	-
Kingston	12	15	2	190	40	14.61	-	-	5
Kingstown	1	2	0	38	36	19.00	-	-	-
Pointe-a-Pierre	2	3	0	61	31	20.33	-	-	1
Port of Spain	12	18	3	351	71	23.40	-	2	7
St Catherine's	1	1	1	49	49*	-	-	-	-
St George's	1	2	1	71	55*	71.00	-	1	1
St John's	6	9	1	234	76	29.25	-	2	2
Totals	**70**	**91**	**13**	**2068**	**89**	**26.51**	**-**	**13**	**33**

ENGLAND	M	I	NO	R	HS	Ave	100	50	Ct
Arundel	2	3	0	57	34	19.00	-	-	-
Basingstoke	8	7	1	123	64	20.50	-	2	5
Bath	1	1	0	14	14	14.00	-	-	-
Bletchley	2	3	0	34	17	11.33	-	-	1
Bournemouth	33	45	1	959	112	21.79	1	4	15
Bradford	1	1	0	4	4	4.00	-	-	-
Bristol	6	8	1	201	68*	28.71	-	1	3
Canterbury	5	6	0	58	20	9.66-	-	-	4
Cardiff	3	2	0	13	10	6.50	-	-	-
Chelmsford	3	4	0	132	76	33.00	-	1	-
Cheltenham	3	6	0	90	39	15.00	-	-	1
Chesterfield	1	1	0	11	11	11.00	-	-	-
Derby	5	4	2	38	27*	19.00	-	-	1
Eastbourne	2	4	1	100	42	33.33	-	-	1
Edgbaston	6	7	2	86	32*	17.20	-	-	2
Folkestone	1	2	0	20	15	10.00	-	-	2
Gloucester	2	1	1	61	61*	-	-	1	-
Guildford	1	1	0	22	22	22.00	-	-	-
Headingley	8	10	1	265	117	29.44	1	-	3
Heanor	1	1	0	26	26	26.00	-	-	-
Horsham	1	1	1	0	0*	-	-	-	-
Hove	4	6	0	38	18	6.33	-	-	1
Ilford	2	4	0	15	9	3.75	-	-	-
Kennington Oval	8	13	2	310	51*	28.18	-	1	3
Leicester	6	5	0	195	112	39.00	1	-	1
Liverpool	2	3	1	65	26*	32.50	-	-	1
Lord's	8	10	0	221	99	22.10	-	1	1
Maidstone	2	3	0	37	22	12.33	-	-	1
Middlesbrough	2	3	1	138	60	69.00	-	2	3
Northampton	4	3	1	19	10*	9.50	-	-	-
Nuneaton	1	1	0	2	2	2.00	-	-	-
Old Trafford	7	7	3	221	86	55.25	-	1	1
The Parks	1	1	0	25	25	25.00	-	-	-
Pontypridd	1	1	0	51	51	51.00	-	1	-
Portsmouth	22	29	5	545	70	22.70	-	2	8
Scarborough	2	0	0	0	0	-	-	-	-
Southampton	46	60	10	1276	116*	25.52	2	5	19
Southend-on-Sea	1	2	1	10	6	10.00	-	-	1
Stockton-on-Tees	1	0	0	0	0	-	-	-	1
Swansea	5	3	2	137	75*	137.00	-	1	4
Taunton	11	12	2	237	58	23.70	-	1	1
Trent Bridge	9	12	0	308	72	25.66	-	2	-
Tunbridge Wells	1	1	0	61	61	61.00	-	1	-
Uxbridge	1	2	0	38	29	19.00	-	-	-
Wellingborough	1	2	1	101	72*	101.00	-	1	-
Weston-super-Mare	2	2	1	39	38	39.00	-	-	1
Worcester	7	8	1	243	58	34.71	-	2	1
Totals	**252**	**311**	**42**	**6646**	**117**	**24.70**	**5**	**30**	**85**

AUSTRALIA	M	I	NO	R	HS	Ave	100	50	Ct
Adelaide	5	7	2	133	66	26.60	-	1	-
Brisbane	4	3	0	69	57	23.00	-	1	2
Devonport	1	1	0	1	1	1.00	-	-	-
Melbourne	2	3	0	81	55	27.00	-	1	1
Perth	4	7	1	118	31	19.66	-	-	2
Sydney	2	4	1	44	32*	14.66	-	-	-
Totals	**18**	**25**	**4**	**446**	**66**	**21.23**	**-**	**3**	**5**

INDIA	M	I	NO	R	HS	Ave	100	50	Ct
Ahmedabad	2	4	0	50	29	12.50	-	-	1
Bangalore	1	2	0	5	5	2.50	-	-	-
Baroda	1	1	0	59	59	59.00	-	1	1
Bombay (Mumbai)	1	1	0	4	4	4.00	-	-	-
Calcutta	2	3	0	56	54	18.66	-	1	2
Delhi	1	1	0	17	17	17.00	-	-	-
Hyderabad	2	2	0	81	61	40.50	-	1	1
Jamshedpur	1	0	0	0	0	-	-	-	2
Jullundur	1	2	1	38	26*	38.00	-	-	-
Kanpur	2	2	1	93	92	93.00	-	1	-
Madras (Chennai)	1	1	0	38	38	38.00	-	-	-
Pune	1	1	0	12	12	12.00	-	-	-
Totals	**16**	**20**	**2**	**453**	**92**	**25.16**	**-**	**4**	**7**

NEW ZEALAND	M	I	NO	R	HS	Ave	100	50	Ct
Auckland	1	1	0	6	6	6.00	-	-	-
Christchurch	1	2	0	47	45	23.50	-	-	-
Hamilton	1	1	0	7	7	7.00	-	-	-
Lower Hutt	1	2	1	13	13*	13.00	-	-	2
Wellington	1	1	0	30	30	30.00	-	-	-
Totals	**5**	**7**	**1**	**103**	**45**	**17.16**	**-**	**-**	**2**

PAKISTAN	M	I	NO	R	HS	Ave	100	50	Ct
Bahawalpur	1	-	-	-	-	-	-	-	-
Faisalabad	3	5	0	36	20	7.20	-	-	-
Karachi	3	5	0	38	21	7.60	-	-	-
Lahore	3	4	1	60	27	20.00	-	-	1
Multan	1	1	0	3	3	3.00	-	-	-
Peshawar	1	1	0	13	13	13.00	-	-	1
Rawalpindi	1	1	1	16	16*	-	-	-	-
Sukkur	1	2	0	44	24	22.00	-	-	-
Totals	**14**	**19**	**2**	**210**	**27**	**12.35**	**-**	**-**	**2**

SOUTH AFRICA	M	I	NO	R	HS	Ave	100	50	Ct
Bloemfontein	2	4	2	183	99*	91.50	-	2	1
CapeTown	2	3	0	54	35	18.00	-	-	2
Centurion	1	-	-	-	-	-	-	-	-
Durban	13	16	4	292	47	24.33	-	-	4
East London	3	3	1	32	18	16.00	-	-	1
Johannesburg	2	4	1	111	82*	37.00	-	1	1
Pietermaritzburg	2	2	1	123	120*	123.00	1	-	1
Port Elizabeth	2	2	0	15	13	7.50	-	-	1
Stellenbosch	1	2	0	81	73	40.50	-	1	-
Totals	**28**	**36**	**9**	**891**	**120***	**33.00**	**1**	**4**	**11**

SRI LANKA	M	I	NO	R	HS	Ave	100	50	Ct
Colombo	2	3	0	12	9	4.00	-	-	-
Totals	**2**	**3**	**0**	**12**	**9**	**4.00**	**-**	**-**	**-**

ZIMBABWE	M	I	NO	R	HS	Ave	100	50	Ct
Bulawayo	1	2	0	128	109	64.00	1	-	-
Salisbury (Harare)	2	2	0	47	34	23.50	-	-	-
Totals	**3**	**4**	**0**	**175**	**109**	**43.75**	**1**	**-**	**-**

Record at Each Venue (Bowling)

WEST INDIES	O	M	R	W	BB	Ave	5i	10m
Bridgetown	972.4	185	2853	158	7-80	18.05	7	2
Essequibo	19	2	46	1	1-39	46.00	-	-
Georgetown	110	19	304	14	4-110	21.71	-	-
Kingston	354.1	75	947	52	6-82	18.21	3	-
Kingstown	43	9	126	4	3-58	31.50	-	-
Pointe-a-Pierre	61	18	149	7	3-48	21.28	-	-
Port of Spain	448.4	98	1191	61	6-38	19.52	4	1
St Catherine's	44.1	10	124	7	6-75	17.71	-	-
St George's	43	12	109	9	5-55	12.11	1	-
St John's	209.1	48	574	29	4-54	19.79	-	-
Totals	**2304.5**	**476**	**6423**	**342**	**7-80**	**18.78**	**16**	**3**

ENGLAND	O	M	R	W	BB	Ave	5i	10m
Arundel	41	10	97	6	3-35	16.16	-	-
Basingstoke	187.5	50	499	28	5-39	17.82	1	-
Bath	25.1	8	71	3	3-71	23.66	-	-
Bletchley	56.4	13	135	10	4-36	13.50	-	-
Bournemouth	1126.2	338	2539	168	7-29	15.11	10	-
Bradford	27	8	64	4	2-16	16.00	-	-
Bristol	105.5	24	286	11	4-14	26.00	-	-
Canterbury	121	38	243	11	3-34	22.09	-	-
Cardiff	73	26	137	7	2-23	19.57	-	-
Chelmsford	84	19	252	10	6-103	25.20	1	-
Cheltenham	86.5	25	204	8	4-44	25.50	-	-
Chesterfield	33.5	12	72	6	4-52	12.00	-	-
Derby	138	35	370	23	6-60	16.08	3	-
Eastbourne	87	28	188	15	7-48	12.53	1	1
Edgbaston	196.2	49	499	26	6-50	19.19	1	-
Folkestone	39.1	8	77	4	3-46	19.25	-	-
Gloucester	32	4	104	8	5-49	13.00	1	-
Heanor	32	6	90	2	1-38	45.00	-	-
Headingley	244.5	70	546	37	7-53	14.75	1	-
Horsham	10	6	9	1	1-9	9.00	-	-
Hove	83	21	221	7	3-40	31.57	-	-
Ilford	74	24	174	10	4-26	17.40	-	-
Kennington Oval	265	65	650	28	7-38	23.21	2	1
Leicester	130	38	317	18	6-57	17.61	1	-
Liverpool	75	12	217	13	6-64	16.69	1	-
Lord's	249	51	667	34	6-32	19.61	2	1
Maidstone	96	23	217	17	6-55	12.76	1	1
Middlesbrough	52	19	110	7	5-48	15.71	1	-
Northampton	128	41	263	20	5-36	13.15	1	-
Nuneaton	23	13	22	2	2-14	11.00	-	-
Old Trafford	191.2	55	505	26	7-22	19.42	1	-
The Parks	6	2	12	0	-	-	-	-
Pontypridd	45.2	14	92	11	6-47	8.36	2	1
Portsmouth	760.1	215	1871	100	7-47	18.71	5	1
Scarborough	37	8	136	5	3-60	27.20	-	-
Southampton	1381.3	356	3649	159	8-71	22.94	9	1
Southend-on-Sea	45.2	10	124	10	6-73	12.40	1	1
Swansea	97	31	260	19	6-54	13.68	1	-
Taunton	265	60	733	42	6-46	17.45	4	-
Trent Bridge	322.4	82	733	30	6-69	24.43	1	-
Tunbridge Wells	21	3	64	2	2-64	32.00	-	-
Uxbridge	37	8	115	7	4-67	16.42	-	-
Wellingborough	24	6	54	2	2-39	27.00	-	-
Weston-super-Mare	55	12	137	5	3-47	27.40	-	-
Worcester	219.4	60	544	32	7-56	17.00	1	-
Totals	**7431.3**	**2006**	**18369**	**994**	**8-71**	**18.47**	**54**	**8**

AUSTRALIA	O	M	R	W	BB	Ave	5i	10m
Adelaide	152.5	33	430	22	5-38	19.54	2	1
Brisbane	136.5	33	349	22	5-31	15.86	2	-
Devonport	25	7	57	3	2-32	19.00	-	-
Melbourne	90.5	21	202	6	5-86	33.66	1	-
Perth	127	25	404	13	4-68	31.07	-	-
Sydney	76	20	157	6	5-29	26.16	1	-
Totals	**608.3**	**139**	**1599**	**72**	**5-29**	**22.20**	**6**	**1**

INDIA	O	M	R	W	BB	Ave	5i	10m
Ahmedabad	69	20	163	11	6-42	14.81	1	-
Bangalore	18	2	53	1	1-53	53.00	-	-
Baroda	19	0	46	1	1-46	46.00	-	-
Bombay (Mumbai)	45	9	135	4	3-88	33.75	-	-
Calcutta	63	17	191	10	6-37	19.10	1	-
Delhi	42	5	157	4	3-52	39.25	-	-
Hyderabad	52	14	136	9	4-45	15.11	-	-
Jamshedpur	35.3	10	125	11	6-71	11.36	2	1
Jullundur	14	4	41	2	2-41	20.50	-	-
Kanpur	66	17	189	9	4-19	21.00	-	-
Madras (Chennai)	26	8	72	5	5-72	14.40	1	-
Pune	29	12	50	4	4-50	12.50	-	-
Totals	**478.3**	**118**	**1358**	**71**	**6-37**	**19.12**	**5**	**1**

NEW ZEALAND	O	M	R	W	BB	Ave	5i	10m
Auckland	50	10	114	6	4-43	19.00	-	-
Christchurch	27	2	75	1	1-75	75.00	-	-
Hamilton	22	4	66	0	-	-	-	-
Lower Hutt	33	9	83	7	5-43	11.85	1	-
Wellington	42	9	100	2	2-57	50.00	-	-
Totals	**174**	**34**	**438**	**16**	**5-43**	**27.37**	**1**	**-**

PAKISTAN	O	M	R	W	BB	Ave	5i	10m
Bahawalpur	15	2	49	2	2-49	24.50	-	-
Faisalabad	67	7	249	15	4-24	16.60	-	-
Karachi	112	21	236	10	3-31	23.60	-	-
Lahore	86.5	21	221	9	5-33	24.55	1	-
Multan	12	1	45	1	1-45	45.00	-	-
Peshawar	14.2	1	58	1	1-14	58.00	-	-
Rawalpindi	17	3	61	1	1-61	61.00	-	-
Sukkur	23.3	5	39	9	5-9	4.33	1	-
Totals	**347.4**	**61**	**958**	**48**	**5-9**	**19.95**	**2**	**-**

SOUTH AFRICA	O	M	R	W	BB	Ave	5i	10m
Bloemfontein	68	17	217	1	1-104	217.00	-	-
Cape Town	78	20	171	8	3-56	21.37	-	-
Centurion	23.1	5	51	2	2-51	25.50	-	-
Durban	446.2	158	934	44	4-40	21.22	-	-
East London	84.3	24	184	6	4-48	30.66	-	-
Johannesburg	72	23	150	12	6-45	12.50	1	-
Pietermaritzburg	94.4	30	191	12	4-36	15.91	-	-
Port Elizabeth	64	11	139	8	3-40	17.37	-	-
Stellenbosch	43	19	81	3	2-57	27.00	-	-
Totals	**973.4**	**307**	**2118**	**96**	**6-45**	**22.06**	**1**	**-**

SRI LANKA	O	M	R	W	BB	Ave	5i	10m
Colombo	42	16	93	5	4-32	18.60	-	-
Totals	**42**	**16**	**93**	**5**	**4-32**	**18.60**	**-**	**-**

ZIMBABWE	O	M	R	W	BB	Ave	5i	10m
Bulawayo	22	7	46	1	1-46	46.00	-	-
Salisbury (Harare)	58.4	13	146	6	4-39	24.33	-	-
Totals	**80.4**	**20**	**192**	**7**	**4-39**	**27.42**	**-**	**-**

Record for Each Team (Batting and Fielding)

	M	I	NO	R	HS	Ave	100	50	Ct
Barbados	37	49	7	1270	89	30.23	-	9	21
West Indians	125	155	20	2723	92	20.17	-	15	36
Hampshire	210	269	37	5847	117	25.20	-	26	76
Young West Indians	4	6	0	233	109	38.83	1	-	-
West Indian XI	2	1	0	40	40	40.00	-	-	-
M.C.C.	1	-	-	-	-	-	-	-	1
Natal	28	36	9	891	120*	33.00	1	4	11
President's XI	1	-	-	-	-	-	-	-	-
Total	**408**	**516**	**73**	**11004**	**120***	**24.83**	**7**	**54**	**145**

Record for Each Team (Bowling)

	O	M	R	W	BB	Ave	5i	10m
Barbados	1134.5	254	3146	180	6-38	17.47	8	1
West Indians	3866.4	845	10365	528	7-22	19.63	31	5
Hampshire	6268	1727	15401	826	8-71	18.64	45	7
Young West Indians	123.4	33	294	11	4-39	26.72	-	-
West Indian XI	36	9	101	3	2-76	33.66	-	-
M.C.C.	22.3	3	63	4	3-53	15.75	-	-
Natal	973.4	307	2118	96	6-45	22.06	1	-
President's XI	16	2	60	3	3-60	20.00	-	-
Total	**12441.2**	**3180**	**31548**	**1651**	**8-71**	**19.10**	**85**	**13**

Modes of Dismissals (Batting)

Bowled 95;   Caught 272;   LBW 51;   Run Out 16;   Stumped 9;   Not Out 73

Modes of Dismissals (Bowling)

Bowled 351;   Caught 954;   LBW 343;   Hit Wicket 2;   Stumped 1

First-Class Centuries (7)

109	Young West Indies	v Zimbabwe	Bulawayo	October 1981
116*	Hampshire	v Lancashire	Southampton	June 1982
100*	Hampshire	v Surrey	Southampton	July 1983
112	Hampshire	v Kent	Bournemouth	August 1983
117	Hampshire	v Yorkshire	Headingley	May 1990
112	Hampshire	v Leicestershire	Leicester	June 1990
120*	Natal	v Western Province	Pietermaritzburg	December 1993

Five Wickets in an Innings (85)

6-77	Barbados	v Jamaica	Bridgetown	January 1978
6-71	West Indians	v East Zone	Jamshedpur	December 1978
5-54	West Indians	v East Zone	Jamshedpur	December 1978
6-42	West Indians	v Karnataka	Ahmedabad	February 1979
6-82	Barbados	v Jamaica	Kingston	March 1979
5-39	Barbados	v Guyana	Bridgetown	April 1979
5-56	Hampshire	v Gloucestershire	Southampton	July 1979
5-43	West Indians	v Wellington	Lower Hutt	February 1980
6-38	Barbados	v Trinidad & Tobago	Port of Spain	March 1980
7-56	West Indians	v Worcestershire	Worcester	May 1980
6-54	West Indians	v Glamorgan	Swansea	June 1980
5-39	Hampshire	v Worcestershire	Bournemouth	August 1980

5-9	Hampshire	v Gauhati	Sukkur	November 1980
6-75	Barbados	v Jamaica	St Catherine's	February 1981
6-57	Hampshire	v Leicestershire	Leicester	May 1981
5-64	Hampshire	v Nottinghamshire	Bournemouth	June 1981
5-60	Hampshire	v Surrey	Portsmouth	July 1981
5-68	Hampshire	v Somerset	Taunton	August 1981
6-62	Hampshire	v Sussex	Bournemouth	August 1981
5-31	West Indians	v Queensland	Brisbane	December 1981
5-84	Hampshire	v Kent	Bournemouth	June 1982
7-38	Hampshire	v Surrey	Kennington Oval	June 1982
5-48	Hampshire	v Lancashire	Southampton	June 1982
6-55	Hampshire	v Kent	Maidstone	July 1982
5-37	Hampshire	v Somerset	Bournemouth	July 1982
7-48	Hampshire	v Sussex	Eastbourne	August 1982
6-103	Hampshire	v Essex	Chelmsford	August 1982
8-71	Hampshire	v Worcestershire	Southampton	August 1982
5-33	Hampshire	v Gloucestershire	Bournemouth	August 1982
6-41	Hampshire	v Yorkshire	Bournemouth	August 1982
6-60	Hampshire	v Derbyshire	Derby	September 1982
5-74	Hampshire	v Warwickshire	Southampton	September 1982
5-37	West Indies	v India	Port of Spain	March 1983
6-58	Hampshire	v Worcestershire	Southampton	May 1983
5-64	Hampshire	v Lancashire	Liverpool	July 1983
6-73	Hampshire	v Essex	Southend-on-Sea	July 1983
7-29	Hampshire	v Somerset	Bournemouth	August 1983
6-46	Hampshire	v Somerset	Taunton	August 1983
6-37	West Indies	v India	Calcutta	December 1983
5-72	West Indies	v India	Madras	December 1983
5-42	West Indies	v Australia	Bridgetown	March 1984
5-51	West Indies	v Australia	Kingston	April 1984
5-31	West Indians	v Somerset	Taunton	May 1984
6-85	West Indies	v England	Lord's	June 1984
7-53	West Indies	v England	Headingley	July 1984
5-35	West Indies	v England	Kennington Oval	August 1984
5-82	West Indies	v Australia	Brisbane	November 1984
5-69	West Indies	v Australia	Adelaide	December 1984
5-38	West Indies	v Australia	Adelaide	December 1984
5-86	West Indies	v Australia	Melbourne	December 1984
7-80	West Indies	v New Zealand	Bridgetown	April 1985
5-48	Hampshire	v Yorkshire	Middlesbrough	June 1985
6-50	Hampshire	v Warwickshire	Edgbaston	June 1985
5-68	Hampshire	v Middlesex	Bournemouth	June 1985
6-42	Hampshire	v Essex	Southampton	June 1985
7-59	Hampshire	v Worcestershire	Portsmouth	July 1985
6-85	Barbados	v Windward Islands	Bridgetown	January 1986
6-51	Hampshire	v Gloucestershire	Bournemouth	May 1986
5-38	Hampshire	v Nottinghamshire	Southampton	May 1986
5-40	Hampshire	v Somerset	Taunton	July 1986
5-22	Hampshire	v Warwickshire	Portsmouth	July 1986
5-49	Hampshire	v Derbyshire	Derby	August 1986
5-33	West Indies	v Pakistan	Lahore	November 1986
5-49	Hampshire	v Gloucestershire	Gloucester	July 1987
5-55	Barbados	v Windward Islands	St George's	February 1988
5-24	Barbados	v Jamaica	Kingston	February 1988
5-65	West Indies	v Pakistan	Bridgetown	April 1988
6-69	West Indies	v England	Trent Bridge	June 1988
6-32	West Indies	v England	Lord's	June 1988
7-22	West Indies	v England	Old Trafford	June 1988
5-29	West Indies	v Australia	Sydney	January 1989
5-60	West Indies	v India	Bridgetown	April 1989
5-34	West Indies	v India	Port of Spain	April 1989
6-55	West Indies	v India	Port of Spain	April 1989
5-39	Hampshire	v Surrey	Basingstoke	June 1989
5-36	Hampshire	v Northamptonshire	Northampton	July 1989

6-69	Hampshire	v Derbyshire	Derby	August 1989
5-68	Hampshire	v Glamorgan	Southampton	September 1989
5-64	Hampshire	v Nottinghamshire	Portsmouth	July 1990
7-47	Hampshire	v Derbyshire	Portsmouth	July 1990
5-45	Hampshire	v Glamorgan	Pontypridd	September 1990
6-47	Hampshire	v Glamorgan	Pontypridd	September 1990
6-58	Hampshire	v Surrey	Southampton	May 1992
6-45	Natal	v Gauhati	Johannesburg	January 1993
5-62	Hampshire	v Glamorgan	Swansea	August 1993

Ten Wickets in a Match (13)

11-125	West Indians	v East Zone	Jamshedpur	December 1978
10-76	Hampshire	v Surrey	Kennington Oval	June 1982
10-109	Hampshire	v Kent	Maidstone	July 1982
11-107	Hampshire	v Sussex	Eastbourne	August 1982
11-128	Hampshire	v Worcestershire	Southampton	August 1982
10-124	Hampshire	v Essex	Southend-on-Sea	July 1983
10-107	West Indies	v Australia	Brisbane	November 1984
11-120	West Indies	v New Zealand	Bridgetown	April 1985
10-124	Barbados	v Windward Islands	Bridgetown	January 1986
10-92	West Indies	v England	Lord's	June 1988
11-89	West Indies	v India	Port of Spain	April 1989
10-107	Hampshire	v Derbyshire	Portsmouth	July 1990
11-92	Hampshire	v Glamorgan	Pontypridd	September 1990

Malcolm Marshall in One-Day Cricket

Malcolm Marshall's Test match and first-class record stands comparison with any bowler in cricket's history. At first glance his limited overs record is less impressive. In 408 first-class matches he took 1651 wickets with five or more wickets in an innings on 85 occasions. He played slightly more limited-overs matches and took just 496 wickets. He never took more than five wickets in an innings and only did that on five occasions.

The reality is more complex. For much of his county career, Marshall carried a fairly weak Hampshire attack and on many occasions, opposition batsmen were content to 'see him off' and take their runs from the other end. For example, in a remarkable NatWest semi-final performance in 1983 Marshall took 4-15 in 12 overs against Kent and still finished on a (well-beaten) losing side.

In international cricket the opposite was true as bowlers like Roberts, Holding, Garner and Ambrose would tend to share the wickets with Marshall. It is also reasonable to assume that his incisive mind and naturally attacking approach were less excited by the demands of limited overs cricket which is so often the batsman's game. In his autobiography Marshall wrote of playing 17 limited overs internationals in the 1984/5 season which he "found a real bore".

Nonetheless he did sometimes care enormously about success in the shorter form of the game. In 1979 he was a member of the West Indies squad which won the World Cup although he did not play in any matches. Four years later, he took 10 wickets in five matches as West Indies reached another Lord's final. He then took 2-24 in 11 overs as India were dismissed for 183 but was required to bat when Greenidge, Haynes, Lloyd, Richards, Gomes and Bacchus were dismissed for 76. He and Dujon added 43 for the seventh wicket but it was insufficient. The favourites were beaten and Marshall recorded how he and his team-mates went from "disbelief to fury".

Two years later Marshall had some consolation as Hampshire won the Sunday League in a close match at The Oval but he was away touring with West Indies as his county side won Lord's finals in 1988 and 1991. The strength of his commitment to Hampshire's limited overs campaigns was clear after a one run defeat against Northamptonshire in the NatWest semi-final of 1990. In the quarter final he had figures of 4-17 against Yorkshire and he was clearly determined to win a final with his county. In the semi-final, Northamptonshire batted first and Marshall conceded least runs as they reached 284 in their 60 overs. Hampshire lost Terry and the Smith brothers for 55 before Marshall and Gower added 141 for the fifth wicket and Marshall and Nicholas 50 for the fifth. It was not enough as Hampshire failed on the last ball to reach Lord's. Marshall was named Man-of-the-Match for the first time in this competition but was too upset to accept the award.

Two years later his performances were central to Hampshire's third triumph at Lord's. During the Benson & Hedges Cup, runs came at under three an over from Marshall's bowling and there was a wicket every 30 balls. In the final he contributed 29* and 3-33 as Hampshire beat Kent by 41 runs and although Robin Smith was named Man-of-the Match, Marshall was the popular hero.

Marshall's innings in that match was his first above 20 in 24 innings in the shorter form of the game and he was somewhat inconsistent as a batsman despite his ability to hit the ball very hard. Nonetheless there were eight half-centuries in his career which is not insignificant for a man who often batted in the lower half of the innings. Perhaps his innings against Northamptonshire suggested what might have been had he batted in a higher position.

His first limited overs half century in Adelaide in 1984 took West Indies to the narrowest possible victory over Pakistan. His score of 56 followed 3-28 in nine overs. He seemed to enjoy these opponents and in 1986 produced a similar performance with 66 and 2-18 in eight overs in another West Indies victory. His most consistent batting spell came with 51, 35 and 41 in three consecutive innings for Hampshire in July 1987 but his average never reached much above 15 per innings.

By the time of his Benson & Hedges success with Hampshire, Marshall's West Indies career had finished. He subsequently appeared in limited overs matches in South Africa and was a member of the unfortunate Natal side which lost a Benson & Hedges Final at Durban by one run, nine months after Hampshire's victory. In the following season he enjoyed a run of good scores for Natal in the same competition, averaging almost 30 for the season but Natal again lost the final by a far greater margin. His limited overs career ended in South Africa in 1996 while in the year before that he had appeared five times on the losing side for Scotland in the English Benson & Hedges Cup.

1977/1978

1. Geddes/Grant Harrison Line Cup - Barbados v Jamaica, Bridgetown, February 13 (Jamaica won by two wickets)

| c L.N.Wright b R.R.Wynter | 0 | 194 | 8 | 4 | 12 | 0 | | 195-8 |

2. Geddes/Grant Harrison Line Cup - Barbados v Windward Islands, Roseau, February 25 (Barbados won by 16 runs)

| b F.A.Thorpe | 5 | 203-9 | - | - | - | - | | 187 |

SEASON'S AVERAGES

Batting and Fielding	M	I	NO	Runs	HS	Ave	100	50	Ct
Geddes/Grant Cup	2	2	0	5	5	2.50	-	-	-

Bowling	O	M	R	W	BB	Ave	5i
Geddes/Grant Cup	8	4	12	0	-	-	-

1978/1979

3. Geddes/Grant Harrison Line Cup - Barbados v Leeward Islands, St John's, March 22 (Leeward Islands won by three wickets)

run out	2	165-8	10	2	19	4	A.L.Kelly b	169-7
							J.C.Adams lbw	
							K.Fredericks b	
							S.A.Liburd lbw	

SEASON'S AVERAGES

Batting and Fielding	M	I	NO	Runs	HS	Ave	100	50	Ct
Geddes/Grant Cup	1	1	0	2	2	2.00	-	-	-
Career - Geddes/Grant Cup	3	3	0	7	5	2.33	-	-	-

Bowling	O	M	R	W	BB	Ave	5i
Geddes/Grant Cup	10	2	19	4	4-19	4.75	-
Career - Geddes/Grant Cup	18	6	31	4	4-19	7.75	-

1979

4. Benson & Hedges Cup - Hampshire v Derbyshire, Derby, April 28 (Derbyshire won by 21 runs)

| b M.Hendrick | 15 | 169 | 11 | 4 | 38 | 1 | P.N.Kirsten b | 190-6 |

5. Sunday League - Hampshire v Middlesex, Lord's, May 6 (Middlesex won by 12 runs)

| c J.E.Emburey b A.A.Jones | 20 | 151 | 8 | 0 | 29 | 2 | G.D.Barlow c N.G.Cowley | 163-7 |
| | | | | | | | R.O.Butcher c T.E.Jesty | |

6. Benson & Hedges Cup - Hampshire v Warwickshire, Bournemouth, May 12 (Warwickshire won by 73 runs)

| b S.P.Perryman | 6 | 132 | 11 | 2 | 42 | 1 | J.Whitehouse b | 205-6 |

7. Sunday League - Hampshire v Essex, Southampton, May 13 (Hampshire won by seven wickets)
did not bat   -   173-3   8   1   26   0   172-5

8. Benson & Hedges Cup - Hampshire v Lancashire, Old Trafford, May 19 (Lancashire won by seven wickets)
·   c B.Wood b W.Hogg   13   202   11   4   26   0   206-3

9. Benson & Hedges Cup - Hampshire v Leicestershire, Southampton, May 23 (Leicestershire won by eight wickets)
did not bat   -   169-5   9   0   19   2   D.I.Gower b   172-2
                                    J.C.Balderstone c J.M.Rice

10. Sunday League - Hampshire v Kent, Canterbury, May 27 (Kent won by 20 runs)
c C.J.Tavare b R.W.Hills   4   101-9   4   0   19   0   121-6

11. Sunday League - Hampshire v Somerset, Taunton, June 3 (Somerset won by three wickets)
did not bat   -   148-6   8   0   26   0   154-7

12. Gillette Cup - Hampshire v Gloucestershire, Bristol, June 27 (Hampshire won by 55 runs)
not out   10   273-6   10   0   43   0   218

13. Sunday League - Hampshire v Leicestershire, Portsmouth, July 1 (Leicestershire won by three wickets)
not out   5   134-7   8   2   24   4   B.Dudleston hit wkt   136-7
                                N.E.Briers c G.R.Stephenson
                                R.W.Tolchard c G.R.Stephenson
                                P.B.Clift c G.R.Stephenson

14. Sunday League - Hampshire v Gloucestershire, Basingstoke, July 8 (Hampshire won by 20 runs)
did not bat   -   159-6   7.1   3   14   3   Sadiq Mohammad
                                           c V.P.Terry   139
                                B.M.Brain b
                                A.J.Brassington b

15. Sunday League - Hampshire v Yorkshire, Headingley, July 15 (Hampshire won by 42 runs)
did not bat   -   255-6   8   0   38   0   213-8

16. Gillette Cup - Hampshire v Middlesex, Lord's, July 18 (Middlesex won by two wickets)
not out   21   193   11.5   4   28   0   196-8

17. Sunday League - Hampshire v Glamorgan, Portsmouth, July 22 (Hampshire won by 12 runs)
not out   0   179-9   8   2   13   5   A.Jones c C.G.Greenidge   167-6
                                J.A.Hopkins c C.G.Greenidge
                                R.C.Ontong c G.R.Stephenson
                                D.A.Francis b
                                P.D.Swart b

18. Sunday League - Hampshire v Warwickshire, Edgbaston, July 29 (Hampshire won by 1 run)
did not bat   -   250-5   8   0   31   1   C.Maynard b   249-8

19. Sunday League - Hampshire v Worcestershire, Worcester, August 5 (Worcestershire won by 58 runs)
run out   6   167   8   0   33   2   Younis Ahmed b   225-4
                                E.J.O.Hemsley c G.R.Stephenson

20. Sunday League - Hampshire v Surrey, Bournemouth, August 12 (Surrey won by eight wickets)
not out   1   121-7   8   0   15   0   122-2

21. Sunday League - Hampshire v Lancashire, Old Trafford, August 19 (Lancashire won by eight wickets)
c J.Abrahams b P.G.Lee   1   153   7.2   1   15   0   154-2

22. Sunday League - Hampshire v Sussex, Southampton, August 26 (Hampshire won by eight wickets)
did not bat   -   115-2   8   1   12   2   G.D.Mendis
                                      c G.R.Stephenson   114   1
                                P.W.G.Parker b

SEASON'S AVERAGES

Batting and Fielding	M	I	NO	Runs	HS	Ave	100	50	Ct
Gillette Cup	2	2	2	31	21*	-	-	-	-
Sunday League	13	7	3	37	20	9.25	-	-	1
Benson & Hedges Cup	4	3	0	34	15	11.33	-	-	-
Career - One Day Matches	22	15	5	109	21*	10.90	-	-	1

Bowling	O	M	R	W	BB	Ave	5i
Gillette Cup	21.5	4	71	0	-	-	-
Sunday League	98.3	10	295	19	5-13	15.52	1
Benson & Hedges Cup	42	10	125	4	2-19	31.25	-
Career - One Day Matches	180.2	30	522	27	5-13	19.33	1

1979/80

23. Geddes/Grant Harrison Line Cup - Barbados v Trinidad & Tobago, Port of Spain, February 26 (Trinidad & Tobago won by four wickets)
c D.L.Murray
b R.R.Jumadeen   0   71   4   1   13   1   D.L.Murray c R.L.Skeete   72-6

24. Geddes/Grant Harrison Line Cup - Barbados v Leeward Islands, Bridgetown, April 22 (Leeward Islands won by 57 runs)
c V.A.Eddy b D.R.Parry   23   148   10   0   46   2   J.C.Allen c and b   205-5   2
     V.A.Eddy c G.N.Reifer

SEASON'S AVERAGES

Batting and Fielding	M	I	NO	Runs	HS	Ave	100	50	Ct
Geddes/Grant Cup	2	2	0	23	23	11.50	-	-	2
Career - Geddes/Grant Cup	5	5	0	30	23	6.00	-	-	2
Career - One Day Matches	24	17	5	132	23	11.00	-	-	3

Bowling	O	M	R	W	BB	Ave	5i
Geddes/Grant Cup	14	1	59	3	2-46	19.66	-
Career - Geddes/Grant Cup	32	7	90	7	4-19	12.85	-
Career - One Day Matches	194.2	31	581	30	5-13	19.36	1

1980 – West Indies in England

25. International - WEST INDIES v ENGLAND, Headingley, May 28 (West Indies won by 24 runs)
b I.T.Botham   6   198   11   2   28   3   P.Willey c I.V.A.Richards   174
     I.T.Botham c D.L.Murray
     C.M.Old b

26. International - WEST INDIES v ENGLAND, Lord's, May 30 (England won by three wickets)
b R.G.D.Willis   0   235-9   11   1   45   1   G.A.Gooch
     c S.F.A.F.Bacchus   236-7

SEASON'S AVERAGES

Batting and Fielding	M	I	NO	Runs	HS	Ave	100	50	Ct
Internationals	2	2	0	6	6	3.00	-	-	-
Career - One Day Matches	26	19	5	138	23	9.85	-	-	3

Bowling	O	M	R	W	BB	Ave	5i
Internationals	22	3	73	4	3-28	18.25	-
Career - One Day Matches	216.2	34	654	34	5-13	19.23	1

1980

27. Sunday League - Hampshire v Northamptonshire, Wellingborough, August 17 (Hampshire won by three wickets)
not out   4   117-7   8   4   7   1   P.Willey lbw   114

28. Sunday League - Hampshire v Derbyshire, Southampton, August 24 (Hampshire won by 5 runs)
not out   3   231-6   8   3   28   1   G.Miller b   226-8

SEASON'S AVERAGES

Batting and Fielding	M	I	NO	Runs	HS	Ave	100	50	Ct
Sunday League	2	2	2	7	4*	-	-	-	-
Career - Sunday League	15	9	5	44	20	11.00	-	-	1
Career - One Day Matches	28	21	7	145	23	10.35	-	-	3

Bowling	O	M	R	W	BB	Ave	5i
Sunday League	16	7	35	2	1-7	17.50	-
Career - Sunday League	114.3	17	330	21	5-13	15.71	1
Career - One Day Matches	232.2	41	689	36	5-13	19.13	1

1980/81 – West Indies in Pakistan

29. International - WEST INDIES v PAKISTAN, Karachi, November 27 (West Indies won by four wickets)
run out   0   128-6   8   0   34   0   127-9   1

30. International - WEST INDIES v PAKISTAN, Sialkot, December 5 (West Indies won by seven wickets)
did not bat   -   201-3   8   1   38   0   200-4   1

31. International - WEST INDIES v PAKISTAN, Lahore, December 19 (West Indies won by 7 runs)
run out   12   170-8   6   0   27   0   163-6

SEASON'S AVERAGES

Batting and Fielding	M	I	NO	Runs	HS	Ave	100	50	Ct
Internationals	3	2	0	12	12	6.00	-	-	2
Career - Internationals	5	4	0	18	12	4.50	-	-	2
Career - One Day Matches	31	23	7	157	23	9.81	-	-	5

Bowling	O	M	R	W	BB	Ave	5i
Internationals	22	1	99	0	-	-	-
Career - Internationals	44	4	172	4	3-28	43.00	-
Career - One Day Matches	254.2	42	788	36	5-13	21.88	1

1980/81

32. Geddes/Grant Harrison Line Cup - Barbados v Guyana, Bridgetown, January 14 (Barbados won by six wickets)
did not bat   -   178-4   9.4   4   20   3   R.Gomes   c A.L.Padmore   176   1
                                                     R.A.Harper   c D.A.Murray
                                                       R.F.Joseph   c D.A.Murray

SEASON'S AVERAGES

Batting and Fielding	M	I	NO	Runs	HS	Ave	100	50	Ct
Geddes/Grant Cup	1	-	-	-	-	-	-	-	1
Career - Geddes/Grant Cup	6	5	0	30	23	6.00	-	-	3
Career - One Day Matches	32	23	7	157	23	9.81	-	-	6

Bowling	O	M	R	W	BB	Ave	5i
Geddes/Grant Cup	9.4	4	20	3	3-20	6.66	-
Career - Geddes/Grant Cup	41.4	11	110	10	4-19	11.00	-
Career - One Day Matches	264	46	808	39	5-13	20.71	1

1981

33. Benson & Hedges Cup - Hampshire v Middlesex, Lord's, May 9 (Hampshire won by one wicket)
c M.W.W.Selvey
     b J.R.Thomson   0   176-9   10   3   18   0   175

34. Benson & Hedges Cup - Hampshire v Minor Counties, Southampton, May 13 (Minor Counties won by 3 runs)
c N.T.O'Brien b S.G.Plumb   10   179   11   2   37   1   F.E.Collyer   c Nicholas   182-7

35. Benson & Hedges Cup - Hampshire v Surrey, Bournemouth, May 16 (No result)
did not bat   -   143-5

36. Sunday League - Hampshire v Glamorgan, Bournemouth, May 17 (Hampshire won by 21 runs)
did not bat   -   112-2   4   1   11   0   91-7   1

37. Benson & Hedges Cup - Hampshire v Sussex, Hove, May 30 (Sussex won by three wickets)
    run out   18   194   11   5   11   3   G.D.Mendis c R.J.Parks   198-7
                                                                  I.A.Greig   c R.J.Parks
                                                                  I.J.Gould   b

38. Sunday League - Hampshire v Sussex, Basingstoke, May 31 (Sussex won by seven wickets)
    not out   18   163-6   7   1   24   0   164-3

39. Sunday League - Hampshire v Derbyshire, Derby, June 14 (Derbyshire won by five wickets)
    not out   7   179-7   8   0   28   0   180-5

40. Sunday League - Hampshire v Gloucestershire, Portsmouth, June 21 (Hampshire won by seven wickets)
    did not bat   -   184-3   8   1   22   0   180-8

41. Sunday League - Hampshire v Lancashire, Old Trafford, June 28 (Hampshire won by two wickets)
    b P.J.W.Allott   8   152-8   8   2   25   0   151-9   1

42. Sunday League - Hampshire v Nottinghamshire, Portsmouth, July 5 (Hampshire won by eight wickets)
    did not bat   -   125-2   8   1   20   1   E.E.Hemmings b   123-8

43. NatWest Trophy - Hampshire v Cheshire, Southampton, July 11 (Hampshire won by six wickets)
    did not bat   -   138-4   9   1   27   0   137

44. Sunday League - Hampshire v Worcestershire, Worcester, July 12 (Worcestershire won by six wickets)
    c D.J.Humphries
                 b A.P.Pridgeon 5   213-8   7   0   37   1   Younis Ahmed
                                                                  c C.G.Greenidge   214-4

45. Sunday League - Hampshire v Surrey, Southampton, July 19 (Hampshire won by four wickets)
    did not bat   -   171-6   8   0   27   3   G.R.J.Roope c D.R.Turner 167-8
                                                                  C.J.Richards c R.J.Parks
                                                                  I.R.Payne   b

46. NatWest Trophy - Hampshire v Glamorgan, Cardiff, July 22 (Hampshire won by 30 runs)
    not out   2   176-7   9.5   1   15   2   E.W.Jones   b   146
                                                                  B.J.Lloyd   b

47. Sunday League - Hampshire v Warwickshire, Edgbaston, July 26 (Warwickshire won by six wickets)
    b A.M.Ferreira   13   242-9   7   0   47   1   D.L.Amiss c V.P.Terry   246-4

48. Sunday League - Hampshire v Kent, Canterbury, August 2 (Kent won by 90 runs)
    b C.S.Cowdrey   17   140   8   0   30   0   230-4

49. NatWest Trophy - Hampshire v Lancashire, Southampton, August 5 (Lancashire won by three wickets)
    not out   16   167-9   12   1   17   1   J.Simmons c R.J.Parks   169-7

50. Sunday League - Hampshire v Yorkshire, Middlesbrough, August 9 (Yorkshire won by 36 runs)
    did not bat   -   81-6   3   0   11   0   117-6

51. Sunday League - Hampshire v Essex, Southampton, August 16 (Hampshire won by seven wickets)
    did not bat   -   198-3   8   2   13   1   B.R.Hardie b   194-4

52. Sunday League - Hampshire v Somerset, Taunton, August 23 (Somerset won by 149 runs)
    c I.T.Botham
                 b N.F.M.Popplewell 20   137   8   1   31   2   P.W.Denning b   286-7
                                                                  N.F.M.Popplewell c R.J.Parks

SEASON'S AVERAGES

Batting and Fielding	M	I	NO	Runs	HS	Ave	100	50	Ct
NatWest Trophy	3	2	2	18	16*	-	-	-	-
Sunday League	13	7	2	88	20	17.60	-	-	2
Benson & Hedges Cup	4	3	0	28	18	9.33	-	-	-
Career - Gillette Cup/NWT	5	4	4	49	21*	-	-	-	-
Career - Sunday League	28	16	7	132	20	14.66	-	-	3
Career - Benson & Hedges Cup	8	6	0	62	18	10.33	-	-	-
Career - One Day Matches	52	35	11	291	23	12.12	-	-	8

Bowling	O	M	R	W	BB	Ave	5i
NatWest Trophy	30.5	3	59	3	2-15	19.66	-
Sunday League	92	9	326	9	3-27	36.22	-
Benson & Hedges Cup	32	10	66	4	3-11	16.50	-
Career - Gillette Cup/NWT	52.4	7	130	3	2-15	43.33	-
Career - Sunday League	206.3	26	656	30	5-13	21.86	1
Career - B & H Cup	74	20	191	8	3-11	23.87	-
Career - One Day Matches	418.5	68	1259	55	5-13	22.89	1

1981/82 – Young West Indies in Zimbabwe

53. Young West Indies v Zimbabwe, Bulawayo, October 18 (Zimbabwe won by 53 runs)
   b A.J.Traicos   1   174   10   3   28   0   227-5   1
54. Young West Indies v Zimbabwe, Umtali, October 21 (Young West Indies won by 118 runs)
   b K.M.Curran   8   283   8   3   11   3   C.Scott c D.L.Haynes   165
                                                            L.de Grandhomme b
                                                            A.J.Pycroft b
55. Young West Indies v Zimbabwe, Salisbury, October 25 (Young West Indies won by 126 runs)
   b V.B.Hogg   2   231-7   10   2   23   2   G.Patterson b   105
                                                            L.de Grandhomme c T.Mohammed

SEASON'S AVERAGES

Batting and Fielding	M	I	NO	Runs	HS	Ave	100	50	Ct
YWI in Zimbabwe	3	3	0	11	8	3.66	-	-	1
Career - One Day Matches	55	38	11	302	23	11.18	-	-	9

Bowling	O	M	R	W	BB	Ave	5i
YWI in Zimbabwe	28	8	62	5	3-11	12.40	-
Career - One Day Matches	446.5	76	1321	60	5-13	22.01	1

1981/82 – Benson & Hedges World Series in Australia

56. International - WEST INDIES v PAKISTAN, Melbourne, November 21 (West Indies won by 18 runs)
   not out   9   245-8   10   1   27   2   Mudassar Nazar b   227-6
                                                            Mansoor Akhtar b
57. International - WEST INDIES v AUSTRALIA, Sydney, November 24 (Australia won by seven wickets)
   not out   16   236-8   10   0   45   0   237-3
58. International - WEST INDIES v PAKISTAN, Adelaide, December 5 (Pakistan won by 8 runs)
   b Wasim Raja   20   132   9   0   18   2   Javed Miandad lbw   140
                                                            Imran Khan c D.A.Murray
59. International - WEST INDIES v PAKISTAN, Perth, December 19 (West Indies won by seven wickets)
   did not bat   -   161-3   9.4   0   33   2   Mudassar Nazar
                                                                c I.V.A.Richards   160
                                                            Sikander Bakht c P.J.L.Dujon
60. International - WEST INDIES v AUSTRALIA, Perth, December 20 (West Indies won by eight wickets)
   did not bat   -   190-2   10   0   31   3   B.M.Laird lbw   188
                                                            A.R.Border c S.F.A.F.Bacchus
                                                            K.J.Hughes c M.A.Holding
61. International - WEST INDIES v AUSTRALIA, Melbourne, January 10 (West Indies won by five wickets)
   not out   5   147-5   5   0   12   1   A.R.Border b   146
62. International - WEST INDIES v PAKISTAN, Sydney, January 12 (West Indies won by seven wickets)
   did not bat   -   192-3   10   1   33   1   Mohsin Khan b   191-7
63. International - WEST INDIES v AUSTRALIA, Sydney, January 19 (Australia won on faster scoring rate)
   not out   32   189   10   0   43   1   R.W.Marsh c C.G.Greenidge 168-7

SEASON'S AVERAGES

Batting and Fielding	M	I	NO	Runs	HS	Ave	100	50	Ct
Internationals	8	5	4	82	32*	82.00	-	-	-
Career - Internationals	13	9	4	100	32*	20.00	-	-	2
Career - One Day Matches	63	43	15	384	32*	13.71	-	-	9

Bowling	O	M	R	W	BB	Ave	5i
Internationals	73.4	2	242	12	3-31	20.16	-
Career - Internationals	117.4	6	414	16	3-28	25.87	-
Career - One Day Matches	520.3	78	1563	72	5-13	21.70	1

1982

64. Benson & Hedges Cup - Hampshire v Kent, Canterbury, May 8 (Kent won by 19 runs)
c A.P.E.Knott b G.R.Dilley 21 198   11   1   40   1 G.W.Johnson b   217-9

65. Sunday League - Hampshire v Nottinghamshire, Trent Bridge, May 9 (Hampshire won by 15 runs)
not out   30 201-6   8   1   16   2 D.W.Randall
                                                             c C.G.Greenidge   186-7
                                                             R.T.Robinson b

66. Benson & Hedges Cup - Hampshire v Sussex, Bournemouth, May 15 (Sussex won by 119 runs)
not out   9 129   11   3   35   2 J.R.T.Barclay c T.E.Jesty   248-9
                                                             A.C.S.Pigott b

67. Sunday League - Hampshire v Middlesex, Bournemouth, May 16 (Middlesex won by four wickets)
c J.M.Brearley
     b W.W.Daniel   21 185-7   7   1   32   1 J.M.Brearley c R.J.Parks   186-6

68. Benson & Hedges Cup - Hampshire v Essex, Chelmsford, May 22 (Essex won by one wicket)
b R.E.East   14 130   11   2   29   2 G.A.Gooch c M.C.J.Nicholas 131-9
                                                             K.W.R.Fletcher c R.J.Parks

69. Sunday League - Hampshire v Essex, Chelmsford, May 23 (Hampshire won on faster scoring rate)
c B.R.Hardie b N.A.Foster   2 144-7   7   2   15   2 G.A.Gooch b   52-5
                                                             B.R.Hardie lbw

70. Benson & Hedges Cup - Hampshire v Surrey, Southampton, May 27 (Surrey won by 13 runs)
c D.M.Smith b R.D.Jackman 10 194-7   11   0   34   1 G.R.J.Roope b   207-8

71. Sunday League - Hampshire v Leicestershire, Leicester, June 6 (Leicestershire won by 9 runs)
b K.Higgs   46 202-8   8   3   24   0   211-5

72. Sunday League - Hampshire v Derbyshire, Portsmouth, June 13 (Hampshire won by one wicket)
run out   0 194-9   8   1   27   0   193-5

73. Sunday League - Hampshire v Kent, Basingstoke, June 27 (Hampshire won on faster scoring rate)
did not bat   - 116-4   8   0   31   5 L.Potter b   84-9
                                                             R.A.Woolmer c T.M.Tremlett
                                                             C.S.Cowdrey lbw
                                                             G.R.Dilley c R.J.Parks
                                                             C.Penn lbw

74. Sunday League - Hampshire v Glamorgan, Cardiff, July 11 (Hampshire won by eight wickets)
did not bat   - 165-2   8   2   24   1 J.A.Hopkins c R.J.Parks   164-8   1

75. NatWest Trophy - Hampshire v Derbyshire, Southampton, July 14 (Hampshire won by six wickets)
did not bat   - 242-4   12   1   48   0   239-5   1

76. Sunday League - Hampshire v Lancashire, Southampton, July 18 (Match tied)
run out   8 215-9   7   1   43   1 D.P.Hughes c J.M.Rice   215-5

77. Sunday League - Hampshire v Gloucestershire, Bristol, July 25 (Gloucestershire won by eight wickets)
b F.D.Stephenson   13 145-9   6   1   33   0   146-2

78. Sunday League - Hampshire v Somerset, Portsmouth, August 1 (Hampshire won by eight wickets)
did not bat   - 180-4   8   2   27   0   177-6   2

79. NatWest Trophy - Hampshire v Surrey, Southampton, August 4 (Surrey won by eight wickets)
b R.D.Jackman   0 119   7   0   29   0   120-2

80. Sunday League - Hampshire v Sussex, Eastbourne, August 8 (Sussex won by 13 runs)
c C.P.Phillipson
     b G.S.le Roux   2 179   8   0   37   0   192-7

81. Sunday League - Hampshire v Worcestershire, Southampton, August 15 (Worcestershire won by 11 runs)
b A.P.Pridgeon   29 225   8   1   29   0   236-1

82. Sunday League - Hampshire v Northamptonshire, Northampton, August 22 (Northamptonshire won by 82 runs)
b T.M.Lamb   32 123   8   1   18   2 P.Willey c R.J.Parks   205-8
                                                             A.J.Lamb c R.J.Parks

83. Sunday League - Hampshire v Yorkshire, Southampton, August 29 (Hampshire won by 14 runs)
did not bat   - 248-4   8   1   21   2 G.Boycott b   234
                                                             K.Sharp c C.G.Greenidge

84. Sunday League - Hampshire v Surrey, Kennington Oval, September 5 (Match tied)
b R.D.V.Knight   2 139-9   8   3   17   3 G.P.Howarth c R.J.Parks   139-9   1
                                                             I.R.Payne c R.J.Parks
                                                             K.Mackintosh b

85. Sunday League - Hampshire v Warwickshire, Bournemouth, September 12 (Hampshire won by four wickets)
b R.G.D.Willis   19 170-6   8   0   37   1 A.M.Ferreira c and b   166-6   1

SEASON'S AVERAGES

Batting and Fielding	M	I	NO	Runs	HS	Ave	100	50	Ct
NatWest Trophy	2	1	0	0	0	0.00	-	-	1
Sunday League	16	12	1	204	46	18.54	-	-	5
Benson & Hedges Cup	4	4	1	54	21	18.00	-	-	-
Career - Gillette Cup/NWT	7	5	4	49	21*	49.00	-	-	1
Career - Sunday League	44	28	8	336	46	16.00	-	-	8
Career - B & H Cup	12	10	1	116	21	12.88	-	-	-
Career - One Day Matches	85	60	17	642	46	14.93	-	-	15

Bowling	O	M	R	W	BB	Ave	5i
NatWest Trophy	19	1	77	0	-	-	-
Sunday League	123	20	431	20	5-31	21.55	1
Benson & Hedges Cup	44	6	138	6	2-29	23.00	-
Career - Gillette Cup/NWT	71.4	8	207	3	2-15	69.00	-
Career - Sunday League	329.3	46	1087	50	5-13	21.74	2
Career - B & H Cup	118	26	329	14	3-11	23.50	-
Career - One Day Matches	706.3	105	2209	98	5-13	22.54	2

1982/83

86. Geddes/Grant Harrison Line Cup Barbados v Leeward Islands, Bridgetown, January 19 (Barbados won by four wickets)
b E.A.E.Baptiste 2 238-6 8 0 35 1 R.B.Richardson c R.L.Skeete 234-4

87. Geddes/Grant Harrison Line Cup Barbados v Guyana, Bridgetown, February 2 (Guyana won by 45 runs)
c L.A.Lambert b G.E.Charles 3 199-9 10 1 38 5 A.A.Lyght c C.G.Greenidge 244-8
S.F.A.F.Bacchus c N.A.Phillips
W.H.White c C.G.Greenidge
K.Singh c R.L.Skeete
R.A.Harper hit wkt

88. International - WEST INDIES v INDIA, Port of Spain, March 9 (West Indies won by 52 runs)
did not bat - 215-4 8 0 25 0 163-7

89. International - WEST INDIES v INDIA, Berbice, March 29 (India won by 27 runs)
c B.S.Sandhu b R.J.Shastri 5 255-9 . 7 0 23 1 R.J.Shastri c P.J.L.Dujon 282-5

90. International - WEST INDIES v INDIA, St George's, April 7 (West Indies won by seven wickets)
did not bat - 167-3 7 2 25 1 R.J.Shastri c P.J.L.Dujon 166

SEASON'S AVERAGES

Batting and Fielding	M	I	NO	Runs	HS	Ave	100	50	Ct
Internationals	3	1	0	5	5	5.00	-	-	-
Geddes/Grant Cup	2	2	0	5	3	2.50	-	-	-
Career - Internationals	16	10	4	105	32*	17.50	-	-	2
Career - Geddes/Grant Cup	8	7	0	35	23	5.00	-	-	3
Career - One Day Matches	90	63	17	652	46	16.54	-	-	15

Bowling	O	M	R	W	BB	Ave	5i
Internationals	22	2	73	2	1-23	36.50	-
Geddes/Grant Cup	18	1	73	6	5-38	12.16	1
Career - Internationals	139.4	8	487	18	3-28	27.05	-
Career - Geddes/Grant Cup	59.4	12	183	16	5-38	11.43	1
Career - One Day Matches	746.3	108	2355	106	5-13	22.21	3

1983

91. Sunday League - Hampshire v Essex, Southampton, May 8 (Hampshire won by 15 runs)
not out   25   214-6   8   2   22   2   K.R.Pont c N.G.Cowley   199-8
                                                                S.Turner c N.E.J.Pocock

92. Benson & Hedges Cup - Hampshire v Somerset, Taunton, May 17, 18 (Hampshire won by 22 runs)
c I.T.Botham b C.H.Dredge   9   138   11   2   22   3   J.W.Lloyds c D.R.Turner   116   1
                                                   V.J.Marks c N.E.J.Pocock
                                                   C.H.Dredge b

93. Benson & Hedges Cup - Hampshire v Minor Counties, Bournemouth, May 19, 20 (Hampshire won by six wickets)
did not bat   -   169-4   11   1   38   2   S.G.Plumb b   168-9   1
                                                 F.E.Collyer c N.E.J.Pocock

94. Sunday League - Hampshire v Northamptonshire, Bournemouth, May 22 (Hampshire won by seven wickets)
did not bat   -   173-3   8   0   17   0   172-7

95. Benson & Hedges Cup - Hampshire v Sussex, Hove, May 23 (Hampshire won by three wickets)
b G.S.le Roux   2   174-7   10   3   21   0   171

96. Sunday League - Hampshire v Kent, Canterbury, May 29 (Kent won by 65 runs)
not out   27   133   8   0   18   0   198-7

97. Benson & Hedges Cup - Hampshire v Kent, Canterbury, June 1, 2 (Kent won by 5 runs)
b R.M.Ellison   8   193-9   11   4   26   4   R.A.Woolmer c V.P.Terry   198-9   1
                                                 C.S.Cowdrey c M.C.J.Nicholas
                                                 A.P.E.Knott c R.J.Parks
                                                 G.W.Johnson c R.J.Parks

98. Sunday League - Hampshire v Yorkshire, Middlesbrough, June 5 (Yorkshire won by six wickets)
run out   18   255-9   8   0   23   0   257-4

99. NatWest Trophy - Hampshire v Hertfordshire, Hitchin, June 29 (Hampshire won by nine wickets)
did not bat   -   163-1   12   2   23   1   B.G.Evans c R.J.Parks   159-6

100. Sunday League - Hampshire v Lancashire, Old Trafford, July 3 (Hampshire won by 58 runs)
did not bat   -   268-4   8   0   22   1   C.Maynard b   210-9   1

101. Sunday League - Hampshire v Surrey, Portsmouth, July 10 (Hampshire won by 104 runs)
did not bat   -   292-1   7   2   14   0   188-5

102. Sunday League - Hampshire v Nottinghamshire, Portsmouth, July 17 (Hampshire won by 56 runs)
not out   27   242-6   6   0   15   0   186-6

103. NatWest Trophy - Hampshire v Glamorgan, Swansea, July 20 (Hampshire won by 156 runs)
not out   15   294-5   6   3   6   1   J.A.Hopkins c N.E.J.Pocock   138

104. Sunday League - Hampshire v Somerset, Taunton, July 24 (Somerset won by seven wickets)
b I.T.Botham   1   93-7   6   0   35   1   P.M.Roebuck c R.J.Parks   97-3

105. Sunday League - Hampshire v Gloucestershire, Bournemouth, July 31 (Gloucestershire won by eight wickets)
did not bat   -   145-2   7.3   0   35   1   B.C.Broad b   148-2

106. NatWest Trophy - Hampshire v Gloucestershire, Bristol, August 3 (Hampshire won by six wickets)
did not bat   -   256-4   12   4   37   2   P.Bainbridge   252-8   1
                                                   c M.C.J.Nicholas
                                                 R.C.Russell b

107. NatWest Trophy - Hampshire v Kent, Canterbury, August 17 (Kent won by 71 runs)
c G.W.Johnson
b C.S.Cowdrey   0   102   12   6   15   4   N.R.Taylor c R.J.Parks   173
                                                 D.G.Aslett c N.E.J.Pocock
                                                 A.P.E.Knott c R.J.Parks
                                                 G.W.Johnson c T.E.Jesty

108. Sunday League - Hampshire v Worcestershire, Worcester, August 21 (Hampshire won on faster run rate)
c T.S.Curtis b A.P.Pridgeon 17   239-5   4   1   6   0   29-2

109. Sunday League - Hampshire v Sussex, Southampton, August 28 (Hampshire won by four wickets)
lbw b A.C.S.Pigott   35   194-6   8   2   19   3   I.J.Gould c R.J.Parks   193-8   1
                                                 A.P.Wells c R.J.Parks
                                                 C.P.Phillipson c R.J.Parks

110. Sunday League - Hampshire v Derbyshire, Derby, September 4 (Derbyshire won by 8 runs)
lbw b P.G.Newman   0   135   8   2   11   1   M.A.Holding c N.G.Cowley   143-9

SEASON'S AVERAGES

Batting and Fielding	M	I	NO	Runs	HS	Ave	100	50	Ct
NatWest Trophy	4	2	1	15	15*	15.00	-	-	1
Sunday League	12	8	3	150	35	30.00	-	-	2
Benson & Hedges Cup	4	3	0	19	9	6.33	-	-	3
Career - Gillette Cup/NWT	11	7	5	64	21*	32.00	-	-	2
Career - Sunday League	56	36	11	486	46	19.44	-	-	10
Career - B & H Cup	16	13	1	135	21	11.25	-	-	3
Career - One Day Matches	110	76	21	836	46	15.20	-	-	21

Bowling	O	M	R	W	BB	Ave	5i
NatWest Trophy	42	15	81	8	4-15	10.12	-
Sunday League	86.3	9	237	9	3-19	26.33	-
Benson & Hedges Cup	43	10	107	9	4-26	11.88	-
Career - Gillette Cup/NWT	113.4	23	288	11	4-15	26.18	-
Career - Sunday League	416	55	1324	59	5-13	22.44	2
Career - B & H Cup	161	36	436	23	4-26	18.95	-
Career - One Day Matches	918	142	2780	132	5-13	21.06	3

1983 – Prudential World Cup in England

111. International - WEST INDIES v INDIA, Old Trafford, June 9, 10 (India won by 34 runs)
st S.M.H.Kirmani
c R.J.Shastri   2   228   12   1   48   2   S.M.Gavaskar c P.J.L.Dujon   262-8
R.M.H.Binny   lbw

112. International - WEST INDIES v INDIA, Kennington Oval, June 15 (West Indies won by 66 runs)
run out   4   282-9   11   3   20   1   S.M.H.Kirmani b   216

113. International - WEST INDIES v AUSTRALIA, Lord's, June 18 (West Indies won by seven wickets)
did not bat   -   276-3   12   0   36   2   G.M.Wood b   273-6
T.M.Chappell c P.J.L.Dujon

114. International - WEST INDIES v ZIMBABWE, Edgbaston, June 20 (West Indies won by ten wickets)
did not bat   -   172-0   12   3   19   2   R.D.Brown c C.H.Lloyd   171
A.J.Pycroft c P.J.L.Dujon

115. International - WEST INDIES v PAKISTAN, Kennington Oval, June 22 (West Indies won by eight wickets)
did not bat   -   188-2   12   2   28   3   Imran Khan c P.J.L.Dujon   184-8
Wasim Raja lbw
Shahid Mahboob c I.V.A.Richards

116. International - WEST INDIES v INDIA, Lord's, June 25 (India won by 43 runs)
c S.M.Gavaskar
b M.Amarnath   18   140   11   1   24   2   K.Srikkanth lbw   183
Madan Lal b

SEASON'S AVERAGES

Batting and Fielding	M	I	NO	Runs	HS	Ave	100	50	Ct
Internationals	6	3	0	24	18	8.00	-	-	-
Career - Internationals	22	13	4	129	32*	14.33	-	-	2
Career - One Day Matches	116	79	21	860	46	14.82	-	-	21

Bowling	O	M	R	W	BB	Ave	5i
Internationals	70	10	175	12	3-28	14.58	-
Career - Internationals	209.4	18	662	30	3-28	22.06	-
Career - One Day Matches	988	152	2955	144	5-13	20.52	3

1983/84 – West Indies in India

117. International - WEST INDIES v INDIA, Srinagar, October 13 (West Indies won on faster scoring rate)
did not bat   - 108-0   7.2   2   13   2   S.M.Gavaskar
                                          c I.V.A.Richards   176   1
                            B.S.Sandhu   c I.V.A.Richards

118. International - WEST INDIES v INDIA, Baroda, November 9 (West Indies won by four wickets)
b Madan Lal   3   217-6⁻   9   0   34   1   Kapil Dev b   214-6

119. International - WEST INDIES v INDIA, Indore, December 1 (West Indies won by eight wickets)
did not bat   - 241-2   9   1   27   0   240-7

120. International - WEST INDIES v INDIA, Jamshedpur, December 7 (West Indies won by 104 runs)
b Kapil Dev   5   333-8   6   0   18   0   229-5

121. International - WEST INDIES v INDIA, Gauhati, December 17 (West Indies won by six wickets)
not out   10   182-4   5   2   8   0   178-7

SEASON'S AVERAGES

Batting and Fielding	M	I	NO	Runs	HS	Ave	100	50	Ct
Internationals	5	3	1	18	10*	9.00	-	-	1
Career - Internationals	27	16	5	147	32*	13.36	-	-	3
Career - One Day Matches	121	82	22	878	46	14.63	-	-	22

Bowling	O	M	R	W	BB	Ave	5i
Internationals	36.2	5	100	3	2-13	33.33	-
Career - Internationals	246	23	762	33	3-28	23.09	-
Career - One Day Matches	1024.2	157	3055	147	5-13	20.78	3

1983/84 – Benson and Hedges World Series in Australia

122. International - WEST INDIES v AUSTRALIA, Melbourne, January 8 (West Indies won by 27 runs)
run out   9   221-7   9   2   25   2   W.B.Phillips c and b   194   1
                            G.N.Yallop c C.H.Lloyd

123. International - WEST INDIES v PAKISTAN, Melbourne, January 12 (Pakistan won by 97 runs)
c Azeem Hafeez
     b Sarfraz Nawaz   20   111   6   0   27   1   Javed Miandad b   208-8

124. International - WEST INDIES v PAKISTAN, Sydney, January 19 (West Indies won by five wickets)
not out   16   185-5   6   4   5   1   Mohsin Khan c P.J.L.Dujon 184-8

125. International - WEST INDIES v AUSTRALIA, Melbourne, January 22 (West Indies won by 26 runs)
b G.F.Lawson   1   252-6   10   0   49   1   J.N.Maguire b   226

126. International - WEST INDIES v PAKISTAN, Adelaide, January 28 (West Indies won by one wicket)
not out   56   180-9   9   1   28   3   Mansoor Akhtar
                                    c P.J.L.Dujon   177-8
                            Javed Miandad c P.J.L.Dujon
                            Salim Malik b

127. International - WEST INDIES v AUSTRALIA, Adelaide, January 29 (West Indies won by six wickets)
did not bat   - 169-4   10   3   21   1   S.B.Smith b   165-7

128. International - WEST INDIES v PAKISTAN, Perth, February 4 (West Indies won by seven wickets)
did not bat   - 183-3   6   0   20   0   182-7   1

129. International - WEST INDIES v AUSTRALIA, Perth, February 5 (Australia won by 14 runs)
c R.W.Marsh
     b C.G.Rackemann   2   197   10   2   27   2   K.C.Wessels c W.W.Daniel 211-8
                            K.J.Hughes c R.B.Richardson

130. International - WEST INDIES v AUSTRALIA, Sydney, February 8 (West Indies won by nine wickets)
did not bat   - 161-1   9   1   24   2   K.J.Hughes b   160
                            D.M.Jones b

131. International - WEST INDIES v AUSTRALIA, Melbourne, February 11 (Match tied)
did not bat   - 222-5   10   1   27   1   K.J.Hughes lbw   222-9   1

132. International - WEST INDIES v AUSTRALIA, Melbourne, February 12 (West Indies won by six wickets)
not out   6   213-4   10   0   44   0   212-8

SEASON'S AVERAGES

Batting and Fielding	M	I	NO	Runs	HS	Ave	100	50	Ct
Internationals	11	7	3	110	56*	27.50	-	1	3
Career - Internationals	38	23	8	257	56*	17.13	-	1	6
Career - One Day Matches	132	89	25	988	56*	15.43	-	1	25

Bowling	O	M	R	W	BB	Ave	5i
Internationals	95	14	297	14	3-28	21.21	-
Career - Internationals	341	37	1059	47	3-28	22.53	-
Career - One Day Matches	1119.2	171	3352	161	5-13	20.81	3

1983/84

133. International - WEST INDIES v AUSTRALIA, Port of Spain, March 14 (Australia won by four wickets)
run out   0   190-6   9   0   52   0   194-6

134. International - WEST INDIES v AUSTRALIA, Castries, April 19 (West Indies won by seven wickets)
did not bat   -   208-3   10   2   34   4   W.B.Phillips b   206-9   2
D.W.Hookes c P.J.L.Dujon
D.M.Jones c and b
T.G.Hogan c and b

135. International - WEST INDIES v AUSTRALIA, Kingston, April 26 (West Indies won by nine wickets)
did not bat   -   211-1   10   1   26   2   D.W.Hookes b   209-7
G.R.J.Matthews b

SEASON'S AVERAGES

Batting and Fielding	M	I	NO	Runs	HS	Ave	100	50	Ct
Internationals	3	1	0	0	0	0.00	-	-	2
Career - Internationals	41	24	8	257	56*	16.06	-	1	8
Career - One Day Matches	135	90	25	988	56*	15.20	-	1	27

Bowling	O	M	R	W	BB	Ave	5i
Internationals	29	3	112	6	4-34	18.66	-
Career - Internationals	370	40	1171	53	4-34	22.09	-
Career - One Day Matches	1148.2	174	3464	167	5-13	20.74	3

1984 – West Indies in England

136. International - WEST INDIES v ENGLAND, Old Trafford, May 31 (West Indies won by 104 runs)
run out   4   272-9   6   1   20   1   D.I.Gower c C.G.Greenidge   168

137. International - WEST INDIES v ENGLAND, Trent Bridge, June 2 (England won by three wickets)
run out   20   179   10   1   30   1   D.I.Gower lbw   180-7

138. International - WEST INDIES v ENGLAND, Lord's, June 4 (West Indies won by eight wickets)
did not bat   -   197-2   11   0   38   3   D.I.Gower b   196
D.W.Randall c P.J.L.Dujon
D.L.Bairstow b

SEASON'S AVERAGES

Batting and Fielding	M	I	NO	Runs	HS	Ave	100	50	Ct
Internationals	3	2	0	24	20	12.00	-	-	-
Career - Internationals	44	26	8	281	56*	15.61	-	1	8
Career - One Day Matches	138	92	25	1012	56*	15.10	-	1	27

Bowling	O	M	R	W	BB	Ave	5i
Internationals	27	2	88	5	3-38	17.60	-
Career - Internationals	397	42	1259	58	4-34	21.70	-
Career - One Day Matches	1175.2	176	3552	172	5-13	20.65	3

1984/85 – Benson and Hedges World Series in Australia

139. International - WEST INDIES v AUSTRALIA, Melbourne, January 6 (West Indies won by seven wickets)
did not bat   -   241-3   10   0   32   1   D.C.Boon b   240-6

140. International - WEST INDIES v SRI LANKA, Hobart, January 10 (West Indies won by eight wickets)
did not bat   -   198-2   10   3   37   0   197-7

141. International - WEST INDIES v SRI LANKA, Brisbane, January 12 (West Indies won by 90 runs)
not out   1   270-6   5   2   9   0   180

142. International - WEST INDIES v AUSTRALIA, Brisbane, January 13 (West Indies won by five wickets)
did not bat   -   195-5   10   2   42   1   M.J.Bennett c A.L.Logie   191

143. International - WEST INDIES v AUSTRALIA, Sydney, January 15 (West Indies won by five wickets)
did not bat   -   201-5   10   0   38   1   S.P.O'Donnell b   200-5

144. International - WEST INDIES v SRI LANKA, Sydney, January 17 (West Indies won by 65 runs)
did not bat   -   267-3   10   1   33   1   S.A.R.Silva c C.G.Greenidge 202-5

145. International - WEST INDIES v AUSTRALIA, Melbourne, January 20 (West Indies won by 65 runs)
not out   2   271-7   9   1   29   2   G.M.Wood c P.J.L.Dujon   206-9
                                               D.M.Jones c D.L.Haynes

146. International - WEST INDIES v AUSTRALIA, Adelaide, January 27 (West Indies won by six wickets)
did not bat   -   201-4   10   1   35   2   A.R.Border lbw   200-9
                                               G.F.Lawson hit wkt

147. International - WEST INDIES v SRI LANKA, Perth, February 2 (West Indies won by 82 runs)
not out   2   309-6   6   0   17   0   227-6

148. International - WEST INDIES v AUSTRALIA, Sydney, February 6 (Australia won by 26 runs)
b R.J.McCurdy   43   221   10   0   55   1   K.C.Wessels c P.J.L.Dujon   247-6

149. International - WEST INDIES v AUSTRALIA, Melbourne, February 10 (West Indies won by four wickets)
not out   0   273-6   10   0   64   1   A.R.Border c P.J.L.Dujon   271-3

150. International - WEST INDIES v AUSTRALIA, Sydney, February 12 (West Indies won by seven wickets)
did not bat   -   179-3   10   0   37   0   178

SEASON'S AVERAGES

Batting and Fielding	M	I	NO	Runs	HS	Ave	100	50	Ct
Internationals	12	5	4	48	43	48.00	-	-	-
Career - Internationals	56	31	12	329	56*	17.31	-	1	8
Career - One Day Matches	150	97	29	1060	56*	15.58	-	1	27

Bowling	O	M	R	W	BB	Ave	5i
Internationals	110	10	428	10	2-29	42.80	-
Career - Internationals	507	52	1687	68	4-34	24.80	-
Career - One Day Matches	1285.2	186	3980	182	5-13	21.86	3

1984/85 – Benson and Hedges World Championships in Australia

151. International - WEST INDIES v NEW ZEALAND, Sydney, February (19), 21 (No result)
did not bat   -   6   1   13   0   57-2

152. International - WEST INDIES v SRI LANKA, Melbourne, February 27 (West Indies won by eight wickets)
did not bat   -   136-2   10   1   26   0   135-7

153. International - WEST INDIES v PAKISTAN, Melbourne, March 6 (Pakistan won by seven wickets)
c Javed Miandad
     b Mudassar Nazar   10   159   9   2   25   1   Mudassar Nazar c A.L.Logie 160-3

154. International - WEST INDIES v NEW ZEALAND, Sydney, March 9 (West Indies won by six wickets)
did not bat   -   139-4   10   1   32   1   R.J.Hadlee b   138-9

SEASON'S AVERAGES

Batting and Fielding	M	I	NO	Runs	HS	Ave	100	50	Ct
Internationals	4	1	0	10	10	10.00	-	-	-
Career - Internationals	60	32	12	339	56*	16.95	-	1	8
Career - One Day Matches	154	98	29	1070	56*	15.50	-	1	27

Bowling	O	M	R	W	BB	Ave	5i
Internationals	35	5	96	2	1-25	48.00	-
Career - Internationals	542	57	1783	70	4-34	25.47	-
Career - One Day Matches	1320.2	191	4076	184	5-13	22.15	3

1985

155. Benson & Hedges Cup - Hampshire v Glamorgan, Southampton, May 14, 15 (Hampshire won by 116 runs)
c T.Davies b J.G.Thomas   10   294-9   8   2   18   2   G.C.Holmes c D.R.Turner   178   1
Younis Ahmed c and b

156. Benson & Hedges Cup - Hampshire v Somerset, Southampton, May 16 (Hampshire won by seven wickets)
did not bat   -   169-3   11   1   32   2   I.T.Botham b   167-8
R.J.Harden c R.J.Parks

157. Benson & Hedges Cup - Hampshire v Minor Counties, Reading, May 18 (Hampshire won by 135 runs)
c A.S.Barnard b S.G.Plumb   2   264-8   4   1   10   1   G.R.J.Roope lbw   129

158. Sunday League - Hampshire v Surrey, Southampton, May 19 (Hampshire won by 48 runs)
c G.S.Clinton
b G.Monkhouse   14   208-7   8   1   32   1   M.A.Lynch b   160-9

159. Sunday League - Hampshire v Yorkshire, Middlesbrough, June 2 (Yorkshire won by 6 wickets)
c S.D.Fletcher b C.Shaw   1   257-6   8   1   39   0   259-4   1

160. Benson & Hedges Cup - Hampshire v Leicestershire, Southampton, June 5 (Leicestershire won by 4 runs)
lbw b L.B.Taylor   25   239   11   1   38   1   J.C.Balderstone lbw   243-4   1

161. Sunday League - Hampshire v Warwickshire, Edgbaston, June 9 (Warwickshire won by five wickets)
c G.C.Small b N.Gifford   11   175-8   8   0   37   2   D.L.Amiss c R.J.Parks   176-5
G.W.Humpage b

162. Sunday League - Hampshire v Sussex, Hove, June 16 (Hampshire won by nine wickets)
did not bat   -   239-1   8   0   46   0   238-4

163. Sunday League - Hampshire v Essex, Bournemouth, June 30 (Hampshire won by eight wickets)
did not bat   -   162-2   8   1   24   3   B.R.Hardie b   161-9
D.R.Pringle c R.J.Parks
K.W.R.Fletcher b

164. NatWest Trophy - Hampshire v Berkshire, Southampton, July 3 (Hampshire won by 187 runs)
did not bat   -   339-4   3   2   1   0   152

165. Sunday League - Hampshire v Lancashire, Old Trafford, July 7 (Hampshire won by 3 runs)
b P.J.W.Allott   0   235-5   8   0   37   1   M.Watkinson b   232

166. NatWest Trophy - Hampshire v Leicestershire, Southampton, July 17 (Hampshire won by four wickets)
b G.J.Parsons   1   213-6   12   0   45   1   P.B.Clift b   212-6

167. NatWest Trophy - Hampshire v Somerset, Taunton, August 7, 8 (Hampshire won by 149 runs)
not out   2   299-5   9   2   17   2   N.F.M.Popplewell b   150
I.T.Botham c R.J.Parks

168. Sunday League - Hampshire v Leicestershire, Leicester, August 18 (No result)
4   0   7   1   I.P.Butcher b   18-1

169. NatWest Trophy - Hampshire v Essex, Southampton, August 21, 22 (Essex won by losing fewer wickets
with scores level)
b J.K.Lever   29   224-8   12   1   41   0   224-7

170. Sunday League - Hampshire v Gloucestershire, Bournemouth, August 25 (Hampshire won on faster scoring
rate)
did not bat   -   88-2   8   2   18   2   J.W.Lloyds c R.J.Parks   152-8
C.W.J.Athey c T.M.Tremlett

171. Sunday League - Hampshire v Middlesex, Southampton, September 1 (Hampshire won by six wickets)
did not bat   -   149-4   7.5   0   35   1   G.D.Rose b   146

172. Sunday League - Hampshire v Derbyshire, Southampton, September 8 (Derbyshire won by 7 runs)
b R.J.Finney   4   179   8   1   29   1   B.Roberts lbw   186-8

173. Sunday League - Hampshire v Nottinghamshire, Trent Bridge, September 15 (Hampshire won by 36 runs)
   b C.E.B.Rice   33 243-5   8   0   39   2   D.J.R.Martindale c R.J.Parks 207
                                                             B.N.French b

SEASON'S AVERAGES

Batting and Fielding	M	I	NO	Runs	HS	Ave	100	50	Ct
NatWest Trophy	4	3	1	32	29	16.00	-	-	-
Sunday League	11	6	0	63	33	10.50	-	-	1
Benson & Hedges Cup	4	3	0	37	25	12.33	-	-	2
Career - Gillette Cup/NWT	15	10	6	96	29	24.00	-	-	2
Career - Sunday League	67	42	11	549	46	17.70	-	-	11
Career - B & H Cup	20	16	1	172	25	11.46	-	-	5
Career - One Day Matches	173	110	30	1202	56*	15.02	-	1	30

Bowling	O	M	R	W	BB	Ave	5i
NatWest Trophy	36	5	104	3	2-17	34.66	-
Sunday League	83.5	6	343	14	3-24	24.50	-
Benson & Hedges Cup	34	5	98	6	2-18	16.33	-
Career - Gillette Cup/NWT	149.4	28	392	14	4-15	28.00	-
Career - Sunday League	499.5	61	1667	73	5-13	22.83	2
Career - B & H Cup	195	41	534	29	4-26	18.41	-
Career - One Day Matches	1474.1	207	4621	207	5-13	22.32	3

1985/86 – Rothmans Three Nations Trophy in Sharjah

174. International - WEST INDIES v PAKISTAN, Sharjah, November 15 (West Indies won by seven wickets)
   did not bat   - 199-3   8   1   30   1   Javed Miandad b   196-4
175. International - WEST INDIES v INDIA, Sharjah, November 22 (West Indies won by eight wickets)
   did not bat   - 186-2   9   2   35   0   180-4

SEASON'S AVERAGES

Batting and Fielding	M	I	NO	Runs	HS	Ave	100	50	Ct
Internationals	2	-	-	-	-	-	-	-	-
Career - Internationals	62	32	12	339	56*	16.95	-	1	8
Career - One Day Matches	175	110	30	1202	56*	15.02	-	1	30

Bowling	O	M	R	W	BB	Ave	5i
Internationals	17	3	65	1	1-30	65.00	-
Career - Internationals	559	60	1848	71	4-34	26.02	-
Career - One Day Matches	1491.1	210	4686	208	5-13	22.52	3

1985/86 – West Indies in Pakistan

176. International - WEST INDIES v PAKISTAN, Gujranwala, November 27 (West Indies won by eight wickets)
   did not bat   - 224-2   8   0   47   0   218-5
177. International - WEST INDIES v PAKISTAN, Lahore, November 29 (Pakistan won by six wickets)
   b Wasim Akram   1 173   7.3   0   38   0   175-4
178. International - WEST INDIES v PAKISTAN, Peshawar, December 2 (West Indies won by 40 runs)
   did not bat   - 201-5   8   1   36   3   Mohsin Khan c R.A.Harper 161
                                                           Abdul Qadir b
                                                           Mohsin Kamal b
179. International - WEST INDIES v PAKISTAN, Rawalpindi, December 4 (Pakistan won by five wickets)
   c Zulqarnain
          b Wasim Akram 20 199-8   8   2   27   0   203-5

180. International - WEST INDIES v PAKISTAN, Karachi, December 6 (West Indies won by eight wickets)
did not bat   - 128-2   8   1   25   2   Mohsin Khan
                                                        c R.B.Richardson   127-7
                                                        Ramiz Raja c P.J.L.Dujon

SEASON'S AVERAGES

Batting and Fielding	M	I	NO	Runs	HS	Ave	100	50	Ct
Internationals	5	2	0	21	20	10.50	-	-	-
Career - Internationals	67	34	12	360	56*	16.36	-	1	8
Career - One Day Matches	180	112	30	1223	56*	14.91	-	1	30

Bowling	O	M	R	W	BB	Ave	5i
Internationals	39.3	4	173	5	3-36	34.60	-
Career - Internationals	598.3	64	2021	76	4-34	26.59	-
Career - One Day Matches	1530.4	214	4859	213	5-13	22.81	3

1985/86

181. Geddes/Grant Harrison Line Cup – Barbados v Windward Islands, Bridgetown, January 15 (Barbados won
by 171 runs)
did not bat   - 276-3   7   0   19   3   L.D.John c C.A.Best   105-7
                                                        L.A.Lewis c M.C.Worrell
                                                        J.D.Charles c D.L.Haynes

182. International - WEST INDIES v ENGLAND, Kingston, February 18 (West Indies won by six wickets)
did not bat   - 146-4   10   1   23   4   G.A.Gooch b   145-8
                                                        M.W.Gatting b
                                                        A.J.Lamb c C.G.Greenidge
                                                        P.Willey c R.B.Richardson

183. International - WEST INDIES v ENGLAND, Port of Spain, March 4 (England won by five wickets)
did not bat   - 229-3   10   1   59   0   230-5

184. International - WEST INDIES v ENGLAND, Bridgetown, March 19 (West Indies won by 135 runs)
c and b I.T.Botham   9   249-7   6   2   14   3   R.T.Robinson
                                                        c R.B.Richardson   114   1
                                                        W.N.Slack c P.J.L.Dujon
                                                        I.T.Botham c J.Garner

185. International - WEST INDIES v ENGLAND, Port of Spain, March 31 (West Indies won by eight wickets)
did not bat   - 166-2   9   0   37   4   G.A.Gooch c I.V.A.Richards 165-9
                                                        R.T.Robinson b
                                                        P.Willey c C.G.Greenidge
                                                        P.R.Downton c C.G.Greenidge

SEASON'S AVERAGES

Batting and Fielding	M	I	NO	Runs	HS	Ave	100	50	Ct
Internationals	4	1	0	9	9	9.00	-	-	1
Geddes/Grant Cup	1	-	-	-	-	-	-	-	-
Career - Internationals	71	35	12	369	56*	16.04	-	1	9
Career - Geddes/Grant Cup	9	7	0	35	23	5.00	-	-	3
Career - One Day Matches	185	113	30	1232	56*	14.84	-	1	31

Bowling	O	M	R	W	BB	Ave	5i
Internationals	35	4	133	11	4-23	12.09	-
Geddes/Grant Cup	7	0	19	3	3-19	6.33	-
Career - Internationals	633.3	68	2154	87	4-23	24.75	-
Career - Geddes/Grant Cup	66.4	12	202	19	5-38	10.63	1
Career - One Day Matches	1572.4	218	5011	227	5-13	22.07	3

1986

186. Sunday League - Hampshire v Glamorgan, Cardiff, May 4 (Hampshire won by 20 runs)
c G.C.Holmes b J.G.Thomas 14   242-6   8   0   35   1   J.A.Hopkins lbw   222-7

187. Benson & Hedges Cup - Hampshire v Middlesex, Southampton, May 10 (Middlesex won by seven wickets)
run out   2   77-5   2   0   8   0   80-3

188. Sunday League - Hampshire v Northamptonshire, Southampton, May 11 (Hampshire won by 4 runs)
c R.J.Bailey b N.A.Mallender 4   158-8   8   2   27   0   154-8

189. Benson & Hedges Cup - Hampshire v Surrey, Kennington Oval, May 13 (Hampshire won by three wickets)
b P.I.Pocock   2   240-7   11   1   34   1   S.T.Clarke b   239-7

190. Benson & Hedges Cup - Hampshire v Kent, Southampton, May 15 (Kent won by 63 runs)
c C.J.Tavare
    b D.L.Underwood   33   187-9   11   4   25   1   C.S.Cowdrey c C.L.Smith   250-5

191. Sunday League - Hampshire v Nottinghamshire, Southampton, June 1 (Nottinghamshire won by seven wickets)
did not bat   -   197-5   8   0   28   0   200-3

192. Sunday League - Hampshire v Essex, Ilford, June 15 (Hampshire won by six wickets)
did not bat   -   257-4   8   1   30   2   G.A.Gooch b   256-5
                                                  D.R.Pringle c M.C.J.Nicholas

193. Sunday League - Hampshire v Kent, Basingstoke, June 22 (Hampshire won by four wickets)
c and b D.L.Underwood   4   150-6   8   0   44   0   149-9   1

194. NatWest Trophy - Hampshire v Hertfordshire, Southampton, June 25 (Hampshire won by four wickets)
not out   15   124-4   12   4   12   1   W.G.Merry c R.J.Parks   122

195. Sunday League - Hampshire v Worcestershire, Worcester, June 29 (Hampshire won by nine wickets)
did not bat   -   183-1   8   0   24   1   D.N.Patel c and b   182-8   1

196. Sunday League - Hampshire v Somerset, Taunton, July 6 (Hampshire won by eight wickets)
did not bat   -   104-2   7   1   20   1   T.Gard c R.J.Parks   103   1

197. NatWest Trophy - Hampshire v Worcestershire, Southampton, July 9 (Worcestershire won by 66 runs)
run out   32   212   12   1   50   1   D.B.D'Oliveira c R.J.Parks   278-5

198. Sunday League - Hampshire v Warwickshire, Portsmouth, July 20 (Hampshire won by six wickets)
not out   39   154-4   8   0   29   2   D.L.Amiss lbw   152
                                                N.Gifford c V.P.Terry

199. Sunday League - Hampshire v Leicestershire, Southampton, July 27 (Hampshire won on faster scoring rate)
not out   2   276-3   8   0   27   2   J.C.Balderstone hit wkt   184-7
                                                P.D.Bowler b

200. Sunday League - Hampshire v Sussex, Bournemouth, August 10 (Sussex won on faster scoring rate)
did not bat   -   221-6   8   0   34   0   199-3

201. Sunday League - Hampshire v Middlesex, Lord's, August 17 (Middlesex won by eight wickets)
did not bat   -   195-5   8   0   42   0   200-2

202. Sunday League - Hampshire v Yorkshire, Bournemouth, August 24 (Hampshire won by seven wickets)
did not bat   -   197-3   8   0   28   1   S.N.Hartley c C.G.Greenidge 196-7

203. Sunday League - Hampshire v Derbyshire, Heanor, August 31 (Hampshire won by 73 runs)
b M.A.Holding   5   257-6   6   0   33   1   M.A.Holding b   184

204. Sunday League - Hampshire v Surrey, Kennington Oval, September 7 (Hampshire won by 3 runs)
c C.J.Richards b M.P.Bicknell 1   149-8   8   0   27   2   G.S.Clinton c R.A.Smith   146-8

SEASON'S AVERAGES

Batting and Fielding	M	I	NO	Runs	HS	Ave	100	50	Ct
NatWest Trophy	2	2	1	47	32	47.00	-	-	-
Sunday League	14	7	2	69	39*	13.80	-	-	3
Benson & Hedges Cup	3	3	0	37	33	12.33	-	-	-
Career - Gillette Cup/NWT	17	12	7	143	32	28.60	-	-	2
Career - Sunday League	81	49	13	618	46	17.16	-	-	14
Career - B & H Cup	23	19	1	209	33	11.61	-	-	5
Career - One Day Matches	204	125	33	1385	56*	15.05	-	1	34

Bowling	O	M	R	W	BB	Ave	5i
NatWest Trophy	24	5	62	2	1-12	31.00	-
Sunday League	109	4	428	13	2-27	32.92	-
Benson & Hedges Cup	24	5	67	2	1-25	33.50	-
Career - Gillette Cup/NWT	173.4	33	454	16	4-15	28.37	-
Career - Sunday League	608.5	65	2095	86	5-13	24.36	2
Career - B & H Cup	219	46	601	31	4-26	19.38	-
Career - One Day Matches	1729.4	232	5568	244	5-13	22.81	3

1986/87 – West Indies in Pakistan

205. International - WEST INDIES v PAKISTAN, Peshawar, October 17 (West Indies won by four wickets)
not out   0   165-6   9   1   21   1   Mohsin Khan   lbw   164-7

206. International - WEST INDIES v PAKISTAN, Gujranwala, November 4 (West Indies won on faster scoring rate)
run out   66   196-7   8   2   18   2   Mohsin Khan   b   155-6
                                                 Asif Mujtaba   c R.B.Richardson

207. International - WEST INDIES v PAKISTAN, Sialkot, November 14 (West Indies won by four wickets)
not out   1   151-6   9   2   29   2   Javed Miandad   b   148-7
                                                 Ijaz Ahmed   b

208. International - WEST INDIES v PAKISTAN, Multan, November 17 (West Indies won by 89 runs)
did not bat   -   202-5   5   1   7   1   Sajid Ali   lbw   113

SEASON'S AVERAGES

Batting and Fielding	M	I	NO	Runs	HS	Ave	100	50	Ct
Internationals	4	3	2	67	66	67.00	-	1	-
Career - Internationals	75	38	14	436	66	18.16	-	2	9
Career - One Day Matches	208	128	35	1452	66	16.78	-	2	34

Bowling	O	M	R	W	BB	Ave	5i
Internationals	31	6	75	6	2-18	12.50	-
Career - Internationals	664.3	74	2229	93	4-23	23.96	-
Career - One Day Matches	1760.4	238	5643	250	5-13	22.57	3

1986/87 – Champions Trophy in Sharjah

209. International - WEST INDIES v PAKISTAN, Sharjah, November 28 (West Indies won by nine wickets)
did not bat   -   145-1   8   1   16   0   143

210. International - WEST INDIES v INDIA, Sharjah, November 30 (West Indies won by 33 runs)
run out   10   198-8   9   2   25   2   K.Srikkanth   b   165-8
                                                 Madan Lal   b

211. International - WEST INDIES v SRI LANKA, Sharjah, December 3 (West Indies won by 193 runs)
not out   3   248-5   5   1   16   1   R.S.Mahanama   c P.J.L.Dujon   55

SEASON'S AVERAGES

Batting and Fielding	M	I	NO	Runs	HS	Ave	100	50	Ct
Internationals	3	2	1	13	10	13.00	-	-	-
Career - Internationals	78	40	15	449	66	17.96	-	2	9
Career - One Day Matches	211	130	36	1465	66	15.58	-	2	34

Bowling	O	M	R	W	BB	Ave	5i
Internationals	22	4	57	3	2-25	19.00	-
Career - Internationals	686.3	78	2286	96	4-23	23.81	-
Career - One Day Matches	1782.4	242	5700	253	5-13	22.52	3

1986/87 – Benson and Hedges Perth Challenge in Australia

212. International - WEST INDIES v ENGLAND, Perth, January 3 (England won by 19 runs)
    b G.R.Dilley   7   209   10   1   30   2   B.C.Broad c J.Garner   228-9
                                                      A.J.Lamb c R.A.Harper

SEASON'S AVERAGES

Batting and Fielding	M	I	NO	Runs	HS	Ave	100	50	Ct
Internationals	1	1	0	7	7	7.00	-	-	-
Career - Internationals	79	41	15	456	66	17.53	-	2	9
Career - One Day Matches	212	131	36	1472	66	15.49	-	2	34

Bowling	O	M	R	W	BB	Ave	5i
Internationals	10	1	30	2	2-30	15.00	-
Career - Internationals	696.3	79	2316	98	4-23	23.63	-
Career - One Day Matches	1792.4	243	5730	255	5-13	22.30	3

1986/87 – Benson and Hedges World Series in Australia

213. International - WEST INDIES v ENGLAND, Brisbane, January 17 (England won by six wickets)
    b G.R.Dilley   13 154   5   1   11   0   156-4

214. International - WEST INDIES v AUSTRALIA, Melbourne, January 20 (West Indies won by seven wickets)
    did not bat   - 182-3   9   0   40   2   D.M.Jones lbw   181-6
                                                      S.P.O'Donnell c M.A.Holding

215. International - WEST INDIES v ENGLAND, Adelaide, January 24 (England won by 89 runs)
    c C.W.J.Athey b J.E.Emburey 3 163   9   1   39   1   C.J.Richards b   252-6   1

216. International - WEST INDIES v AUSTRALIA, Adelaide, January 25 (West Indies won by 16 runs)
    did not bat   - 237-5   10   2   34   2   D.M.Wellham c P.J.L.Dujon 221-9
                                                       S.P.O'Donnell c P.J.L.Dujon

217. International - WEST INDIES v AUSTRALIA, Sydney, January 28 (Australia won by 36 runs)
    c S.R.Waugh
            b S.P.O'Donnell 2 158   10   1   29   2   D.M.Wellham c P.J.L.Dujon 194
                                                       P.L.Taylor c P.J.L.Dujon

218. International - WEST INDIES v ENGLAND, Melbourne, January 30 (West Indies won by six wickets)
    did not bat   - 148-4   9.2   2   30   3   D.I.Gower b   147
                                                       C.J.Richards b
                                                       N.A.Foster b

219. International - WEST INDIES v ENGLAND, Devonport, February 3 (England won by 29 runs)
    c C.W.J.Athey
            b P.A.J.DeFreitas 27 148   10   0   31   3   D.I.Gower c T.R.O.Payne 177-9
                                                       C.W.J.Athey lbw
                                                      B.N.French b

SEASON'S AVERAGES

Batting and Fielding	M	I	NO	Runs	HS	Ave	100	50	Ct
Internationals	7	4	0	45	27	11.25	-	-	1
Career - Internationals	86	45	15	501	66	16.70	-	2	10
Career - One Day Matches	219	135	36	1517	66	15.32	-	2	35

Bowling	O	M	R	W	BB	Ave	5i
Internationals	62.2	7	214	13	3-30	16.46	-
Career - Internationals	758.5	86	2530	111	4-23	22.79	-
Career - One Day Matches	1855	250	5944	268	5-13	22.17	3

1987

220. Benson & Hedges Cup - Hampshire v British Universities, The Parks, May 2 (Hampshire won by 93 runs)
b C.Perera   18   300-8   5   1   13   0   207-5

221. Sunday League - Hampshire v Leicestershire, Leicester, May 3 (Hampshire won by 5 runs)
did not bat   -   226-4   8   0   29   0   221-6

222. Benson & Hedges Cup - Hampshire v Middlesex, Southampton, May 9 (Hampshire won by nine wickets)
did not bat   -   193-1   11   2   30   1   P.H.Edmonds   b   192-8

223. Sunday League - Hampshire v Surrey, Southampton, May 10 (Hampshire won by 75 runs)
not out   3   281-5   7   0   34   2   N.J.Falkner c M.C.J.Nicholas 206
                R.J.Doughty b

224. Benson & Hedges Cup - Hampshire v Somerset, Southampton, May 12 (Somerset won by 71 runs)
b G.D.Rose   0   248   11   1   42   0   319-2

225. Benson & Hedges Cup - Hampshire v Essex, Chelmsford, May 14 (Hampshire won by 86 runs)
lbw b N.A.Foster   34   186   10.1   0   33   4   G.A.Gooch b   100   1
                B.R.Hardie c C.G.Greenidge
                H.A.Page b
                N.A.Foster c R.J.Parks

226. Sunday League - Hampshire v Lancashire, Old Trafford, May 24 (Lancashire won by five wickets)
not out   27   175-7   8   1   18   1   J.Abrahams c M.C.J.Nicholas 179-5

227. Benson & Hedges Cup - Hampshire v Yorkshire, Headingley, May 27 (Yorkshire won by nine wickets)
c P.Carrick b P.J.Hartley   24   174-8   9   1   18   1   M.D.Moxon b   178-1

228. Sunday League - Hampshire v Gloucestershire, Southampton, May 31 (Match tied)
b M.W.Alleyne   4   214-9   8   0   35   2   A.W.Stovold b   214-5
                C.W.J.Athey c R.J.Parks

229. Sunday League - Hampshire v Sussex, Horsham, June 7 (Sussex won by one wicket)
c I.C.Waring b G.S.le Roux   7   216-7   8   0   29   0   218-9   1

230. Sunday League - Hampshire v Derbyshire, Southampton, June 14 (Match tied)
c M.A.Holding
    b M.Jean-Jacques   1   206-6   8   0   33   4   K.J.Barnett c A.N.Aymes   206
                M.A.Holding b
                P.G.Newman lbw
                M.Jean-Jacques lbw

231. Sunday League - Hampshire v Middlesex, Basingstoke, June 21 (Hampshire won by seven wickets)
did not bat   -   146-3   8   0   27   3   A.Needham b   143
                M.R.Ramprakash c T.M.Tremlett
                N.F.Williams c T.M.Tremlett

232. NatWest Trophy - Hampshire v Dorset, Southampton, June 24 (Hampshire won by 209 runs)
did not bat   -   304-2   5   1   9   1   G.S.Calway c C.G.Greenidge 95

233. Sunday League - Hampshire v Warwickshire, Edgbaston, June 28 (Hampshire won by 84 runs)
b A.A.Donald   2   210-7   4   0   7   0   126-8

234. NatWest Trophy - Hampshire v Leicestershire, Leicester, July 8 (Leicestershire won by 15 runs)
c P.B.Clift b J.P.Agnew   51   326-9   12   2   32   1   J.J.Whitaker
                        c C.G.Greenidge   341-6

235. Sunday League - Hampshire v Worcestershire, Southampton, July 12 (Worcestershire won by six wickets)
c I.T.Botham b G.R.Dilley   35   183-9   8   2   30   2   T.S.Curtis c R.J.Parks   188-4
                D.B.D'Oliveira c R.J.Parks

236. Sunday League - Hampshire v Essex, Portsmouth, July 26 (Hampshire won by four wickets)
not out   41   125-6   7.5   0   21   3   G.Miller c R.J.Parks   122
                B.R.Hardie lbw
                J.K.Lever c R.J.Parks

237. Sunday League - Hampshire v Glamorgan, Bournemouth, August 9 (Glamorgan won on faster scoring rate)
b S.R.Barwick   2   200-6   7   0   26   0   116-5

238. Sunday League - Hampshire v Nottinghamshire, Trent Bridge, August 16 (Nottinghamshire won by seven wickets)
c and b E.E.Hemmings   2   166-8   8   0   20   1   P.Johnson c R.J.Parks   170-3

SEASON'S AVERAGES

Batting and Fielding	M	I	NO	Runs	HS	Ave	100	50	Ct
NatWest Trophy	2	1	0	51	51	51.00	-	1	-
Sunday League	12	10	3	124	41*	17.71	-	-	1
Benson & Hedges Cup	5	4	0	76	34	19.00	-	-	1
Career - Gillette Cup/NWT	19	13	7	194	51	32.33	-	1	2
Career - Sunday League	93	59	16	742	46	17.25	-	-	15
Career - B & H Cup	28	23	1	285	34	12.95	-	-	6
Career - One Day Matches	238	150	39	1768	66	15.92	-	3	37

Bowling	O	M	R	W	BB	Ave	5i
NatWest Trophy	17	3	41	2	1-9	20.50	-
Sunday League	89.5	3	309	18	4-33	17.16	-
Benson & Hedges Cup	46.1	5	136	6	4-33	22.66	-
Career - Gillette Cup/NWT	190.4	36	495	18	4-15	27.50	-
Career - Sunday League	698.4	68	2404	104	5-13	23.11	2
Career - B & H Cup	265.1	51	737	37	4-26	19.91	-
Career – One Day Matches	2008	261	6430	294	5-13	21.87	3

1987/88

239. Geddes/Grant Harrison Line Cup - Barbados v Trinidad & Tobago, Port of Spain, January 27 (Barbados won on faster scoring rate)
did not bat   -   119-2   8   3   12   2   B.C.Lara c T.R.O.Payne   132-6
R.Nana b

240. Geddes/Grant Harrison Line Cup - Barbados v Guyana, Bridgetown, February 11 (Barbados won by eight wickets)
did not bat   -   164-2   9   1   37   2   C.B.Lambert c A.L.Grant   161
S.Dhaniran c T.R.O.Payne

241. Geddes/Grant Harrison Line Cup - Barbados v Jamaica, Kingston, March 3 (Barbados won by one wicket)
c A.G.Daley b C.A.Walsh   0   219-9   10   1   41   1   W.W.Lewis b   218-8

242. International - WEST INDIES v PAKISTAN, Georgetown, March 30 (West Indies won by seven wickets)
did not bat   -   225-3   10   2   42   1   Shoaib Mohammad
c P.J.L.Dujon   221-7

SEASON'S AVERAGES

Batting and Fielding	M	I	NO	Runs	HS	Ave	100	50	Ct
Internationals	1	-	-	-	-	-	-	-	-
Geddes/Grant Cup	3	1	0	0	0	0.00	-	-	-
Career - Internationals	87	45	15	501	66	16.70	-	2	10
Career - Geddes/Grant Cup	12	8	0	35	23	4.37	-	-	3
Career - One Day Matches	242	151	39	1768	66	15.78	-	3	37

Bowling	O	M	R	W	BB	Ave	5i
Internationals	10	2	42	1	1-42	42.00	-
Geddes/Grant Cup	27	4	90	5	2-12	18.00	-
Career - Internationals	768.5	88	2572	112	4-23	22.96	-
Career - Geddes/Grant Cup	93.4	16	292	24	5-38	12.16	1
Career - One Day Matches	2045	267	6562	300	5-13	21.87	3

1988 – West Indies in England

243. International - WEST INDIES v ENGLAND, Edgbaston, May 19 (England won by six wickets)
c A.J.Lamb b P.A.J.DeFreitas 6   217   11   1   32   1   B.C.Broad c C.G.Greenidge 219-4

244. International - WEST INDIES v ENGLAND, Headingley, May 21 (England won by 47 runs)
c P.R.Downton b G.A.Gooch 1 139 9 1 29 2 M.W.Gatting c C.J.Richards 186-8
M.A.Lynch lbw

245. International - WEST INDIES v ENGLAND, Lord's, May 23, 24 (England won by seven wickets)
b J.E.Emburey 41 178-7 9 2 21 0 180-3

SEASON'S AVERAGES

Batting and Fielding	M	I	NO	Runs	HS	Ave	100	50	Ct
Internationals	3	3	0	48	41	16.00	-	-	-
Career - Internationals	90	48	15	549	66	16.63	-	2	10
Career - One Day Matches	245	154	39	1816	66	15.79	-	3	37

Bowling	O	M	R	W	BB	Ave	5i
Internationals	29	4	82	3	2-29	27.33	-
Career - Internationals	797.5	92	2654	115	4-23	23.07	-
Career - One Day Matches	2074	271	6644	303	5-13	21.92	3

1988/89 – Benson and Hedges World Series in Australia

246. International - WEST INDIES v PAKISTAN, Adelaide, December 10 (West Indies won by 89 runs)
b Imran Khan 20 269-9 10 1 34 4 Sajid Ali c C.G.Greenidge 180-7
Salim Malik b
Ijaz Ahmed c D.Williams
Wasim Akram b

247. International - WEST INDIES v AUSTRALIA, Sydney, December 13 (West Indies won by 1 run)
c sub (G.M.Wood)
b C.J.McDermott 17 220 10 0 40 1 D.C.Boon b 219-8

248. International - WEST INDIES v AUSTRALIA, Melbourne, December 15 (West Indies won by 34 runs)
c I.A.Healy
b C.J.McDermott 19 236 10 0 39 0 202

249. International - WEST INDIES v PAKISTAN, Hobart, December 17 (West Indies won by 17 runs)
did not bat - 244-4 9 1 31 1 Ramiz Raja c A.L.Logie 227-8

250. International - WEST INDIES v PAKISTAN, Perth, January 1 (West Indies won by seven wickets)
did not bat - 142-3 7 0 17 1 Saeed Anwar c C.L.Hooper 140-9

251. International - WEST INDIES v PAKISTAN, Brisbane, January 7 (Pakistan won by 55 runs)
b Wasim Akram 39 203 10 0 34 1 Moin-ul-Atiq
c I.V.A.Richards 258-7

252. International - WEST INDIES v AUSTRALIA, Sydney, January 12 (Australia won by 61 runs)
lbw b P.L.Taylor 1 154-8 10 3 25 2 D.C.Boon c K.L.T.Arthurton 215-5
M.E.Waugh c D.L.Haynes

253. International - WEST INDIES v AUSTRALIA, Melbourne, January 14 (Australia won by 2 runs)
run out 18 202-9 9 1 31 2 G.M.Wood c A.L.Logie 204-9
S.P.O'Donnell b

254. International - WEST INDIES v AUSTRALIA, Sydney, January 16 (West Indies won by 92 runs)
b M.G.Hughes 4 277-9 5 1 30 0 185

255. International - WEST INDIES v AUSTRALIA, Sydney, January 18 (West Indies won by eight wickets - revised target)
did not bat - 111-2 8 0 45 0 226-4

SEASON'S AVERAGES

Batting and Fielding	M	I	NO	Runs	HS	Ave	100	50	Ct
Internationals	10	7	0	118	39	16.85	-	-	-
Career - Internationals	100	55	15	667	66	16.67	-	2	10
Career - One Day Matches	255	161	39	1934	66	15.85	-	3	37

Bowling	O	M	R	W	BB	Ave	5i
Internationals	88	7	326	12	4-34	27.16	-
Career - Internationals	885.5	99	2980	127	4-23	23.46	-
Career - One Day Matches	2163	278	6970	315	5-13	22.12	3

1989

256. Sunday League - Hampshire v Leicestershire, Bournemouth, May 28 (Hampshire won by seven wickets)
did not bat   - 110-3   4.5   0   13   3   P.Willey lbw   107   1
                                                            C.C.Lewis b
                                                            G.J.F.Ferris c R.J.Parks

257. Sunday League - Hampshire v Middlesex, Lord's, June 4 (Match tied)
c J.D.Carr b S.P.Hughes   36   138   8   1   18   2   K.R.Brown c R.J.Parks   138-8   1
                                                            S.P.Hughes c R.J.Parks

258. Sunday League - Hampshire v Warwickshire, Basingstoke, June 11 (Hampshire won on faster scoring rate)
did not bat   - 106-4   8   0   29   0   158-9   3

259. Sunday League - Hampshire v Sussex, Southampton, June 25 (Hampshire won by three wickets)
c A.M.Babington
           b A.C.S.Pigott   31   193-7   8   0   27   1   D.M.Smith b   192-5

260. NatWest Trophy - Hampshire v Cheshire, Chester, June 28 (Hampshire won by 147 runs)
did not bat   - 306-2   10.1   1   40   4   B.Wood c R.J.Parks   159
                                                            D.W.Varey c R.J.Parks
                                                            J.S.Hitchmough b
                                                            S.Dyson b

261. Sunday League - Hampshire v Yorkshire, Southampton, July 2 (Hampshire won by six wickets)
did not bat   - 183-4   8   1   37   0   179-7

262. Sunday League - Hampshire v Northamptonshire, Northampton, July 9 (No result)
                                         6   1   15   0   135-1

263. NatWest Trophy - Hampshire v Glamorgan, Cardiff, July 12 (Hampshire won by seven wickets)
did not bat   - 190-3   12   3   31   1   G.C.Holmes c R.J.Maru   189

264. Sunday League - Hampshire v Gloucestershire, Trowbridge, July 16 (Gloucestershire won by 21 runs)
c M.W.Alleyne
           b M.W.Pooley   14   163   8   0   40   0   184-8

265. Sunday League - Hampshire v Lancashire, Portsmouth, July 23 (Lancashire won by six wickets)
c D.P.Hughes b J.Simmons   14   166-9   8   1   17   2   G.Fowler lbw   168-4
                                                            D.P.Hughes b

266. Sunday League - Hampshire v Glamorgan, Swansea, July 30 (Glamorgan won by 37 runs)
b S.L.Watkin   24   156   8   0   28   2   S.P.James c J.R.Wood   193-9
                                                            S.L.Watkin b

267. NatWest Trophy - Hampshire v Surrey, Kennington Oval, August 2 (Hampshire won by five wickets)
c and b M.P.Bicknell   3   229-5   12   3   40   1   G.S.Clinton c V.P.Terry   228-8

268. NatWest Trophy - Hampshire v Middlesex, Southampton, August 16 (Middlesex won by 3 runs)
not out   17   264-7   12   2   25   1   P.R.Downton c R.A.Smith   267-7

SEASON'S AVERAGES

Batting and Fielding	M	I	NO	Runs	HS	Ave	100	50	Ct
NatWest Trophy	4	2	1	20	17*	20.00	-	-	-
Sunday League	9	5	0	119	36	23.80	-	-	5
Career - Gillette Cup/NWT	23	15	8	214	51	30.57	-	1	2
Career - Sunday League	102	64	16	861	46	17.93	-	-	20
Career - One Day Matches	268	168	40	2073	66	16.23	-	3	42

Bowling	O	M	R	W	BB	Ave	5i
NatWest Trophy	46.1	9	136	7	4-40	19.42	-
Sunday League	66.5	4	224	10	3-13	22.40	-
Career - Gillette Cup/NWT	236.5	45	631	25	4-15	25.24	-
Career - Sunday League	765.3	72	2628	114	5-13	23.05	2
Career - One Day Matches	2275	291	7330	332	5-13	22.07	3

1989/90 – Champions Trophy in Sharjah

269. International - WEST INDIES v INDIA, Sharjah, October 13 (West Indies won by five wickets)
did not bat   - 173-5   10   1   23   0   169
270. International - WEST INDIES v PAKISTAN, Sharjah, October 14 (Pakistan won by 11 runs)
b Wasim Akram   0 239   10   0   41   0   250-8
271. International - WEST INDIES v INDIA, Sharjah, October 16 (India won by 37 runs)
b A.K.Sharma   40 174   10   0   50   1 M.Prabhakar lbw 211-9

SEASON'S AVERAGES

Batting and Fielding	M	I	NO	Runs	HS	Ave	100	50	Ct
Internationals	3	2	0	40	40	20.00	-	-	-
Career - Internationals	103	57	15	707	66	16.83	-	2	10
Career - One Day Matches	271	170	40	2113	66	16.25	-	3	42

Bowling	O	M	R	W	BB	Ave	5i
Internationals	30	1	114	1	1-50	114.00	-
Career - Internationals	915.5	100	3094	128	4-23	24.17	-
Career - One Day Matches	2305	292	7444	333	5-13	22.35	3

1989/90 – World Series (Nehru Cup) in India

272. International - WEST INDIES v AUSTRALIA, Madras, October 21 (Australia won by 99 runs)
c T.M.Alderman
   b A.R.Border   12 142   10   0   31   0   241-6
273. International - WEST INDIES v INDIA, Delhi, October 23 (West Indies won by 20 runs)
c M.Amarnath b C.Sharma   27 196-9   9   0   40   1 K.Srikkanth c P.J.L.Dujon 176
274. International - WEST INDIES v PAKISTAN, Jullundur, October 25 (West Indies won by six wickets)
did not bat   - 226-4   10   1   51   1 Shoaib Mohammad
                                c I.V.A.Richards 222-5
275. International - WEST INDIES v ENGLAND, Gwalior, October 27 (West Indies won by 26 runs)
c R.A.Smith b G.C.Small   16 265-5   10   0   33   4 G.A.Gooch c P.J.L.Dujon 239-8
                            W.Larkins c sub (K.L.T.Arthurton)
                            R.A.Smith c P.J.L.Dujon
                            A.J.Lamb b
276. International - WEST INDIES v INDIA, Bombay, October 30 (West Indies won by eight wickets)
did not bat   - 166-2   10   2   19   1 M.Prabhakar
                            c I.V.A.Richards 165   1
277. International - WEST INDIES v PAKISTAN, Calcutta, November 1 (Pakistan won by four wickets)
not out   10 273-5   10   0   43   0   277-6

SEASON'S AVERAGES

Batting and Fielding	M	I	NO	Runs	HS	Ave	100	50	Ct
Internationals	6	4	1	65	27	21.66	-	-	1
Career - Internationals	109	61	16	772	66	17.15	-	2	11
Career - One Day Matches	277	174	41	2178	66	16.37	-	3	43

Bowling	O	M	R	W	BB	Ave	5i
Internationals	59	3	217	7	4-33	31.00	-
Career - Internationals	974.5	103	3311	135	4-23	24.52	-
Career - One Day Matches	2364	295	7661	340	5-13	22.53	3

1989/90

278. Geddes/Grant Harrison Line Cup – Barbados v Guyana, Bridgetown, January 17 (Barbados won by seven wickets)
did not bat   - 117-3   6   0   23   1 R.A.Harper lbw 116-9

279. Geddes/Grant Harrison Line Cup – Barbados v Trinidad & Tobago, Port of Spain, February 10 (Trinidad & Tobago won by five wickets)
lbw b I.R.Bishop   24   178-9   10   2   33   1   B.C.Lara b   180-5

280. International - WEST INDIES v ENGLAND, Port of Spain, February 14 (No result)
b G.C.Small   9   208-8   6   1   12   1   W.Larkins c C.A.Best   26-1

281. International - WEST INDIES v ENGLAND, Port of Spain, February 17 (No result)
did not bat   -   13-0

282. International - WEST INDIES v ENGLAND, Kingston, March 3 (West Indies won by three wickets)
did not bat   -   216-7   10   1   39   1   R.C.Russell b   214-8   1

283. International - WEST INDIES v ENGLAND, Bridgetown, April 3 (West Indies won by four wickets)
did not bat   -   217-6   8   0   50   0   214-3

SEASON'S AVERAGES

Batting and Fielding	M	I	NO	Runs	HS	Ave	100	50	Ct
Internationals	4	1	0	9	9	9.00	-	-	1
Geddes/Grant Cup	2	1	0	24	24	24.00	-	-	-
Career - Internationals	113	62	16	781	66	16.97	-	2	12
Career - Geddes/Grant Cup	14	9	0	59	24	6.55	-	-	3
Career - One Day Matches	283	176	41	2211	66	16.37	-	3	44

Bowling	O	M	R	W	BB	Ave	5i
Internationals	24	2	101	2	1-12	50.50	-
Geddes/Grant Cup	16	2	56	2	1-23	28.00	-
Career - Internationals	998.5	105	3412	137	4-23	24.90	-
Career - Geddes/Grant Cup	109.4	18	348	26	5-38	13.38	1
Career - One Day Matches	2404	299	7818	344	5-13	22.72	3

1990

284. Benson & Hedges Cup - Hampshire v Yorkshire, Southampton, April 24 (Yorkshire won by seven wickets)
run out   24   206-6   10   0   28   0   208-3

285. Sunday League - Hampshire v Kent, Canterbury, April 29 (Kent won by 53 runs)
c M.V.Fleming b R.P.Davis   3   160-8   8   0   41   0   213-6

286. Benson & Hedges Cup - Hampshire v Surrey, Kennington Oval, May 1 (Surrey won by 87 runs)
c D.M.Ward b M.P.Bicknell 31   244   11   1   52   0   331-5

287. Sunday League - Hampshire v Gloucestershire, Southampton, May 6 (No result)
not out   6   224-6

288. Benson & Hedges Cup - Hampshire v Lancashire, Old Trafford, May 8 (No result)
did not bat   -   99-1   4   0   45   0   145-5

289. Sunday League - Hampshire v Somerset, Taunton, May 13 (Somerset won by five wickets)
did not bat   -   246-3   8   0   53   2   G.D.Rose c V.P.Terry   247-5
C.J.Tavare c R.J.Parks

290. Sunday League - Hampshire v Yorkshire, Headingley, May 27 (Hampshire won by 36 runs)
b D.Byas   10   184-7   7   1   32   1   C.S.Pickles c R.J.Maru   148

291. Sunday League - Hampshire v Leicestershire, Leicester, June 3 (Hampshire won by five wickets)
c A.D.Mullally   b J.D.R.Benson   44   169-5   8   1   23   1   G.J.F.Ferris lbw   166-8

292. Sunday League - Hampshire v Middlesex, Basingstoke, June 10 (Middlesex won by seven wickets)
c R.O.Butcher b S.P.Hughes 46   140   8   0   19   0   144-3

293. Sunday League - Hampshire v Glamorgan, Bournemouth, June 17 (Hampshire won by 64 runs)
c C.P.Metson b S.L.Watkin   1   234-6   5   0   23   0   170-7

294. Sunday League - Hampshire v Lancashire, Old Trafford, June 24 (No result)
1   3-0   1   0   3   0   3-0

295. NatWest Trophy - Hampshire v Leicestershire, Leicester, June 27 (Hampshire won by 1 run)
c N.E.Briers b J.P.Agnew   6   226-7   12   2   32   0   225-8

296. Sunday League - Hampshire v Sussex, Hove, July 1 (Sussex won on faster scoring rate)
c N.J.Lenham b C.M.Wells   19   151   7   0   50   1   C.M.Wells b   244-5

297. Sunday League - Hampshire v Essex, Southampton, July 8 (Hampshire won by seven wickets)
not out   43   200-3   8   0   33   2   B.R.Hardie   c R.J.Parks   196
                                                           N.A.Foster   c D.I.Gower

298. NatWest Trophy - Hampshire v Essex, Chelmsford, July 11 (Hampshire won by losing fewer wickets with
scores level)
b D.R.Pringle   9   307-5   12   0   45   2   P.J.Prichard   c D.I.Gower   307-6
                                                           M.E.Waugh   c R.J.Parks

299. Sunday League - Hampshire v Nottinghamshire, Southampton, July 15 (Hampshire won by 7 runs)
run out   7   267-4   8   0   36   2   P.Johnson   c R.J.Parks   260-8
                                                           K.E.Cooper   b

300. Sunday League - Hampshire v Derbyshire, Portsmouth, July 22 (Hampshire won by 189 runs)
run out   1   250-5   4   2   4   1   J.E.Morris   c R.J.Parks   61

301. Sunday League - Hampshire v Warwickshire, Edgbaston, July 29 (Hampshire won by three wickets)
run out   24   183-7   8   0   36   2   A.J.Moles   c R.J.Parks   179-6
                                                           T.M.Moody   b

302. NatWest Trophy - Hampshire v Yorkshire, Southampton, August 1 (Hampshire won by 111 runs)
c A.Sidebottom b P.J.Hartley 4 229-9   8   1   17   4   A.A.Metcalfe   c R.J.Maru   118
                                                           S.A.Kellett   b
                                                           P.W.Jarvis   c C.A.Connor
                                                           S.D.Fletcher   c R.J.Parks

303. Sunday League - Hampshire v Northamptonshire, Bournemouth, August 5 (Hampshire won by six wickets)
not out   17   210-4   8   1   33   1   A.Fordham   c R.J.Scott   208-4   1

304. Sunday League - Hampshire v Worcestershire, Worcester, August 12 (Hampshire won by 20 runs)
c P.J.Newport b S.R.Lampitt 38 207-6   8   0   22   1   R.K.Illingworth   b   187

305. NatWest Trophy - Hampshire v Northamptonshire, Southampton, August 15 (Northamptonshire won by 1
run)
c and b N.G.B.Cook   77   283   12   3   37   1   D.Ripley   c R.J.Maru   284

306. Sunday League - Hampshire v Surrey, Southampton, August 26 (Surrey won by 4 runs)
lbw b Waqar Younis   0   244-9   8   0   50   0   248-5

SEASON'S AVERAGES

Batting and Fielding	M	I	NO	Runs	HS	Ave	100	50	Ct
NatWest Trophy	4	4	0	96	77	24.00	-	1	-
Sunday League	16	14	3	259	46	23.54	-	-	1
Benson & Hedges Cup	3	2	0	55	31	27.50	-	-	-
Career - Gillette Cup/NWT	27	19	8	310	77	28.18	-	2	2
Career - Sunday League	118	78	19	1120	46	18.98	-	-	21
Career - B & H Cup	31	25	1	340	34	14.16	-	-	6
Career - One Day Matches	306	196	44	2621	77	17.24	-	4	45

Bowling	O	M	R	W	BB	Ave	5i
NatWest Trophy	44	6	131	7	4-17	18.71	-
Sunday League	104	5	458	14	2-33	32.71	-
Benson & Hedges Cup	25	1	125	0	-	-	-
Career - Gillette Cup/NWT	280.5	51	762	32	4-15	23.81	-
Career - Sunday League	869.3	77	3086	128	5-13	24.10	2
Career - B & H Cup	290.1	52	862	37	4-26	23.29	-
Career - One Day Matches	2577	311	8532	365	5-13	23.37	3

1990/91 – West Indies in Pakistan

307. International - WEST INDIES v PAKISTAN, Karachi, November 9 (Pakistan won by 6 runs)
not out   26   205-7   8   0   30   0   211-5

308. International - WEST INDIES v PAKISTAN, Lahore, November 11 (Pakistan won by five wickets)
b Mushtaq Ahmed   4   176-7   8   1   36   1   Javed Miandad   c P.J.L.Dujon 177-5

SEASON'S AVERAGES

Batting and Fielding	M	I	NO	Runs	HS	Ave	100	50	Ct
Internationals	2	2	1	30	26*	30.00	-	-	-
Career - Internationals	115	64	17	811	66	17.25	-	2	12
Career - One Day Matches	308	198	45	2651	77	17.32	-	4	45

Bowling	O	M	R	W	BB	Ave	5i
Internationals	16	1	66	1	1-36	66.00	-
Career - Internationals	1014.5	106	3478	138	4-23	25.20	-
Career - One Day Matches	2593	312	8598	366	5-13	23.49	3

1990/91

309. Geddes/Grant Shield - Barbados v Guyana, Bridgetown, January 9 (Barbados won by 99 runs)
c S.N.Mohammed
b L.A.Joseph 2 203-8 8 1 17 5 C.L.Hooper c C.O.Browne 104
M.A.Harper c C.O.Browne
R.A.Harper c D.L.Haynes
I.D.Harper c R.I.C.Holder
S.N.Mohammed b

310. Geddes/Grant Shield - Barbados v Leeward Islands, St John's, January 16 (Leeward Islands won by four wickets)
b K.C.Benjamin 12 237-7 9 1 29 2 R.B.Richardson
c E.A.Moseley 238-6 2
K.LT.Arthurton b

311. International - WEST INDIES v AUSTRALIA, Kingston, February 26 (Australia won by 35 runs)
run out 1 209 6 0 27 0
244-4

312. International - WEST INDIES v AUSTRALIA, Port of Spain, March 9 (Australia won by 45 runs)
c D.C.Boon b C.J.McDermott 5 127 6 0 37 0
172-9

313. International - WEST INDIES v AUSTRALIA, Bridgetown, March 13 (Australia won by 37 runs)
c M.R.Whitney
b C.J.McDermott 19 246 10 1 67 1 D.M.Jones c C.A.Walsh 283-6

SEASON'S AVERAGES

Batting and Fielding	M	I	NO	Runs	HS	Ave	100	50	Ct
Internationals	3	3	0	25	19	8.33	-	-	-
Geddes/Grant Shield	2	2	0	14	12	7.00	-	-	2
Career - Internationals	118	67	17	836	66	16.72	-	2	12
Career - G/G Shield	16	11	0	73	24	6.63	-	-	5
Career - One Day Matches	313	203	45	2690	77	17.02	-	4	47

Bowling	O	M	R	W	BB	Ave	5i
Internationals	22	1	131	1	1-67	131.00	-
Geddes/Grant Shield	17	2	46	7	5-17	6.57	1
Career - Internationals	1036.5	107	3609	139	4-23	25.96	-
Career - G/G Shield	126.4	20	394	33	5-17	11.93	2
Career - One Day Matches	2632	315	8775	374	5-13	23.46	4

1991 – West Indies in England

314. International - WEST INDIES v ENGLAND, Edgbaston, May 23, 24 (England won by one wicket)
c C.C.Lewis
b P.A.J.DeFreitas 17 173-8 11 1 32 2 G.A.Hick c R.B.Richardson 175-9
P.A.J.DeFreitas c R.B.Richardson

315. International - WEST INDIES v ENGLAND, Old Trafford, May 25 (England won by 9 runs)
c and b D.R.Pringle 22 261-8 10 0 45 0
270-4

316. International - WEST INDIES v ENGLAND, Lord's, May 27 (England won by seven wickets)
c P.A.J.DeFreitas
       b D.V.Lawrence 13 264-9   11   1   49 1 M.A.Atherton c P.J.L.Dujon 265-3

SEASON'S AVERAGES

Batting and Fielding	M	I	NO	Runs	HS	Ave	100	50	Ct
Internationals	3	3	0	52	22	17.33	-	-	-
Career - Internationals	121	70	17	888	66	16.75	-	2	12
Career - One Day Matches	316	206	45	2742	77	17.03	-	4	47

Bowling	O	M	R	W	BB	Ave	5i
Internationals	32	2	126	3	2-32	42.00	-
Career - Internationals	1068.5	109	3735	142	4-23	26.30	-
Career - One Day Matches	2664	317	8901	377	5-13	23.61	4

1991/92 – West Indies in Pakistan

317. International - WEST INDIES v PAKISTAN, Lahore, November 22 (Match tied)
not out   2 186-5   8   0   39 3 Ramiz Raja c D.Williams   186-9
                                        Inzamam-ul-Haq b
                                        Wasim Akram b

318. International - WEST INDIES v PAKISTAN, Faisalabad, November 24 (West Indies won by 17 runs)
not out   7 204-5   8   0   44 2 Wasim Akram b   187-8   1
                                        Waqar Younis c and b

SEASON'S AVERAGES

Batting and Fielding	M	I	NO	Runs	HS	Ave	100	50	Ct
Internationals	2	2	2	9	7	-	-	-	1
Career - Internationals	123	72	19	897	66	16.92	-	2	13
Career - One Day Matches	318	208	47	2751	77	17.08	-	4	48

Bowling	O	M	R	W	BB	Ave	5i
Internationals	16	.0	83	5	3-39	16.60	-
Career - Internationals	1084.5	109	3818	147	4-23	25.97	-
Career - One Day Matches	2680	317	8984	382	5-13	23.51	4

1991/92 – Benson and Hedges World Series in Australia

319. International - WEST INDIES v INDIA, Perth, December 6 (Match tied)
c K.S.More b S.T.Banerjee 7 126   10   2   23 2 R.J.Shastri c B.C.Lara   126
                                        Kapil Dev c R.B.Richardson

320. International - WEST INDIES v AUSTRALIA, Melbourne, December 12 (Australia won by 9 runs)
run out   3 164   10   4   18 4 G.R.Marsh c R.B.Richardson 173-9
                                        D.C.Boon b
                                        D.M.Jones c D.Williams
                                        C.J.McDermott lbw

321. International - WEST INDIES v INDIA, Adelaide, December 14 (India won by 10 runs)
lbw b J.Srinath   17 252   10   0   59 0   262-4

322. International - WEST INDIES v AUSTRALIA, Sydney, December 18 (Australia won by 51 runs)
b M.R.Whitney   7 183   9   2   39 0   234-6

323. International - WEST INDIES v AUSTRALIA, Melbourne, January 9 (No result)
c I.A.Healy b M.R.Whitney 4 160-7

324. International - WEST INDIES v INDIA, Brisbane, January 11 (West Indies won by six wickets)
did not bat   - 192-4   10   0   30 2 N.S.Sidhu c C.L.Hooper 191   2
                                        M.Azharuddin lbw

325. International - WEST INDIES v AUSTRALIA, Brisbane, January 12 (West Indies won by 12 runs)
c A.R.Border b S.R.Waugh 4 215   9   1   39 0   203

326. International - WEST INDIES v INDIA, Melbourne, January 16 (India won by five wickets)
run out　　　　　　　　0　175-8　10　1　33　0　　　　　　　　176-5

SEASON'S AVERAGES

Batting and Fielding	M	I	NO	Runs	HS	Ave	100	50	Ct
Internationals	8	7	0	42	17	6.00	-	-	2
Career - Internationals	131	79	19	939	66	15.65	-	2	15
Career - One Day Matches	326	215	47	2793	77	16.62	-	4	50

Bowling	O	M	R	W	BB	Ave	5i
Internationals	68	10	241	8	4-18	30.12	-
Career - Internationals	1152.5	119	4059	155	4-18	26.18	-
Career - One Day Matches	2748	327	9225	390	5-13	23.65	4

1991/92 – Benson and Hedges World Cup in Australia and New Zealand

327. International - WEST INDIES v PAKISTAN, Melbourne, February 23 (West Indies won by ten wickets)
did not bat　　　　　　　-　221-0　10　1　53　0　　　　　　220-2
328. International - WEST INDIES v ENGLAND, Melbourne, February 27 (England won by six wickets)
run out　　　　　　　　3　157　　8　0　37　0　　　　　　　160-4
329. International - WEST INDIES v ZIMBABWE, Brisbane, February 29 (West Indies won by 75 runs)
c D.L.Houghton
　　　　b E.A.Brandes　2　264-8　　6　0　23　0　　　　　　189-7
330. International - WEST INDIES v SOUTH AFRICA, Christchurch, March 5 (South Africa won by 64 runs)
c J.N.Rhodes b R.P.Snell　6　136　　10　1　26　2　K.C.Wessels c D.L.Haynes　200-8
　　　　　　　　　　　　　　　　　　　　　　　　　　P.N.Kirsten c D.Williams
331. International - WEST INDIES v NEW ZEALAND, Auckland, March 8 (New Zealand won by five wickets)
b G.R.Larsen　　　　　5　203-7　　9　1　35　0　　　　　　206-5

SEASON'S AVERAGES

Batting and Fielding	M	I	NO	Runs	HS	Ave	100	50	Ct
Internationals	5	4	0	16	6	4.00	-	-	-
Career - Internationals	136	83	19	955	66	14.92	-	2	15
Career - One Day Matches	331	219	47	2809	77	16.33	-	4	50

Bowling	O	M	R	W	BB	Ave	5i
Internationals	43	3	174	2	2-26	87.00	-
Career - Internationals	1195.5	122	4233	157	4-18	26.96	-
Career - One Day Matches	2791	330	9399	392	5-13	23.97	4

1992

332. Sunday League - Hampshire v Gloucestershire, Southampton, April 19 (Hampshire won by six wickets)
not out　　　　　　　　0　151-4　　8　0　34　2　C.W.J.Athey b　　　150-6
　　　　　　　　　　　　　　　　　　　　　　　　　J.T.C.Vaughan c S.D.Udal
333. Benson & Hedges Cup - Hampshire v Essex, Southampton, April 23 (Hampshire won by 41 runs)
c M.A.Garnham b M.C.Ilott　1　177　　11　3　20　4　G.A.Gooch lbw　　　136
　　　　　　　　　　　　　　　　　　　　　　　　　J.P.Stephenson lbw
　　　　　　　　　　　　　　　　　　　　　　　　　M.E.Waugh lbw
　　　　　　　　　　　　　　　　　　　　　　　　　N.Hussain c V.P.Terry
334. Benson & Hedges Cup - Hampshire v Northamptonshire, Southampton, April (30), May 1 (Hampshire won by 6 runs)
c A.J.Lamb b C.E.L.Ambrose 4　197-6　　7　0　34　1　K.M.Curran b　　　191-5

335. Benson & Hedges Cup - Hampshire v Lancashire, Old Trafford, May 2 (Hampshire won by 38 runs)
did not bat   -   241-4   10   3   28   3   G.D.Mendis   c A.N.Aymes   203
                                                     G.D.Lloyd   c R.A.Smith
                                                     I.D.Austin b

336. Sunday League - Hampshire v Lancashire, Old Trafford, May 3 (Lancashire won by four wickets)
b P.A.J.DeFreitas   7   209-7   8   0   31   0   210-6   1

337. Benson & Hedges Cup - Hampshire v Scotland, Hamilton Crescent, Glasgow, May (5), 6 (No result)
did not bat   -   16-2   7   3   17   0   151-5

338. Sunday League - Hampshire v Somerset, Taunton, May 17 (Somerset won by 97 runs)
run out   2   87   8   0   29   1   R.J.Harden   b   184-7

339. Sunday League - Hampshire v Yorkshire, Headingley May 24 (Hampshire won by 59 runs)
c C.White b D.Gough   19   211-5   4   0   15   1   D.Byas   c J.R.Ayling   152

340. Benson & Hedges Cup - Hampshire v Middlesex, Southampton, May 27 (Hampshire won by six wickets)
did not bat   -   207-4   5   2   11   0   206

341. Sunday League - Hampshire v Surrey, Basingstoke, June 7 (Surrey won by nine wickets)
c J.D.Robinson
    b M.P.Bicknell   5   153   8   0   30   0   157-1

342. Benson & Hedges Cup - Hampshire v Somerset, Southampton, June 10 (Hampshire won by six wickets)
did not bat   -   219-4   11   3   37   1   M.N.Lathwell   c A.N.Aymes   218-8

343. Sunday League - Hampshire v Warwickshire, Edgbaston, June 14 (Warwickshire won by 40 runs)
c P.C.L.Holloway
    b D.R.Brown   9   186   8   0   36   2   D.P.Ostler   c R.J.Maru   226-6
                                                     T.L.Penney   c D.I.Gower

344. Sunday League - Hampshire v Essex, Bournemouth, June 21 (Hampshire won by eight wickets)
did not bat   -   178-2   8   1   34   2   D.R.Pringle   c R.J.Parks   175-6
                                                     N.A.Foster   lbw

345. NatWest Trophy - Hampshire v Dorset, Southampton, June 24 (Hampshire won by nine wickets)
did not bat   -   219-1   12   3   26   0   218-3   1

346. Sunday League - Hampshire v Nottinghamshire, Southampton, July 5 (Hampshire won by 24 runs)
not out   13   172-7   7   0   26   2   P.Johnson   c R.J.Parks   148-9
                                                     W.A.Dessaur   c R.J.Parks

347. NatWest Trophy - Hampshire v Kent, Southampton, July 9 (Kent won by two wickets)
c R.P.Davis b M.V.Fleming   7   243-9   12   0   43   2   M.V.Fleming   c R.J.Parks   244-8
                                                     S.A.Marsh   b

348. Benson & Hedges Cup - Hampshire v Kent, Lord's, July 11, 12 (Hampshire won by 41 runs)
not out   29   253-5   10   1   33   3   T.R.Ward   c R.J.Parks   212
                                                     G.R.Cowdrey   c D.I.Gower
                                                     R.P.Davis   c D.I.Gower

349. Sunday League - Hampshire v Glamorgan, Portsmouth, July 19 (Glamorgan won by seven wickets)
st C.P.Metson b S.R.Barwick 0   129   8   1   29   0   133-3   1

350. Sunday League - Hampshire v Worcestershire, Worcester, July 26 (Hampshire won by six wickets)
not out   23   177-4   8   1   19   2   D.B.D'Oliveira   c J.R.Wood   176-5
                                                     A.C.H.Seymour   c and b

351. Sunday League - Hampshire v Middlesex, Southampton, August 2 (Hampshire won by five wickets)
b J.E.Emburey   18   182-5   8   0   44   1   P.N.Weekes   c A.N.Aymes   181-7   1

352. Sunday League - Hampshire v Sussex, Hove, August 3 (Hampshire won by eight wickets)
did not bat   -   210-2   8   0   33   2   J.W.Hall   b   206-7
                                                     A.P.Wells   c D.I.Gower

353. Sunday League - Hampshire v Kent, Canterbury, August 9 (Kent won by six wickets)
lbw b M.J.McCague   19   172-9   8   0   41   1   C.L.Hooper   c S.D.Udal   176-4

354. Sunday League - Hampshire v Northamptonshire, Bournemouth, August 16 (Hampshire won by 81 runs)
did not bat   -   255-3   8   0   23   1   K.M.Curran   c R.A.Smith   174   2

355. Sunday League - Hampshire v Derbyshire, Southampton, August 23 (Hampshire won on faster scoring rate)
did not bat   -   120-3   5   0   29   0   143-2

SEASON'S AVERAGES

Batting and Fielding	M	I	NO	Runs	HS	Ave	100	50	Ct
NatWest Trophy	2	1	0	7	7	7.00	-	-	1
Sunday League	15	11	3	115	23*	14.37	-	-	6
Benson & Hedges Cup	7	3	1	34	29*	17.00	-	-	-
Career - Gillette Cup/NWT	29	20	8	317	77	26.41	-	2	3
Career - Sunday League	133	89	22	1235	46	18.43	-	-	27
Career - B & H Cup	38	28	2	374	34	14.38	-	-	6
Career - One Day Matches	355	234	51	2965	77	16.20	-	4	57

Bowling	O	M	R	W	BB	Ave	5i
NatWest Trophy	24	3	69	2	2-43	34.50	-
Sunday League	112	3	453	17	2-19	26.64	-
Benson & Hedges Cup	61	15	180	12	4-20	15.00	-
Career - Gillette Cup/NWT	304.5	54	831	34	4-15	24.44	-
Career - Sunday League	981.3	80	3539	145	5-13	24.40	2
Career - B & H Cup	351.1	67	1042	49	4-20	21.26	-
Career - One Day Matches	2988	351	10101	423	5-13	23.87	4

1992/93

356. Total Power Series - Natal v Western Transvaal, Potchefstroom, October 3 (Natal won by 199 runs)
did not bat   -   307-5   9.1   2   21   5   H.G.Prinsloo c E.L.R.Stewart 108
     A.J. van Deventer c E.L.R.Stewart
     J.P.B.Mulder c N.E.Wright
     R.Meyer b
     D.J. van Schalkwyk b

357. Benson & Hedges Series - Natal v Border, East London, October 9 (Natal won by 19 runs)
lbw b O.D.Gibson   50   183-9   8.3   2   20   1   O.D.Gibson c R.A.Lyle   164

358. Benson & Hedges Series - Natal v Transvaal, Johannesburg, October 16 (Natal won by five wickets)
did not bat   -   203-5   8   0   36   0   201-5

359. Benson & Hedges Series - Natal v Western Province, Durban, October 21 (Natal won by four wickets)
b B.M.McMillan   26   188-6   9   0   43   2   T.N.Lazard c N.E.Wright   186-5
     K.C.Jackson c E.L.R.Stewart

360. Total Power Series - Natal v Northern Transvaal, Durban, January 17 (Natal won by 43 runs)
b T.Bosch   7   228   9   4   11   0   185

361. Total Power Series - Natal v Eastern Province, Port Elizabeth, January 24 (Eastern Province won by six wickets)
c D.J.Richardson
  b E.A.E.Baptiste   0   184-9   11   2   20   2   P.G.Amm c C.E.B.Rice   187-4
     M.W.Rushmere c E.L.R.Stewart

362. Total Power Series - Natal v Eastern Province, Port Elizabeth, January 30 (Eastern Province won by 26 runs)
run out   30   158   9.4   3   22   2   M.W.Rushmere c N.E.Wright184-8
     M.C.Venter c A.C.Hudson

363. Benson & Hedges Series - Natal v Northern Transvaal, Durban, March 10 (Natal won by two wickets)
lbw b M.J.R.Rindell   1   181-8   9   1   32   1   S.Elworthy c & b   178-9   1

364. Benson & Hedges Series - Natal v Impalas, Durban, March 12 (Natal won on faster run rate)
not out   16   204-8   9   1   15   4   M.J.Cann c E.L.R.Stewart   49-6
     D.Jordaan b
     F.J.C.Cronje c E.L.R.Stewart
     A.Hoffmann c E.L.R.Stewart

365. Benson & Hedges Series - Natal v Orange Free State, Bloemfontein, March 17 (Natal won by one wicket)
lbw b C.J.P.G. van Zyl   8   196-9   9   1   34   0   195-8

366. Benson & Hedges Series - Natal v Eastern Province, Durban, March 26 (Eastern Province won by 29 runs)
run out   4   164   7   1   24   1   E.A.E.Baptiste
     c E.L.R.Stewart   133   1

367. Benson & Hedges Series - Natal v Western Province, Cape Town, March 30 (Natal won by 39 runs)
did not bat   -   173-5   7.5   3   15   4   F.B.Touzei lbw   134
                                            G.Kirsten b
                                            H.H.Gibbs c J.N.Rhodes
                                            M.W.Pringle c J.N.Rhodes

368. Benson & Hedges Series - Natal v Western Province, Durban, April 2 (Natal won by four wickets)
not out   3   165-6   9   1   30   2   M.W.Pringle c P.L.Symcox   164-9   1
                                            C.R.Matthews c E.L.R.Stewart

369. Benson & Hedges Series - Natal v Transvaal, Durban, April 7 (Transvaal won by 1 run)
c J.A.Teeger b R.P.Snell   0   192-8   9   2   24   2   B.M.White c A.C.Hudson   193-7
                                            D.R.Laing c J.N.Rhodes

SEASON'S AVERAGES

Batting and Fielding	M	I	NO	Runs	HS	Ave	100	50	Ct
Total Power Series	4	3	0	37	30	12.33	-	-	-
Benson & Hedges Series	10	8	2	108	50	18.00	-	1	3
Career - One Day Matches	369	245	53	3110	77	16.19	-	5	68

Bowling	O	M	R	W	BB	Ave	5i
Total Power Series	38.5	11	74	9	5-21	8.22	1
Benson & Hedges Series	85.2	12	273	17	4-15	16.05	-
Career - Total Power Series	38.5	11	74	9	5-21	8.22	1
Career - B & H Series	85.2	12	273	17	4-15	16.05	-
Career - One Day Matches	3112.1	374	10448	449	5-13	23.26	5

1993

370. Benson & Hedges Cup - Hampshire v Combined Universities, Southampton, April 24 (Hampshire won by nine wickets)
did not bat   -   178-1   11   4   24   2   G.M.Charlesworth b   177-7   1
                                            J.C.Hallett c A.N.Aymes

371. Benson & Hedges Cup - Hampshire v Durham, Stockton-on-Tees, May 11 (Hampshire won by three wickets)
b A.C.Cummins   4   197-7   11   1   29   2   G.Fowler c R.A.Smith   196-5
                                            P.W.G.Parker c A.N.Aymes

372. Sunday League - Hampshire v Durham, Stockton-on-Tees, May 16 (No result)
b A.C.Cummins   3   127-6   5   1   12   0   48-0

373. Sunday League - Hampshire v Yorkshire, Southampton, May 23 (Yorkshire won by 30 runs)
run out   59   170   10   3   26   2   A.A.Metcalfe c V.P.Terry   200-8
                                            M.J.Foster b

374. Benson & Hedges Cup - Hampshire v Northamptonshire, Southampton, May 25 (Northamptonshire won by seven wickets)
lbw b J.P.Taylor   9   223-7   11   1   48   0   227-3

375. Sunday League - Hampshire v Kent, Basingstoke, June 13 (Kent won by seven wickets)
c C.L.Hooper b M.A.Ealham 27   198   5   0   35   0   202-3

376. Sunday League - Hampshire v Northamptonshire, Northampton, June 20 (Northamptonshire won by four wickets)
did not bat   -   226-2   9.4   0   46   1   N.A.Felton lbw   229-6

377. NatWest Trophy - Hampshire v Staffordshire, Stone, June 23 (Hampshire won by seven wickets)
did not bat   -   166-3   11.1   0   28   0   165

378. Sunday League - Hampshire v Gloucestershire, Bristol, July 4 (Gloucestershire won by 24 runs)
run out   0   216   10   1   44   0   240-7

379. NatWest Trophy - Hampshire v Sussex, Hove, July 7 (Sussex won by nine wickets)
not out   31   248-4   12   0   36   0   252-1

380. Sunday League - Hampshire v Somerset, Southampton, July 11 (Hampshire won by seven wickets)
did not bat   -   215-3   10   2   26   1   A.R.Caddick c A.N.Aymes   214   2

381. Sunday League - Hampshire v Warwickshire, Southampton, August 1 (Hampshire won by nine wickets)
did not bat   -   233-1   10   0   50   0   232-6

382. Sunday League - Hampshire v Lancashire, Southampton, August 15 (Lancashire won by six wickets)
lbw b P.A.J.DeFreitas   6   158   9   1   25   1   N.J.Speak b   159-4
383. Sunday League - Hampshire v Glamorgan, Swansea, August 22 (Glamorgan won by six wickets)
c C.P.Metson b R.P.Lefebvre 8   207-8   9.3   2   32   0   209-4

SEASON'S AVERAGES

Batting and Fielding	M	I	NO	Runs	HS	Ave	100	50	Ct
NatWest Trophy	2	1	1	31	31*	-	-	-	-
Sunday League	9	6	0	103	59	17.16	-	1	2
Benson & Hedges Cup	3	2	0	13	9	6.50	-	-	1
Career - Gillette Cup/NWT	31	21	9	348	77	29.00	-	2	3
Career - Sunday League	142	95	22	1338	59	18.32	-	1	29
Career - B & H Cup	41	30	2	387	34	13.82	-	-	7
Career - One Day Matches	383	254	54	3257	77	16.28	-	6	63

Bowling	O	M	R	W	BB	Ave	5i
NatWest Trophy	23.1	0	64	0	-	-	-
Sunday League	78.1	10	296	5	2-26	59.20	-
Benson & Hedges Cup	33	6	101	4	2-24	25.25	-
Career - Gillette Cup/NWT	328	54	895	34	4-15	26.32	-
Career - Sunday League	1059.4	90	3835	150	5-13	25.56	2
Career - B & H Cup	384.1	73	1143	53	4-20	21.56	-
Career - One Day Matches	3246.5	390	10909	458	5-13	23.81	5

1993/94

384. Benson & Hedges Series - Natal v Impalas, Springs, October 15 (Natal won by 47 runs)
b L.Botes   3   212-8   9   2   30   0   165-7
385. Benson & Hedges Series - Natal v Boland, Durban, November 12 (Natal won on faster scoring rate)
did not bat   -   154-7   5   2   7   0   99-1
386. Benson & Hedges Series - Natal v Northern Transvaal, Verwoerdburg, December 8 (Northern Transvaal won by 62 runs)
c C.van Noordwyk
b R.E.Bryson   18   185   10   0   45   2   R.F.Pienaar b   247-6
                                       J.J.Strydom c P.W.E.Rawson
387. Benson & Hedges Series - Natal v Transvaal, Johannesburg, December 17 (Natal won on faster scoring rate)
did not bat   -   222-4   7   1   14   1   S.J.Cook lbw   125
388. Benson & Hedges Series - Natal v Orange Free State, Durban, December 20 (Natal won by 26 runs)
c F.D.Stephenson b N.Boje 32   210-8   8.3   2   21   1   P.J.L.Radley c U.H.Goedeke   184
389. Benson & Hedges Series - Natal v Eastern Province, Port Elizabeth, December 23 (Natal won by 59 runs)
c S.C.Pope b R.E.Veenstra 24   192   7.2   1   23   2   P.G.Amm lbw   133   1
                                         R.A.Lyle b
390. Benson & Hedges Series - Natal v Western Province, Durban, January 12 (Natal won by 102 runs)
b M.W.Pringle   63   249-7   7   2   19   3   D.Jordaan lbw   147
                                         C.A.Best c U.H.Goedeke
                                         A.P.Kuiper c sub (R.B.Armstrong)
391. Benson & Hedges Series - Natal v Border, Durban, January 19 (Natal won by 15 runs)
b P.J.Botha   37   234-9   9   2   35   0   219-8
392. Benson & Hedges Series - Natal v Border, East London, February 2 (Border won by three wickets)
c and b K.G.Bauermeister 15   134   10   2   13   2   G.C.Victor c U.H.Goedeke 139-7
                                         P.C.Strydom c U.H.Goedeke
393. Benson & Hedges Series - Natal v Border, Durban, February 4 (Natal won by four wickets)
c S.J.Palframan b S.J.Base   2   186-6   10   0   35   3   P.N.Kirsten
                                       c D.M.Benkenstein   183-9
                                   P.C.Strydom b
                                   K.G.Bauermeister b

94. Benson & Hedges Series - Natal v Border, Durban, February 6 (Natal won by 53 runs)
not out   64   244-6   8.1   1   35   2 B.M.Osborne lbw   191
                                                          S.J.Base c N.C.Johnson

395. Benson & Hedges Series - Natal v Orange Free State, Durban, March 11 (Orange Free State won by seven wickets)
c W.J.Cronje b B.T.Player   8   103   8   1   31   0   108-3

SEASON'S AVERAGES

Batting and Fielding	M	I	NO	Runs	HS	Ave	100	50	Ct
Benson & Hedges Series	12	10	1	266	64*	29.55	-	2	1
Career - B & H Series	22	18	3	374	64*	24.93	-	3	4
Career - One Day Matches	395	264	55	3523	77	16.85	-	8	64

Bowling	O	M	R	W	BB	Ave	5i
Benson & Hedges Series	99	16	308	16	3-19	19.25	-
Career - B & H Series	184.2	28	581	33	4-15	17.60	-
Career - One Day Matches	3345.5	406	11217	474	5-13	23.66	5

1994/95

396. Benson & Hedges Series - Natal v Transvaal, Durban, October 14 (No result)
                                     5   1   8   0   10-3

397. Benson & Hedges Series - Natal v Western Transvaal, Durban, October 21 (Natal won by six wickets)
did not bat   - 128-4   10   3   21   1 A.Cilliers lbw   124-8   1

398. Benson & Hedges Series - Natal v Eastern Transvaal, Springs, October 28 (No result)
did not bat   - 211-6

399. Benson & Hedges Series - Natal v Border, Durban, November 16 (Border won by 6 runs)
b I.L.Howell   0   235   10   0   44   4 P.N.Kirsten c P.L.Symcox 241-7
                                                     D.J.Cullinan c M.L.Bruyns
                                                     P.C.Strydom c P.L.Symcox
                                                       O.D.Gibson c S.M.Pollock

400. Benson & Hedges Series - Natal v Western Province, Durban, February 1 (Western Province won by 25 runs)
lbw b D.G.Payne   10   172   10   1   24   1 D.B.Rundle c M.L.Bruyns 197-9

401. Benson & Hedges Series - Natal v Orange Free State, Bloemfontein, February 10 (Natal won by six wickets)
did not bat   - 137-4   7   2   15   0   135

402. Benson & Hedges Series - Natal v Griqualand West, Kimberley, February 24 (Natal won by seven wickets)
did not bat   - 147-3   9   1   22   1 G.J.Schouten b   145-9

403. Benson & Hedges Series - Natal v Northern Transvaal, Verwoerdburg, March 3 (Natal won by six wickets)
did not bat   - 213-4   10   1   22   1 R.F.Pienaar b   212-7

404. Benson & Hedges Series - Natal v Boland, Paarl, March 8 (Boland won by three wickets)
c L.M.Germishuys
   b W.F.Stelling   25   164   9   2   26   0   165-7

405. Benson & Hedges Series - Natal v Eastern Province, Durban, March 15 (Natal won by six wickets)
did not bat   - 190-4   9   2   26   0   189-5

406. Benson & Hedges Series - Natal v Transvaal, Johannesburg, March 29, 30 (Transvaal won by losing fewer wickets)
c N.Pothas b R.P.Snell   25   236-9   10   0   36   2 R.P.Snell c M.L.Bruyns 236-8
                                                     C.E.Eksteen c M.L.Bruyns

SEASON'S AVERAGES

Batting and Fielding	M	I	NO	Runs	HS	Ave	100	50	Ct
Benson & Hedges Series	11	4	0	60	25	15.00	-	-	1
Career - B & H Series	33	22	3	434	64*	22.84	-	3	5
Career - One Day Matches	406	268	55	3583	77	16.82	-	8	65

Bowling	O	M	R	W	BB	Ave	5i
Benson & Hedges Series	89	12	244	10	4-44	24.40	-
Career - B & H Series	273.2	40	825	43	4-15	19.18	-
Career - One Day Matches	3434.5	418	11461	484	5-13	23.67	5

1995

407. Benson & Hedges Cup - Scotland v Worcestershire, Worcester, April 23 (Worcestershire won by ten wickets)
b N.V.Radford   2   118   7   1   19   0   119-0

408. Benson & Hedges Cup - Scotland v Derbyshire, Glasgow, April 25 (Derbyshire won by 46 runs)
c T.J.G.O'Gorman
b D.E.Malcolm   36   174   11   2   35   2   D.G.Cork b   220-6
P.A.J.DeFreitas c I.M.Stanger

409. Benson & Hedges Cup - Scotland v Yorkshire, Glasgow, May 2 (Yorkshire won by ten wickets)
c R.J.Blakey b P.J.Hartley   0   129   5   0   24   0   130-0

410. Benson & Hedges Cup - Scotland v Northamptonshire, Northampton, May 16 (Northamptonshire won by 153 runs)
c R.J.Warren b T.C.Walton   2   151-5   11   1   47   1   R.J.Warren c I.M.Stanger   304-6

411. NatWest Trophy - Scotland v Nottinghamshire, Trent Bridge, June 27 (Nottinghamshire won by eight wickets)
c G.F.Archer b J.R.Wileman 45   171-9   9   0   32   0   172-2

SEASON'S AVERAGES

Batting and Fielding	M	I	NO	Runs	HS	Ave	100	50	Ct
NatWest Trophy	1	1	0	45	45	45.00	-	-	-
Benson & Hedges Cup	4	4	0	40	36	10.00	-	-	-
Career - NatWest Trophy	32	22	9	393	77	30.23	-	2	3
Career - B & H Cup	45	34	2	427	36	13.34	-	-	7
Career - One Day Matches	411	273	55	3668	77	16.82	-	8	65

Bowling	O	M	R	W	BB	Ave	5i
NatWest Trophy	9	0	32	0	-	-	-
Benson & Hedges Cup	34	4	125	3	2-35	41.66	-
Career – NatWest Trophy	337	54	927	34	4-15	27.26	-
Career - B & H Cup	418.1	77	1268	56	4-20	22.64	-
Career - One Day Matches	3477.3	422	11618	487	5-13	23.85	5

1995/96

412. Benson & Hedges Cup - Natal v Easterns, Durban, October 20 (Natal won by six wickets)
did not bat   - 149-4   6   1   19   1   W.R.Radford c M.L.Bruyns   148

413. Benson & Hedges Cup - Natal v Western Transvaal, Foschville, October 25 (Natal won by 219 runs)
did not bat   - 319-6   5   0   8   1   V.Wandrag c P.L.Symcox   100

414. Benson & Hedges Cup - Natal v Eastern Province, Port Elizabeth, December 13 (Eastern Province won by 3 runs)
b T.G.Shaw   0   188   6   0   23   1   G.C.Victor b   191-7

415. Benson & Hedges Cup - Natal v Boland, Durban, January 20 (Boland won by four wickets)
c T.N.Lazard b W.F.Stelling 23   157   7.3   0   31   0   158-6

416. Benson & Hedges Cup - Natal v Northern Transvaal, Durban, February 2 (Natal won by 2 runs)
not out   3   185-8   9   0   24   2   M.van Jaarsveld c N.C.Johnson   183-8   1
M.J.G.Davis c K.A.Forde

417. Benson & Hedges Cup - Natal v Transvaal, Johannesburg, February 7 (Match tied)
did not bat   - 230-8   9   1   36   1   D.R.Laing c T.Bosch   230-8

418. Benson & Hedges Cup - Natal v Griqualand West, Durban, February 16 (Natal won by 62 runs)
not out   3   190-7   6   2   12   1   M.I.Gidley c K.A.Forde   128-7

419. Benson & Hedges Cup - Natal v Western Province, Cape Town, March 1 (Western Province won by 54 runs)

b E.O.Simons	21	172	9	2	37	2	D.L.Haynes c N.C.Johnson	226-4
							J.B.Cummins b	

SEASON'S AVERAGES

Batting and Fielding	M	I	NO	Runs	HS	Ave	100	50	Ct
Benson & Hedges Series	8	5	2	50	23	16.66	-	-	1
Career - B & H Series	41	27	5	484	64*	22.00	-	3	6
Career - One Day Matches	419	278	57	3718	77	16.82	-	8	66

Bowling	O	M	R	W	BB	Ave	5i
Benson & Hedges Series	57.3	5	190	9	2-24	21.11	-
Career - B & H Series	330.5	45	1015	52	4-15	19.51	-
Career - One Day Matches	3535	427	11808	496	5-13	23.80	5

ACKNOWLEDGEMENTS

I am very grateful to the following, without whom much of this publication would not have seen the light of day:
David Baggett (ACS), Phillip Bailey (ACS), Andrew Samson (RSA), Ray Goble (WI statistician), Gordon Vince (Database), Peter Griffiths (Typesetting) and my son Richard for his unstinting help.

BIBLIOGRAPHY

Hampshire Handbook 1980-1999 – Various editors
The Wisden Book of Test Cricket – Bill Frindall, Headline, 1995
Limited-Overs International Cricket – Bill Frindall, Headline, 1997
South African Cricket Annual 1994-1998
Wisden Cricketers' Almanack 1980-1999